International Perspectives on Teacher R

International Perspectives on English Language Teaching
Series edited by **Sue Garton** and **Keith Richards**

Titles include:

Ema Ushioda (*editor*)
INTERNATIONAL PERSPECTIVES ON MOTIVATION

Sue Garton and Kathleen Graves (*editors*)
INTERNATIONAL PERSPECTIVES ON MATERIALS IN ELT

Sarah Rich (*editor*)
INTERNATIONAL PERSPECTIVES IN TEACHING ENGLISH TO YOUNG LEARNERS

Simon Borg and Hugo Santiago Sanchez (*editors*)
INTERNATIONAL PERSPECTIVES ON TEACHER RESEARCH

Forthcoming titles in the series:
Chris Jenks and Paul Seedhouse (*editors*)
INTERNATIONAL PERSPECTIVES ON ELT CLASSROOM INTERACTION

Hugo Bowles and Alessia Cogo (*editors*)
INTERNATIONAL PERSPECTIVES ON TEACHING ENGLISH AS A LINGUA FRANCA

Thomas S.C. Farrell (*editor*)
INTERNATIONAL PERSPECTIVES ON ENGLISH LANGUAGE TEACHING

International Perspectives on English Language Teaching
Series Standing Order ISBN 978–0230–30850–3 (hardback)
978–0230–30851–0 (paperback)
(*outside North America only*)

You can receive future titles in this series as they are published by placing a standing order. Please contact your bookseller or, in case of difficulty, write to us at the address below with your name and address, the title of the series and the ISBN quoted above.

Customer Services Department, Macmillan Distribution Ltd, Houndmills, Basingstoke, Hampshire RG21 6XS, England

Also by Simon Borg

TEACHER COGNITION AND LANGUAGE EDUCATION
Research and Practice

TEACHER RESEARCH IN LANGUAGE TEACHING
A Critical Analysis

International Perspectives on Teacher Research

Edited by

Simon Borg
ELT Consultant

and

Hugo Santiago Sanchez
University of Bath, UK

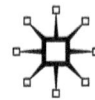

Selection, introduction, and editorial content © Simon Borg
and Hugo Santiago Sanchez 2015
Individual chapters © Respective authors 2015

All rights reserved. No reproduction, copy or transmission of this
publication may be made without written permission.

No portion of this publication may be reproduced, copied or transmitted save with
written permission or in accordance with the provisions of the Copyright, Designs and
Patents Act 1988, or under the terms of any licence permitting limited copying issued
by the Copyright Licensing Agency, Saffron House, 6–10 Kirby Street, London EC1N 8TS.

Any person who does any unauthorized act in relation to this publication may be
liable to criminal prosecution and civil claims for damages.

The authors have asserted their rights to be identified as the authors of this work in
accordance with the Copyright, Designs and Patents Act 1988.

First published 2015 by
PALGRAVE MACMILLAN

Palgrave Macmillan in the UK is an imprint of Macmillan Publishers Limited,
registered in England, company number 785998, of Houndmills, Basingstoke,
Hampshire, RG21 6XS.

Palgrave Macmillan in the US is a division of St Martin's Press LLC,
175 Fifth Avenue, New York, NY 10010.

Palgrave is the global academic imprint of the above companies and has
companies and representatives throughout the world.

Palgrave® and Macmillan® are registered trademarks in the United States,
the United Kingdom, Europe and other countries.

ISBN 978–1–137–37620–6   hardback
ISBN 978–1–137–37621–3   paperback

This book is printed on paper suitable for recycling and made from fully managed and
sustained forest sources. Logging, pulping and manufacturing processes are expected
to conform to the environmental regulations of the country of origin.

A catalogue record for this book is available from the British Library.

A catalog record for this book is available from the Library of Congress.

Typeset by MPS Limited, Chennai, India.

Contents

List of Figures and Tables   ix

Series Editors' Preface   x

Notes on Contributors   xii

List of Abbreviations   xv

1. Key Issues in Doing and Supporting Language Teacher Research   1
   Simon Borg and Hugo Santiago Sanchez

2. Towards New Understandings: Reflections on an Action Research Project with Japanese University Students   14
   Gerald Talandis Jr. and Michael Stout

3. Action Research as a Means of Stepping Out of the Teaching Comfort Zone   29
   Megan Yucel and Vicki Bos

4. Learning to Do Teacher Research Independently: Challenges and Solutions   47
   Jianmei Xie

5. Teacher Research in Video-Based Online Classrooms   57
   Paula Charbonneau-Gowdy

6. Border Crossings: Researching across Contexts for Teacher Professional Development   70
   Patsy Vinogradov

7. Participative Investigation: Narratives in Critical Research in the EFL Classroom   87
   Gerrard Mugford

8. Facilitating Teacher Research: Course Design, Implementation, and Evaluation   98
   Simon Borg

9. Supporting Teacher Research through a Practical In-Service Course   113
   Anisa Saleh Al-Maskari

10. Action Research as a Professional Development Strategy   125
    Servet Çelik and Kenan Dikilitaş

11	Practices and Principles of Pre-Service Action Research *Maureen Rajuan*	139
12	Teacher Research in the English Language Teacher Development Project *Rachel Bowden*	152
13	Encouraging Teacher Research through In-House Activities: The Approach of a Finnish University Language Centre *Tuula Lehtonen, Kari Pitkänen, and Johanna Vaattovaara*	170
14	Teacher Research: Looking Back and Moving Forward *Hugo Santiago Sanchez and Simon Borg*	185

Further Reading   194

Index   199

List of Figures and Tables

Figures

6.1	Learners as problem solvers and related components	78
12.1	ELTDP's reflective cycle	157

Tables

10.1	Outline of the project phases	127
10.2	Sample research proposal	132
10.3	Issues encountered in carrying out action research as a PD strategy	135
11.1	Example of rubric for assessment of final action research project	148
13.1	Organizational structures for research and teaching development at the Helsinki University Language Centre	174
14.1	Benefits of teacher research	189
14.2	Challenges in teacher research	191

Series Editors' Preface

It is by the lodestone of research, informally conceived, that teachers navigate their ways through the tricky waters of language pedagogy. With none of the formal apparatus of the academic and usually with no training in relevant techniques, they combine acute observation of classroom behaviour, informal interviews with students, and sensitive linguistic and documentary analysis to uncover potential solutions to practical challenges. Research is embedded within the quotidian rhythms of their professional lives and usually passes without notice.

In view of this natural orientation, it is perhaps surprising that the history of teacher research has not always been a comfortable one. Huberman's work on teachers' lives revealed, for example, that while teachers who 'tinkered' with their classes tended to be happy in their work, those who had been involved in large-scale projects were the most dissatisfied with their lot. The shift to smaller-scale projects and the direct involvement of teachers in the process of investigation that marked the development of action research offered teachers a stronger sense of investment and control, but even this brought associated challenges. Instead of serving as an opportunity for liberation, it was sometimes appropriated as an instrument of control as teachers were required to undertake research unwillingly and in uncongenial circumstances.

Nevertheless, action research has weathered its storms, resolved its differences, and matured into an accessible and rewarding approach that is welcomed across the globe in circumstances from the meanest to the most richly endowed. Unsurprisingly, it features prominently in this collection, and the range of perspectives involved is a testament to its breadth and depth of penetration into the lived world of teachers. The honesty and immediacy of Talandis and Stout's account of an action research project involving Japanese university students sets the tone for what follows in the collection. This is followed by a chapter by Yucel and Bos that explores the approach as a means of taking teachers outside their comfort zone. The practical outcomes of this are brought out clearly in an account that is richly illustrated with data extracts and strikingly honest in orientation. Charbonneau-Gowdy's chapter takes teacher research into the online world, arguing that deepening our insights into the place of technology in understanding teaching and learning serves as 'a wake-up call'. The chapters by Çelik and Dikilitaş and Rajuan make a strong pairing, the first concerned with action research as a strategy for professional development, drawing general lessons from a richly contextualized local example. Action research in a pre-service setting has received relatively little attention, but the strength of the student teachers' voices emerging from Rajuan's description of a research training course suggests that there is much to be learnt from this context.

There are those who treat educational action research and teacher research as almost synonymous, but in their wide ranging and penetrating overview of the latter Borg and Sanchez paint a richer and more complex picture of the field, placing it in the broader context of professional learning and pointing out not only the potential benefits it brings but also the criticisms levelled at it. While they are able to respond to many of these, some remain intractable. They can find no explanation, for example, that would account for the narrow focus of much teacher research, but they have put together here a collection that takes us much closer to understanding the forces that bear on not only teacher researchers but those who train and mentor them. The chapter by Xie, for example, offers a very personal account of what it means to be a teacher researcher and should be essential reading for anyone setting out on this path.

The collection is also well-served by accounts from those who facilitate teacher research. Vinogradov's dual role as teacher researcher and facilitator is the basis for some thought-provoking observations, while Mugford's engagement with student-teacher researchers in Mexico informs a chapter as impressive in its strong sense of local presence as in the ways in which it draws global lessons from this. Al-Maskari's account of an INSET course in Oman is also replete with valuable detail. The involvement of Borg and Bowden was with broader national initiatives in Pakistan and Malaysia, but their chapters too take the reader into the projects themselves, both offering invaluable insights into what contributes to success. Borg's evaluation draws on a breadth of experience in the field of teacher research that few, if any, can match, while Bowden has assembled a collection of online resources that take the reader to the very heart of the project.

In their introduction, Borg and Sanchez point to worldwide initiatives aimed at promoting teacher research in systematic ways and highlight the importance of support, a theme taken up by Lehtonen, Pitkänen, and Vaattovaara in their compelling account of the transformative power of structural innovation in combination with a collaborative orientation. It is perhaps fitting that the collection should end with an account that extends a consideration of teacher research to wider issues that are important to all institutions of higher education.

Nevertheless, as Sanchez and Borg recognize in their conclusion, however strong the institutional support, teacher research is 'a self-initiated process' – teachers need to be inspired to undertake it. The accounts in this volume are vivid, warts-and-all testimonies to the vibrant blend of frustration and elation that characterizes all research worthy of the name. They chart no easy course through the choppy seas of teacher research, but we hope that their honesty and insight will inspire others to embark on this voyage of a professional lifetime.

Notes on Contributors

Anisa Saleh Al-Maskari works as a regional in-service teacher trainer for the Ministry of Education, Oman, where she is responsible for designing and delivering in-service courses for teachers. She holds degrees from the University of Leeds and Sultan Qaboos University and was one of the first Omani teachers to join the FLTA (Fulbright Teaching Assistants) Program in 2005/06. In 2007, she was awarded Oman's National Prize for the Distinguished Teacher.

Simon Borg has been involved in ELT for over 25 years working as a teacher, teacher educator, lecturer, examiner, researcher, and consultant in a range of international contexts. After 15 years in the School of Education at the University of Leeds, where he was a Professor of TESOL, Simon now works full-time as an ELT consultant. He specializes in teacher education and development, teacher research, and research methods training.

Vicki Bos has a CELTA and an MA in TESOL, and has been teaching in the ESL industry for 12 years. She has taught both English and singing in Australia and overseas, and is currently employed as a language teacher and teacher trainer at ICTE-UQ. She conducts the ICTE-UQ Chorus, as an extra-curricular activity.

Rachel Bowden has worked as a teacher, trainer, teacher trainer, senior teacher and project manager with the British Council in Malaysia, Sri Lanka, Bhutan, Nepal, India and East Malaysia. She is interested in participatory approaches to evaluation within teacher development projects.

Paula Charbonneau-Gowdy is Professor of English as a Foreign Language and teacher educator in the Education Faculty at the Universidad Andres Bello in Santiago, Chile. She was previously Senior Advisor for Learning Development and Technology for the Government of Canada. She has published extensively in the areas of e-learning and distance education, drawing from her ongoing research in pushing the pedagogical boundaries of social learning technologies in traditional and virtual classroom settings.

Servet Çelik is Assistant Professor in the Department of Foreign Language Education at Karadeniz Technical University, Turkey. He also serves as a senior researcher for the Scientific and Technological Research Council of Turkey (TÜBİTAK). He holds a Bachelor's degree in ELT from Gazi University, Turkey; a Masters of Education degree in TESOL from the University of Pennsylvania, and a doctorate in Literacy, Culture, and Language Education from Indiana University at Bloomington.

Kenan Dikilitaş is a teacher trainer at the Foreign Language Preparatory school at Gediz University, Turkey. He holds a BA in English Language Teaching from Selçuk University, Turkey; a Master's degree in English Language Teaching from Çanakkale Onsekiz Mart University, Turkey; and a PhD in English Language Teaching from Yeditepe University, Turkey.

Tuula Lehtonen is a senior lecturer in English and the co-head of the English Unit at the University of Helsinki Language Centre. She holds an MA and an EdD, and she was recently awarded the title of docent by the University of Helsinki. Her research interests include vocabulary learning, personal relevance in language learning, students as users of language at work and language support for students in the many, relatively new English-medium Master's programmes at the University of Helsinki.

Gerrard Mugford works on BA, MA, and PhD programmes at the Universidad de Guadalajara, Mexico. He holds a PhD in TEFL from the Institute of Education, University of London. Current research interests include second-language interpersonal language use and critical linguistics. He has published articles and book chapters on foreign language pragmatics, politeness, impoliteness, and lexical studies.

Kari Pitkänen is a senior lecturer in English at the University of Helsinki Language Centre. He holds a PhD. His research interests include text linguistics, discourse analysis, and developing language support for international students on the English-medium Master's programmes at the University of Helsinki.

Maureen Rajuan is a teacher trainer and a senior lecturer at Achva College of Education in Israel, where she was recently appointed as Head of the English Department. She received her doctorate from the Eindhoven Technical University, School of Education, the Netherlands, in mentoring student teachers. She translates academic manuscripts from Hebrew to English and publishes articles on teacher education.

Hugo Santiago Sanchez has been involved in English language teaching for over 18 years, working as an EFL teacher, lecturer, teacher trainer, and researcher in Argentina and the UK. He specializes in teacher cognition, language awareness, teacher education, and teacher development. At the University of Bath, he is involved in teaching and supervision in the MA TESOL, EdD in Education, and PhD programmes. He is a Fellow of the Higher Education Academy and a member of the editorial board of the *Argentinian Journal of Applied Linguistics*.

Michael Stout is Associate Professor in the Foreign Language Center at the University of Tsukuba. His research interests are CALL, project-based language learning, materials development, learner autonomy, and professional development. He can also be reached on academia.edu.

Gerald Talandis Jr. has been working as an English teacher in Japan since 1993 and is currently an Associate Professor at the University of Toyama. His research interests include pragmatics, materials design, learner autonomy, and professional development. He can be reached on academia.edu.

Johanna Vaattovaara is a senior lecturer in University Pedagogy in the Support Unit for Teaching and Learning at the University of Helsinki Language Centre. She is responsible for university pedagogy training and support for research for Language Centre staff. Her research interests are university language teaching and learning as well as sociolinguistics (linguistic attitudes) and the communication of science.

Patsy Vinogradov lives and works in Minnesota which is home to a considerable population of refugees and immigrants from all over the world. Particularly large numbers come from Laos, Burma, Somalia, Ethiopia, as well as from various countries in Central and South America. Patsy works with teachers and learners in Minnesota's extensive Adult Basic Education (ABE) system, which provides English language, basic skills, and career readiness training to adults. She teaches at Hamline University in St Paul, on the Adult ESL and Adult Basic Education certificate programmes. Her research interests include teacher preparation and development, literacy instruction, and curriculum design for low-literacy learners, those who come to the United States with little or no formal schooling in their home countries. She has earned a Master of Arts in ESL (2000) and a PhD in Education (2013), both from the University of Minnesota.

Jianmei Xie holds a PhD in Education from the Graduate School of Education, University of Exeter. She was trained to be a language teacher and has worked for seven years as a lecturer (in language education) at the Guangdong University of Foreign Studies, China. She has written and presented works on language teaching pedagogy, teacher mentoring, research methods, and quality of educational research. Her research interests include: second-language education, language teacher development, teacher research, educational research, quality of research, and qualitative research methodologies.

Megan Yucel teaches at the Institute of Continuing and TESOL Education of the University of Queensland (ICTE-UQ). She has worked as a teacher, examiner, and test writer in Turkey, the United Kingdom, and Australia. She has the Cambridge DELTA and an MA in Applied Linguistics (TESOL). Her interests include assessment and narrative inquiry.

List of Abbreviations

ABE	adult basic education
APA	American Psychological Association
AR	action research
BA	Bachelor of Arts
BANA	British, Australasia, and North American
EFL	English as a foreign language
ELF	English as a lingua franca
ELICOS	English language intensive courses for overseas students
ELT	English language teaching
ELTDP	English Language Teacher Development Project
ELTR	English language teaching reforms
ESL	English as a second language
ESOL	English for speakers of other languages
ESP: BEP	English for specific purposes: Bridging English programme
ETAI	English Teachers Association in Israel
ICT	information and communication technologies
ICTE	Institute of Continuing and TESOL Education
K–12	kindergarten–12th grade
L1	first language
LC	language centre
MA	Master of Arts
MoD	Ministry of Education
MSF	Médecins sans Frontières
NATO	North Atlantic Treaty Organization
NCSALL	National Center for the Study of Adult Learning and Literacy
PAL	programa abierto de lenguas (open language programme)
PAR	participatory action research
PD	professional development

PDS	professional development schools
PhD	Doctor of Philosophy
RPD	research for professional development
TEFL	teaching English as a foreign language
TESEP	tertiary secondary primary
TESOL	teaching English to speakers of other languages
TL	target language
UH	University of Helsinki
UQ	University of Queensland
ZPD	zone of proximal development

1
Key Issues in Doing and Supporting Language Teacher Research

Simon Borg and Hugo Santiago Sanchez

Introduction

This chapter identifies and discusses key issues in the contemporary literature on teacher research in language teaching and our purpose here is to outline the broader theoretical framework within which the individual chapters which follow are situated. Teacher research in education generally has a long history (see, for example, Noffke 2002; Olson 1990) and is characterized by a substantial body of literature; we will not attempt to provide a comprehensive analysis of this here but rather our focus will be on selected salient themes. After dealing with definitional matters we focus on methodological and practical issues in the conduct of teacher research. We then consider teacher research from the perspective of those who facilitate it, and outline some observations on both the benefits of teacher research and criticisms of it. We conclude with a brief overview of the structure of the book.

Defining teacher research

A minimal definition of teacher research is systematic self-study by teachers (individually or collaboratively) which seeks to achieve real-world impact of some kind and is made public. It is thus *systematic* – like any form of research – and involves *self-study* – the focus of inquiry in teacher research is the teacher and their own work. Its goal is *real-world impact* (i.e. it is not an exercise in generating knowledge for its own sake) and such impact can assume many forms. A wide range of possibilities exist; for example, teacher research may impact on teachers' beliefs, knowledge, attitudes, skills, and classroom practices. It may impact on students' beliefs, knowledge and performance, or on some aspect of institutions more generally. Emancipatory views of teacher research (see Hammersley 2004) extend its impact even further to include challenging and promoting change in inequitable social conditions (we return to this notion of teacher research later).

Finally, teacher research needs to be *made public*, as opposed to being a wholly private activity. Teacher inquiry that remains wholly private should not be called research; this does not imply such activity is not valuable, but research by definition seeks to make a contribution to knowledge and it cannot do so if it is not made public. Private inquiry cannot be scrutinized, reviewed, replicated and built on by others, but research can. Private inquiry, no matter how systematic, is better referred to using terms other than research (e.g. reflective practice).

Teacher research goes by many different names. *Practitioner research* is a broader term that includes not just teachers but practitioners in other fields (e.g. nurses) who engage in systematic self-study. *Action research* (e.g. Burns 2010) denotes a particular methodology for doing teacher research which is typically defined by repeated cycles of planning, action, observation and reflection through which changes to practice are evaluated. *Classroom research* is another term that recurs in the literature; this simply denotes research that is conducted in the classroom (i.e. *where* the research takes place). Thus while most teacher research is also classroom research, the latter may also be carried out by, for example, university researchers who visit classrooms to collect data but who are not doing teacher research (because they are studying others rather than themselves).

Doing teacher research

Teacher research, in common with research generally, requires teachers to identify an issue to examine, to collect information (i.e. data) relevant to it, to examine and interpret that information, and to reach some conclusions. 'Conclusions' is perhaps an unfortunate word in that it suggests a degree of finality that research can never justifiably claim, and therefore the conclusions reached through teacher research are always provisional – i.e. they may be revised as a result of further inquiry.

Teacher research is a methodologically-flexible activity – a wide range of strategies can be used in collecting and analysing data as well as in reporting findings. These strategies can be quantitative, qualitative, or a combination of these (mixed methods research) and the range of specific data collection methods available to teachers is quite extensive, for example: interviews (of various kinds), lesson observation, questionnaires, diaries, group discussions, photos, video, student work, teaching materials, policy documents, drawings, recordings of lessons, note taking, checklists, rating scales, stories, and biographical writing (see, for example, Campbell et al. 2004; Freeman 1998; Kalmbach Phillips and Carr 2010).

Teacher research, then, is not defined by particular research methods and, as in research generally, teachers will choose data collection strategies according to the questions that are being investigated. However, one important practical consideration in teacher research is feasibility, or what Allwright (1997) refers to as sustainability. Teacher research needs to be designed in a way that teachers can manage given the limitations and constraints of their knowledge, skills, and working conditions. A project which requires teachers to invest ten hours a week of their time outside school hours is wholly unfeasible. Similarly, a teacher research project which seeks to collect large volumes of numerical data and to subject these to complex statistical analyses will not succeed. It is essential, then, that decisions to pursue or promote teacher research are based on a sound understanding of what can be feasibly achieved in any given context. This suggests that a feasibility audit may be a useful exercise to engage, addressing questions such as the following:

1. Does the teacher have experience of reflective practice?
2. Do they understand what teacher research is?
3. Are they motivated to do teacher research?
4. Do they have the knowledge required to do research?
5. Do they have the skills required to do research?
6. Will they be able to exercise some autonomy in making decisions about their inquiry?
7. Will they have access to appropriate advice or mentoring?
8. Is the time required for teacher research available?
9. Will the teacher's school support their efforts to do teacher research?
10. Will the teacher have access to a community of teacher researchers?
11. Will the teacher have opportunities to share their work?
12. Will the teacher have access to appropriate resources?
13. Can teacher research be integrated into the teacher's routine practices?
14. Does the project have clear potential benefits?

Clearly, where the answer to the majority of these questions is 'no', then teacher research is not an appropriate option to pursue and other forms of professional development should be considered. In contrast, many 'yes' answers would suggest that the conditions for teacher research are more favourable. Although we are very committed to teacher research, we also recognize that it will not be appropriate in all contexts.

As question 13 above implies, in making teacher research a feasible activity it is important to integrate it as far as possible into the professional practices teachers engage in routinely. We do not believe that teacher research can be accommodated by teachers without any extra commitment (temporal, intellectual, and emotional) on their part; however, teacher research becomes much more feasible when teachers are able to use skills, knowledge, and opportunities which already exist. For example, the observation of learners will be an activity teachers engage in regularly and the skills they have in this respect can be utilized to good effect in the context of teacher research. Interestingly, as Bartlett and Burton (2003) note, teacher researchers may undervalue the research skills they already possess; yet taking full advantage of these is an important way of making teacher research a more feasible activity.

It is also important to stress that, although it is unreasonable to expect teachers to achieve the scale, rigour, or sophistication that full-time researchers can, quality *is* an essential concern in teacher research. We understand the argument (reported by practitioners in Borg 2013) that teacher research – because it stimulates reflection on practice – is a beneficial activity irrespective of the results it produces. However, teacher research extends beyond reflection (Cochran-Smith and Lytle 1999); it seeks to generate understandings which inform practice, and it is thus important that those understandings are trustworthy. This is why quality matters in teacher research – it is not a watered-down, amateurish, or inferior form of inquiry; it has its own distinctive characteristics but shares, with research generally, a commitment to reaching sound conclusions through systematic processes of data collection, analysis, and interpretation, all of which are driven by a concern for specific issues, problems, puzzles, or questions.

What counts as quality in teacher research, though, has been an issue of debate in the literature. One position is to argue that the value of teacher research should be assessed using the same criteria that apply to research generally, though various perspectives also exist on what these generic criteria might be (e.g. Borg 2010a; Denscombe 2002; Pawson et al. 2003). For example, Eisenhart and Howe (1992) specify five quality standards that can be applied to all forms of research; one, for instance, is that the research methods should fit the research questions while another is that clear links should be made to existing knowledge. The latter is a good example of where generic criteria for research quality may not sit comfortably with teacher research; teachers typically do not have easy access to background literature and may lack the time and skills to process this material when they can access it; thus while we would always recommend that teacher researchers do some background reading, we would not expect this to be extensive or deeply analytical in the manner that it is written up. An alternative position is to argue that teacher research, as a distinctive form of inquiry, should be assessed against a unique set of criteria. Anderson and Herr (1999), for example, propose five kinds of validity (outcome, process, democratic, catalytic and dialogic) for evaluating practitioner research (see Oolbekkink-Marchand et al. 2014 for a recent analysis that applies these criteria to secondary school teachers' practitioner research). Another example is McNiff and Whitehead (2009: 319) who assess the quality of action research using the criteria of

> comprehensibility; truth in the sense of providing sufficient evidence to justify the claims being made; rightness in the sense of justifying the normative assumptions in the research; and authenticity in the sense that the

researcher shows over time and in interaction that they are genuinely committed to what they claim to believe in.

Clearly, then, there is no 'correct' answer to what counts as quality in teacher research; it is important, though, that teacher researchers are explicit about which of the available quality criteria they are seeking to address.

One significant methodological advantage that teacher research has over conventional forms of inquiry stems from the extended and intimate contact with the classroom that teachers have. Teachers' professional lives unfold and are enacted on a daily basis in the very settings in which teacher research happens. That affords teachers access to data which exceeds by far that available to any outside researcher visiting a classroom, even over an extended period of time. However, teachers' dual role as researchers and research participants also creates challenges. For example, it can be difficult for teachers to achieve the distance from their experience that is required to examine it critically. Another challenge for teacher researchers relates to their relationships with students and colleagues. In conventional research, the roles of researchers and participants are clearly defined – the former have full responsibility for the study, the latter contribute by providing data, and interactions between the two parties are typically infrequent, short-term, and fairly formal. Teacher research involves a different set of relationships between the researchers and those individuals who form part of their local professional community. For example, teachers work with their students on a daily basis and will seek, in the interests of good pedagogy, to establish good relationships with them. These relationships cannot be dismissed because the teacher researcher feels they need to be 'objective'. Similar questions arise in relation to the roles that students play in teacher research. They may function simply as a source of data; they may, though, assume a more participatory role (e.g. by contributing to the choice of issues to focus on or to how the data will be collected). Students may even be involved in collecting (rather than just providing) data – see, for example, the discussion of exploratory practice in Allwright and Hanks (2009). The same applies to the role of colleagues in teacher research; they may only be asked to provide data or can alternatively be an active part of a group that is collectively responsible for the design, conduct, and reporting of the study. Teacher researchers, then, need to adopt an explicit stance in relation to the members of the educational communities in which inquiry is taking place.

Supporting teacher research

Borg (2010b) claims that teacher research remains a minority activity in the field of language teaching, particularly if those teachers who do research in their classrooms as part of an academic degree are not counted. While it remains the case that teacher research is not a common activity in our field, there is increasing evidence worldwide of initiatives that are seeking to promote it in systematic ways (e.g. the Cambridge English-English UK Action Research Scheme or the Cambridge University Press Teacher Research Scheme). This realization that teacher research needs to be supported is important and represents a step forward from the rather simplistic belief that once teachers have been told about the benefits of teacher research they will then without hesitation proceed to engage fully in it. It is clear that teachers' own backgrounds and the contexts in which language teachers work around the world are often not conducive to teacher research and indeed to professional development more generally; however, with carefully planned support structures it is possible for teacher research to become a productive element in teachers' professional lives. This, then, raises important questions about how the development of teacher researchers can be effectively facilitated.

An important source of insight here is contemporary thinking in the field of teacher professional learning more generally (e.g. Borg 2015; Borko et al. 2010; Darling-Hammond and Lieberman 2012; Muijs et al. 2014; Timperley 2011). Although we would not want to be prescriptive about what constitutes good practice in supporting the professional development of teachers (as Opfer and Pedder 2011 note, varying contexts mean that what 'works' will also vary), there is broad consensus in education generally that professional learning will be more effective when it has these characteristics:

- it is seen by teachers to be relevant to their needs and those of their students;
- teachers are centrally involved in decisions about content and process;
- collaboration and the sharing of expertise among teachers is fostered;
- it is a collective enterprise supported by schools and educational systems more broadly;
- exploration and reflection are emphasized over methodological prescriptivism;
- expert internal and/or external support is available;
- classroom inquiry by teachers is seen as a central professional learning process.

Teacher research, as a strategy which has reflective classroom-based inquiry at its core, is well-aligned with such aspirations. The importance of collaboration is also noted here; in its most basic form, this implies that teacher researchers will benefit from opportunities to talk to colleagues about the work they are doing; collaboration can, though, where appropriate, be significantly scaled up to include teacher research projects in which several teachers in one or more schools are concurrently engaged in exploring an issue of common interest.

Beyond these general recommendations for supporting teacher learning, specific discussions of the practices and principles of teacher research facilitators are not widely available in the literature. Outside language teaching, Levin (2008) discusses ways of preparing PhD students for action research. Taylor et al. (2008) discuss how they teach reflective practice, while Mead (2008) discusses ten attributes that a facilitator of a large-scale action research project requires – for example, not being attached to particular ways of working, a capacity to tolerate uncertainty, a willingness to act decisively when needed, and a determination to insist on what is needed to make the project work. Another relevant resource for facilitators of teacher research is McKernan (1996), who dedicates a chapter of his book to 'Teaching Action Research'. He discusses several courses from different contexts and outlines the principles he follows in his own work. He also highlights key course design issues which merit close attention, such as the duration of the course, how it is assessed, the size of the group, and the teaching and learning approaches that are used.

In language teaching, Anne Burns, who has been involved in supporting action research for many years, particularly in Australia, has written about the design and evaluation of different initiatives she has facilitated (most recently Burns 2014) and these analyses provide consistent support for the central role that an expert mentor can play in fostering teacher research; the importance of institutional support for teacher research is also repeatedly highlighted. Borg (2013) reviews various reports[1] of various teacher research projects and also analyses two he facilitated in order to identify factors in their design and conduct that contributed to positive outcomes. A long list of such factors were identified, including official support, an extended period of time, feasible objectives, a clear structure, an advisor who provided teachers with regular support, a strong practical orientation, concrete outcomes and opportunities for dissemination. The analysis of teachers' needs and concerns was also important in allowing these courses to maximize the effectiveness of the support provided. For example, in one case, early in the project teachers were asked to identify challenges they felt they would face and they noted issues such as time-management, staying on schedule, obtaining relevant books, and designing instruments. An awareness of these potential difficulties allowed the facilitator to consider ways of addressing them.

Overall, then, there is scope for a wider discussion in the literature of the thinking behind the design of teacher research initiatives and of the practices that facilitators on such initiatives adopt to support teachers, particularly in contexts outside university-based programmes.

Benefits of teacher research

In contrast to some of the issues we have discussed so far, the benefits of teacher research have received extensive coverage in the literature, and a very long list of such benefits could be extracted from a wide range of sources. For example (see Borg 2013), teacher research has been reported to impact on teachers' confidence, self-esteem, classroom practices, autonomy, motivation, collegiality, and enthusiasm. The benefits to schools more generally have also been noted (Sharp 2007) and positive impacts on learners have been identified too (Bell et al. 2010). There is no doubt, then, that teacher research is seen to have enormous potential to impact positively on teachers, students, and organizations. More critically, though, much of the evidence that is available comes from self-reports provided by teachers, either in written or oral feedback or through written research reports, and which capture teachers' perspectives at the end of a teacher research course. While such sources of insight into the impacts of teacher research will continue to be important, it would also be valuable to complement them with additional perspectives, such as those of colleagues, students, and head teachers. The benefits of teacher research over time, too, is an issue we need to examine more closely – to what extent are the gains teachers report at the end of a teacher research course sustained in the subsequent months? There are, of course, practical difficulties involved in tracking down teachers months after a course has ended and limitations of funding may often mean that delayed evaluations of this kind are not possible; the general point is, though, that as a field we would benefit from a broader and longer-term analysis of the impacts that teacher research has on teachers, students, and schools.

Criticisms of teacher research

Finally, but not insignificantly, it is important for us to acknowledge some of the criticisms that have been levelled at teacher research. In his analysis of published teacher research in language teaching, Borg (2010b) notes that this is often conducted within the context of academic programmes or by teachers working in universities rather than in schools. The format in which much teacher research is reported also mirrors that used in conventional research reports, which may imply that teacher research is struggling to establish its own identity as a genre of research. Other criticisms relate to the methodological quality of teacher research. In education, Huberman (1996) has questioned the reliability of the methods used in teacher research and of the conclusions that are reached; Ellis (2010) notes similar methodological concerns about work conducted by language teachers. The importance of quality in teacher research has been noted above and it is difficult to defend work which has severe methodological flaws. Criticisms of teacher research, though, will always be based on assumptions about what research is, the standards it should meet, and the purposes it should serve, and it is unfair to judge teacher research against targets which it does not aspire to meet. For example, teacher researchers tend to have local concerns – they want to develop understandings which can contribute to the improvement of their own practices; concerns about the generalizability of the conclusions they reach are secondary. Critiques of teacher research which focus on its lack of generalizability, then, are not justified, particularly when the notions of generalizability being applied are ones which rely on statistical logic. Alternative ways of thinking about generalizability do exist, though, which depend on 'a richness of description and interpretation that makes a particular case interesting and relevant to those in other situations' (Richards 2003: 286). This takes us back to our earlier discussion of the criteria against which teacher research should be assessed.

We will highlight two further criticisms of language teacher research. The first comes from Dörnyei (2007), who claimed that he had never met a teacher who had volunteered to do action research. We hope that several years on, he has been fortunate enough to meet some teachers who have, for many do exist (e.g. on the action research schemes run in the UK and Australia by Cambridge English and its respective partners). A more serious criticism of teacher research in language teaching is that it tends to have a very immediate focus on pedagogical issues in teachers' own classrooms. The context for such an observation is the view that teacher research has the potential to contribute to broader social and political change (see, for example, Kemmis and McTaggart 2008). Teacher research in language teaching, though, very often limits itself to teachers' individual classrooms and fails to make broader connections with the schools these are part of, never mind socio-political concerns more generally. We do not have an explanation for the narrow practical focus of teacher research in our field; it may relate to the fact that for many language teachers, the process of becoming teacher researchers involves such a significant conceptual and attitudinal shift that a consideration of broader and deeper socio-political issues is not feasible. The explanation may also lie more broadly in the culture of English language teaching globally and specifically in the training courses through which individuals gain access to the profession; if an awareness of the socio-political dimensions of language teaching (see, for example, McKay and Rubdy 2011) is not created early in their careers, teachers may not be sensitive to them. In any case, there is a stark contrast between teacher research reports and textbooks in the field of language teaching, on the one hand, and volumes such as, for example, Noffke and Somekh (2009) where there is a strong focus on the broader social and political implications of educational action research. Such observations may extend to much teacher research outside language teaching too, given some criticisms of work done by teachers in the UK (e.g. Elliott and Sarland 1995).

Structure of the book

In this chapter we have highlighted a range of issues which are central to teacher research in language teaching, both from the perspectives of the practitioners who engage in such research as well as of those who are responsible for facilitating such engagement. In the chapters that follow, language teaching professionals from around the world describe and analyse specific examples of their experiences in either doing or supporting teacher research and, through their accounts, provide situated illustrations that shed light on how some of the dilemmas and challenges we have signalled here are realized in practice.

Chapters 2 to 5 focus on the perspectives of teachers as they experience what becoming and being a teacher researcher involve. In Chapter 2, Talandis and Stout provide a reflective account of a year-long collaborative action research project undertaken at a private university in Japan. The authors discuss issues of research design, implementation, and reporting, and address some of the difficulties inherent in simultaneously fulfilling teacher and researcher roles. In Chapter 3, Yucel and Bos report on an action research project conducted in an English language centre attached to a university in Australia. The authors examine how engaging in action research represented stepping out of their comfort zones in different ways, from doing research for the first time to exploring an unconventional method for pronunciation teaching, and how this contributed to the development of relevant teaching and research skills. In Chapter 4, Xie reflects on her experience as a novice teacher of English learning to do research independently in an examination-oriented tertiary education context in China. She explores both the factors that facilitated her learning as well as the challenges she faced and her responses to them. In Chapter 5, Charbonneau-Gowdy describes her experience as a teacher researching her own video-based on-line classroom setting. She details the challenges encountered and the lessons learnt and considers the deeper principles underpinning her approach to action research.

Chapters 6 to 13 focus on the perspectives of those who facilitate teacher research, highlighting the practices and principles they employ in supporting teachers. Chapter 6 acts as a bridge between the two sets of perspectives since Vinogradov adopts the dual role of teacher researcher and facilitator. The author describes a collaborative inquiry conducted in the context of adult ESL education in the United States. and illustrates the impact on professional development of stepping outside one's teaching context, or 'border crossing', to engage in teacher research. In Chapter 7, Mugford reflects on the process of supporting beginning 'non-native' EFL student-teacher researchers in Mexico in defining and evaluating modes of research which were locally relevant. He outlines the challenges and obstacles which these student-teacher researchers met as they engaged in research. In Chapter 8, Borg examines a teacher research initiative that he facilitated with a group of university and college teachers of English in Pakistan. The analysis utilizes a five-point framework through which several factors which contributed to the success of the initiative are highlighted. Al-Maskari, in Chapter 9, reports on a research in-service training course offered to teachers of English in Oman. She discusses the features of the course's structure and processes which contributed to the teachers' positive evaluation of it and the major obstacles to research engagement in the Omani context. This is followed in Chapter 10 by Çelik and Dikilitaş' account of an action research programme with Turkish EFL teachers. The authors outline the procedures followed in the programme, the challenges experienced by the teachers, and the perceived impact of action research on their practices. In Chapter 11, Rajuan provides a description of an action research course in the final year of a pre-service teacher education course in Israel. She details the framework used to support student-teacher learning and discusses how it enables student teachers to integrate theories and principles of education with their classroom practices. Bowden, in Chapter 12, illustrates three case-study examples of teacher research drawn from a large-scale teacher development project in Malaysia. The author presents reflections from mentors on processes, outcomes, challenges and, in particular, on the factors which facilitated teacher research. Finally, in Chapter 13, Lehtonen, Pitkänen, and Vaattovaara discuss the approaches adopted by a university language centre in Finland to encourage teacher engagement with and in research. The authors outline the role which support, collaboration and in-house activities played in promoting research engagement in a traditionally teaching-oriented university department.

Each of the core chapters includes a list of 'engagement priorities' which suggest issues for continuing inquiry in relation to teacher research. The book concludes with a chapter which pulls together key commonalities in the collection, highlighting issues that are central to the continuing development of teacher research in language teaching and identifying some new lines of thinking.

Notes

1. As this chapter went to press two further publications of relevance appeared – Burns & Edwards (2014) and Smith et al. (2014).

References

Allwright, D. (1997). Quality and sustainability in teacher-research. *TESOL Quarterly*, 31(2): 368–370.
Allwright, D. and Hanks, J. (2009). *The Developing Language Learner: An Introduction to Exploratory Practice*. Basingstoke: Palgrave Macmillan.
Anderson, G. L. and Herr, K. (1999). The new paradigm wars: Is there room for rigorous practitioner knowledge in schools and universities? *Educational Researcher*, 28(5): 12–21, 40.
Bartlett, S. and Burton, D. (2003). The professional development of teachers through practitioner research: A discussion using significant cases of best practice research rcholarships. *Teacher Development*, 7(1): 107–120.

Bell, M., Cordingley, P., Isham, C. and Davis, R. (2010). Report of professional practitioner use of research review: practitioner engagement in and/or with research. Coventry: CUREE, GTCE, LSIS & NTRP.

Borg, S. (2010a). Doing good quality research. *JACET Journal, 50*: 9–13.

Borg, S. (2010b). Language teacher research engagement. *Language Teaching, 43*(4): 391–429.

Borg, S. (2013). *Teacher Research in Language Teaching: A Critical Analysis*. Cambridge: Cambridge University Press.

Borg, S. (2015). Researching language teacher education. In B. Paltridge and A. Phakiti (eds). *The Continuum Companion to Research Methods in Applied Linguistics* (Second Edition). London: Bloomsbury.

Borko, H., Jacobs, J. and Koellner, K. (2010). Contemporary approaches to teacher professional development. In P. Peterson, E. Baker and B. McGaw (eds). *International Encyclopedia of Education* (Third Edition). Oxford: Elsevier, pp. 548–556.

Burns, A. (2010). *Doing Action Research in English Language Teaching. A Guide for Practitioners*. New York: Routledge.

Burns, A. (2014). Professional learning in Australian ELICOS: An action research orientation. *English Australia Journal, 29*(2): 3–20.

Burns, A., & Edwards, E. (2014). Introducing innovation through action research in an Australian national programme: Experiences and insights. In D. Hayes (ed.). *Innovations in the Continuing Professional Development of English Language Teachers*. London: British Council, pp. 65–86.

Campbell, A., McNamara, O. and Gilroy, P. (2004). *Practitioner Research and Professional Development in Education*. London: Paul Chapman.

Cochran-Smith, M. and Lytle, S. L. (1999). The teacher research movement: A decade later. *Educational Researcher, 28*(7): 15–25.

Darling-Hammond, L. and Lieberman, A. (2012). *Teacher Education around the World: Changing Policies and Practices*. London: Routledge.

Denscombe, M. (2002). *Ground Rules for Good Research*. Buckingham: Open University Press.

Dörnyei, Z. (2007). *Research Methods in Applied Linguistics*. Oxford: Oxford University Press.

Eisenhart, M. A. and Howe, K. R. (1992). Validity in educational research. In M. D. LeCompte, W. L. Millroy and J. Preissle (eds). *The Handbook of Qualitative Research in Education*. San Diego, CA: Academic Press, pp. 643–680.

Elliott, J. and Sarland, C. (1995). A study of 'teachers as researchers' in the context of award-bearing courses and research degrees. *British Educational Research Journal, 21*(3): 371–385.

Ellis, R. (2010). Second language acquisition, teacher education and language pedagogy. *Language Teaching, 43*(2): 182–201.

Freeman, D. (1998). *Doing Teacher Research*. Boston: Heinle and Heinle.

Hammersley, M. (2004). Action research: A contradiction in terms? *Oxford Review of Education, 30*(2): 165–181.

Huberman, M. (1996). Focus on research moving mainstream: Taking a closer look at teacher research. *Language Arts, 73*(2): 124–140.

Kalmbach Phillips, D. and Carr, K. (2010). *Becoming a Teacher through Action Research* (Second Edition). London: Routledge.

Kemmis, S. and McTaggart, R. (2008). Participatory action research: Communicative action and public sphere. In N. K. Denzin and Y. S. Lincoln (eds). *Strategies of Qualitative Inquiry* (Third Edition.). Los Angeles: Sage Publications, pp. 271–330.

Levin, M. (2008). The praxis of educating action researchers. In P. Reason and H. Bradbury (eds). *The Sage Handbook of Action Research: Participative Inquiry and Practice* (Second Edition). London: Sage Publications, pp. 669–681.

McKay, S. L. and Rubdy, R. (2011). The social and sociolinguistic contexts of language learning and teaching. In M. H. Long and C. J. Doughty (eds). *The Handbook of Language Teaching*. Oxford: Wiley-Blackwell, pp. 9–25.

McKernan, J. (1996). *Curriculum Action Research: A Handbook of Methods and Resources for the Reflective Practitioner* (Second Edition). London: Kogan Page.

McNiff, J. and Whitehead, J. (2009). Demonstrating quality in educational research for social accountability. In S. E. Noffke and B. Somekh (eds). *The Sage Handbook of Educational Action Research*. Thousand Oaks, CA: Sage Publications, pp. 313–323.

Mead, G. (2008). Muddling through: Facing the challenges of managing a large-scale action research project. In P. Reason and H. Bradbury (eds), *The Sage Handbook of Action Research: Participative Inquiry and Practice* (Second Edition). London: Sage Publications, pp. 629–642.

Muijs, D., Kyriakides, L., van der Werf, G., Creemers, B., Timperley, H. and Earl, L. (2014). State of the art – teacher effectiveness and professional learning. *School Effectiveness and School Improvement, 25*(2): 231–256.

Noffke, S. E. (2002). Action research: Towards the next generation. In C. Day, J. Elliott, B. Somekh and R. Winter (eds). *Theory and Practice in Action Research*. Oxford: Symposium Books, pp. 13–26.

Noffke, S. E. and Somekh, B. (eds). (2009). *The Sage Handbook of Educational Action Research*. Thousand Oaks, CA: Sage Publications.

Olson, M. W. (1990). The teacher as researcher: A historical perspective. In M. W. Olson (ed.), *Opening the Door to Classroom Research*. Newark, Delaware: International Reading Association, pp. 1–20.

Oolbekkink-Marchand, H. W., van der Steen, J. and Nijveldt, M. (2014). A study of the quality of practitioner research in secondary education: Impact on teacher and school development. *Educational Action Research, 22*(1): 122–139.

Opfer, V. D. and Pedder, D. (2011). Conceptualizing teacher professional learning. *Review of Educational Research, 81*(3): 376–407.

Pawson, R., Boaz, A., Grayson, L., Long, A. and Barnes, C. (2003). Types and quality of knowledge in social care. Available from: http://www.scie.org.uk/publications/knowledgereviews/kr03.pdf [Accessed 29/07/14.]

Richards, K. (2003). *Qualitative Inquiry in TESOL*. Basingstoke: Palgrave.

Sharp, C. (2007). *Making Research Make a Difference. Teacher Research: A Small-Scale Study to Look at Impact*. Chelmsford: Flare.

Smith, R., Connelly, T. and Rebolledo, P. (2014). Teacher-research as continuing professional development: A project with Chilean secondary school teachers. In D. Hayes (ed.). *Innovations in the Continuing Professional Development of English Language Teachers*. London: British Council, pp. 111–129.

Taylor, S., Rudolph, J. W. and Foldy, E. G. (2008). Teaching reflective practice in the action science/action inquiry tradition: Key stages, concepts and practices. In P. Reason and H. Bradbury (eds). *The Sage Handbook of Action Research: Participative Inquiry and Practice* (Second Edition). London: Sage Publications, pp. 656–668.

Timperley, H. (2011). *Realizing the Power of Professional Learning*. Milton Keynes: Open University Press.

2
Towards New Understandings: Reflections on an Action Research Project with Japanese University Students

Gerald Talandis Jr. and Michael Stout

Introduction

For teachers interested in developing their practice, there is no shortage of information about the basic practical details of designing and carrying out classroom-based research (see, e.g. Burns 2010; Freeman 1998; Wallace 1998). In addition, there are some public reports of teachers reflecting on their own research. Gregson (2004) reports on one experience and provides a fine example of the benefits and challenges of doing teacher research. Her investigation showed that implementing classroom change can lead to unexpected findings, where even failures can lead to important insights. She argues that teacher research is messy and the outcomes take time to unfold. This was certainly true of our investigation as well. Unfortunately, there are not enough reports such as Gregson's in the literature. Given the difficulties inherent in simultaneously fulfilling teacher and researcher roles, reflective accounts can give aspiring teacher researchers opportunities to vicariously learn from peers, make plain the challenges involved, and consider what becoming a teacher researcher actually involves. This is what our chapter aims to do.

Our research experience was a year-long collaborative action research project undertaken at a private university in Japan with 160 first-year students taking required English speaking classes. While teacher research is a general term that describes many types of methodologies, action research is a specific type of teacher research. It is 'very problem-focused in its approach and very practical in its intended outcomes' (Wallace 1998: 15). In addition, as Check and Shutt (2011) point out, it is also a recursive process involving a spiral of adaptable steps that include reflection and investigation of a particular issue. It is then followed by the development, implementation, and progressive refinement of an action plan. Action research is often described as cyclical, but for us, to paraphrase Burns (1999), the reality of action research was not so much a cycle or sequence of cycles, but rather a series of interrelated experiences involving exploring, identifying, planning, collecting data, analysing/reflecting, hypothesizing/speculating, intervening, observing, reporting, writing, and presenting. Action research is often collaborative in nature, as was our project. At every stage we worked together to plan and reflect on lessons, collect data, and finally report on our findings. Our primary aim was to help learners with low proficiency, motivation, and self-esteem speak English with more fluency, accuracy, and pragmatic complexity. Our intervention consisted of shifting from a transactional syllabus designed to prepare students for travel abroad to an interactional one focused on helping them express themselves via personalizable daily life topics and on raising their pragmatic awareness of culturally appropriate conversation.

This chapter is divided into three sections: Context, Insights, and Implications. In the Context section, we will provide a brief overview of English teaching and learning in Japan and a description of the research context at the university where we conducted our action research project. A description of our research process will include highlights of a key unexpected outcome. The Insights section will track the evolution of our project throughout the year and highlight how our understandings grew through the design, implementation, and reporting stages. Finally, in the Implications section, we will discuss how our experience fits into the wider context of English language teacher research and offer up some recommendations based on what we learnt.

Context

EFL education in Japan

While a thorough treatment of EFL education in Japan is beyond the scope of this chapter, a brief overview of several structural, cultural, and social aspects will help orient readers unfamiliar with the Japanese context and serve as an instructive backdrop to our research experience. Historically in Japan, development of English grammar, reading, and writing skills has been prioritized over building oral communication ability (Lee 2010). Pragmatic codes for conducting culturally appropriate communication are rarely emphasized (Harumi 2001), so students get little, if any, specific training in how to conduct conversations. Learners have been and continue to be taught almost exclusively via a grammar-based approach that emphasizes accuracy (Hammond 2007). One result of this emphasis on correctness has been students who feel inhibited and unwilling to take chances with using their knowledge to communicate (Lightbown and Spada 1999). English classrooms are commonly filled with anxious students (Andrade and Williams 2009) that are reticent and orally inactive (King 2013). In addition, the role silence plays in the classroom further compounds this situation. Harumi (2011) notes that, when unsure of their answers or if their ideas differ from classmates, Japanese learners tend towards silence. In addition, silence is often perceived as a positive quality within Japanese classrooms (Hammond 2007). Students wishing to fulfil the culturally defined role of 'good student' are thus inclined to stay quiet and pay studious attention to the teacher.

Another issue impacting instruction of English oral communication is the common Japanese notion of what a university education is really about (Bailey 2004). According to Norris (2004), in contrast to the strict, highly regulated education during the secondary school years where values such as endurance, obedience, and maximum effort are taught, the university years are mainly about giving Japanese youths a chance to mature. It is thus more of a transition period, where students finally have the opportunity to develop their personalities, social skills, and individual responsibility before entering the workforce. As Bailey (2004: 241) describes, a common view is that the university years are a time for students to 'explore their world both socially and culturally, make friends, join clubs, find hobbies, discover politics and art, and discuss issues long into the night with comrades, even if it means missing a morning lecture or two.'

As Norris (2004) notes, there are competing culturally-connected interests to those of foreign teachers and what they expect from students in foreign language classrooms. Dealing effectively with Japanese university students requires awareness and understanding of students' academic, cultural, and social backgrounds (Kemp 1995). According to Kelly (1993), there are three main types of students that populate Japanese university campuses: club, school, and society types. Briefly, club types are heavily involved in their interests and sporting activities, which take up most of their time. They tend to prioritize the learning gained from these experiences (such as a deeper understanding of group dynamics and how to handle responsibility) over what can be learnt in the classroom. School types are more or less the opposite; they are students who work hardest in class and get the highest grades because they value the learning that takes place there. Then there are society types, the students who concentrate their energies on part-time jobs, relationships, travel, and having a good time. In general, society types were not high achievers in high school and tend to have lower self-esteem. The classroom milieu does not suit them well, and they are probably the most difficult type of student for teachers to motivate.

Our research context

At the four-year private university where we taught, English was a required subject for all first-year students. At the beginning of the school year in April, each new student took a placement test that streamlined them into a class at one of three levels: intermediate (roughly equivalent to level A2 on the Common European Framework of Reference), low-intermediate (about A1), and false-beginner (pre-A1). Each class then attended four English lessons per week, one for each skill, each usually taught by a different teacher. With occasional exceptions, the L1 English speaker staff taught speaking, with Japanese lecturers covering the reading, writing, and listening classes. Within each lesson, we were required to cover specific pages of a textbook. After completing these pages, we were free to fill the remaining time as we liked, usually by finding ways to provide more practice on topics covered in the main text. Topics included various transactions such as ordering food in a restaurant, giving directions, buying a train ticket, or shopping for clothes. This created a de facto functional-notional syllabus, one geared towards preparing students for using practical English during travel abroad. However, based on our own perception of the students, most were clearly society types who had priorities other than learning English for situations which they would most likely never encounter. We found ourselves constantly struggling with misbehaving students who did not prepare for class, made little effort during lessons, and were frequently late or absent. Given the demotivation we felt with this situation, it was clear that a new approach was needed.

Our research process

For the 2011–2012 school year, we decided to embark on a year-long collaborative action research project with high hopes of helping our reluctant learners improve their speaking skills. Recognizing that many of our 160 students seemed to prioritize socializing over classroom learning helped us clarify our intervention. If most of them were indeed society types, then perhaps they would find English more relevant if it became a medium through which they could develop their social skills and connections. To better match our syllabus with our students' interests, we came up with the following plan: instead of using our extra time to elaborate on the transactional elements in our required text, we would use it to emphasize interactional English based on personalizable topics, direct instruction of pragmatic and conversational routines, and frequent assessment of speaking ability. We also decided to increase L1 support by providing Japanese translations of all activity directions, vocabulary items, and assessment criteria in hopes of supporting lower-level learners. Finally, to encourage use of English outside of class and promote autonomous learning, students were required to fill out a stamp card by completing various tasks, such as studying vocabulary online, holding conversations with L1 English speaker teachers, and reading graded readers (Taylor et al. 2012).

We sought to assess our intervention from various perspectives because with action research it can be impractical to control for every variable at all times (Wallace 1993). Collecting data from three sources helped to increase the reliability and validity of our research findings. Teacher-written class notes made either during or soon after class helped track our ongoing reflections regarding the progress and effectiveness of the intervention. Questionnaires were administered to gather student self-perceptions of their progress and effort, reactions to course content, and expectations for future success in speaking English. Finally, speaking tests were recorded throughout the year to provide an actual record of student performance. After the spring semester, we reflected on our progress and made a series of adjustments intended to improve results in the fall. Upon completion of our research, we presented our preliminary findings at a large teacher conference in Japan and then submitted a written report for publication to an international journal.

An unexpected outcome

At the end of the first cycle, student questionnaire data indicated a clear trend: as expected, student reactions to the intervention and perceptions of progress were largely positive overall. However, when broken down by class level, a clear trend emerged: the higher the student level, the more positive their reaction. There were clear problems with the pre-A1 students, as only about a third of them felt their English had improved during the spring. Class note entries chronicled numerous instances of continued frustration in dealing with these students. At times it felt like nothing we did worked, as we kept seeing the same sorts of problems: chronic lateness, lack of preparation, minimal effort, and various disruptive behaviours. The changes we made to our intervention prior to the fall semester were largely made with this group in mind. Nevertheless, from our point of view, nothing significantly changed in the fall for most of these students. The new activities we tried were hit and miss, and there was no real feeling on our part that this group had gained anything from our efforts. From the pre-A1 students' perspective, however, after listening to recordings made at the beginning and end of the year, a strong majority (82%) indicated that their English had indeed improved significantly by the end of the course.

In an effort to better understand the perception gap between us and the pre-A1 students, we decided to closely examine their speaking test recordings. By looking carefully at instances of four specific criteria (grammar mistakes, length of 1-second+ pauses, L1 utterances, and use of taught pragmatic expressions), we were able to move beyond our emotional reactions to student progress. Despite not being able to control for variables such as speaking partner or conversation topic, this data-centric comparative analysis pointed towards areas of concrete improvement, however subtle. While their vocabulary was still relatively basic, there was a noticeable lack of grammar errors. Those that occurred were minor and not a cause for confusion. Pauses were still prevalent and noticeable, but they were shorter in length. Most encouragingly, numerous reactive phrases conveyed a sense of interaction and friendliness, indicating that many students had picked up on the pragmatic need for showing interest in their interlocutor. While we took these results with a sense of caution, it did give us an indication that clear progress could be made by even our lowest level students, and that perhaps our intervention did indeed help even amidst some extreme learning conditions. It is possible that in the act of listening to themselves at the beginning and end of the year, the pre-A1 students also noticed their improvement, which led in turn to their positive responses in the final questionnaire.

Insights

In this section we reflect on what we learnt throughout the process of our study. We discuss our research design, the implementation of our intervention, and how insights developed through the reporting of our findings.

Creating our research design

As the school year approached, our attention was focused mainly on getting ready for classes and doing our best with the intervention. We viewed language as a skill that could be learnt and were convinced that, if we just presented a well-constructed, easy-to-follow course which was relevant to our students' interests, they would make an effort and their English would improve. We did a bit of background reading to help us brainstorm ideas for our research design and focus. Marchand (2006), an action research project conducted with Japanese high school students on use of metacognitive expressions for repairing and extending conversations, led us to seriously consider a focus on communicative competence. However, knowing that most of our students were society types with little interest in English, we were also concerned with issues of motivation and classroom behaviour. Given the urgency of preparations, we did not fully think through or commit to any of these ideas.

Based on previous experiences with action research, we knew that multiple sources of data were needed to improve the reliability and validity of results. We chose questionnaires for gauging student reactions to the intervention, but had little idea as to what type to use or what sorts of questions to ask. We decided our lesson notes would track our own reflections, but we did not consider any sort of guiding protocols for how these notes would be written other than to get them done as soon as possible after class. To get a record of actual student performance, each of us chose to record our pre-A1 class in hopes of capturing improvements over time with our least proficient students. We considered recording other classes but feared doing so would prove logistically unmanageable. Without a clear research question to guide our inquiry, however, we were not fully able to conceptualize the connection between these data sets. Our thinking at the time was basically 'let's do a good job with this intervention, collect as much data as we can, and then figure out the details later.'

Upon reflection, we could have improved our research design in several ways. First, a more thorough literature review might have helped us find our focus sooner. While such a review may not be necessary before beginning an action research project (Burns 2010), in our case doing one would have increased our understanding of how to design all aspects of our project and perhaps boosted our confidence in what we were doing. For example, we could have begun designing the questionnaires much sooner instead of waiting until just before administering them. We also could have followed Farrell's (2003) suggestion to negotiate data collection guidelines. Without any structure, our class notes were filled with too many descriptions of classroom management issues. A more analytical focus on our students' developing communicative competence would have been more useful. Finally, while we loosely followed a plan for collecting the test recording data, we overestimated the time required to manage this task and could have collected even more data without any undue inconvenience or disruption to our classes.

Implementing our intervention

As we got deep into the spring semester, it became clear that our lack of focus had affected the implementation of our project in various ways. There was, for example, insufficient systematicity and synchronization with regard to how we collected data. In the midst of a busy semester, without any structure to guide us, we ended up acting on our own abilities and preferences. For class notes, one teacher enjoyed the reflection-in-action process during quiet moments in class and was able to record fresh and immediate observations throughout the year. For the other teacher, however, note-taking was a chore that could only be maintained during the first few months of our project. With the recording data, one teacher stuck to the original plan of recording a single class, feeling that collecting more recordings was unnecessary extra work. In contrast, the other teacher decided to record speaking tests from all his classes, regardless of level. He did so for personal reasons, to increase the reliability of his grades by having the option of reviewing speaking tests after the fact. Eventually, the stockpiling of extra data we thought we would not need at the time proved instrumental in helping us make sense of our research experience.

After the spring semester ended, we reflected upon the first cycle of research and saw that the intervention was not going so well with our pre-A1 students. Many were not preparing as well as they should, nor were they reflecting on their learning. Improving these classes became a priority. The ideas we came up with marked a shift in the focus of our research. While at the beginning of the year we leaned towards a focus on communicative competence, decisions about our project were now largely being driven by pedagogical concerns.

Examples of this shift can be seen in the online questionnaires we decided to administer after speaking tests in the fall semester. The nature of the questions clearly exemplifies our shift in priority. No longer were we much concerned with how well students were reacting to the intervention or to how their communicative competence was developing. Instead, questions not only were designed to help us understand why many students were not preparing for the tests, but were a clear attempt on our part to change their behaviour:

> In order to prepare for this test, I (check all that apply)
> - reviewed the handouts outside of class
> - practised with a classmate
> - practised with an L1 English speaker
> - studied vocabulary using Quizlet
> - studied vocabulary using English Central

Ideally, in this case, we were hoping our students would select all of these options. Similarly constructed questions covering topics such as attendance, preparation, and performance of required elements were intentionally written to impart ideas for more effective test preparation. Unfortunately, we encountered some technical difficulties with these online questionnaires. Since we did not trial the online survey application before using it in class, we made some mistakes that caused us to lose valuable data. We learnt the hard way that utilizing unfamiliar software while in the midst of a study was a bad idea. Looking back, we should have done a practice survey before using it for real.

By the end of the school year, when we administered the final questionnaire, our research focus had shifted back to communicative competence. Technical challenges with the online survey application were overcome, and we were able to gather useful data on student perceptions of progress. Questions focused on key elements of the course, such as usage of pragmatic expressions, taught vocabulary, and grammatical accuracy. We discovered that this form of questionnaire design had intrinsic value as a pedagogic exercise, as students were able to self-evaluate their own progress. This was important to us, as it pointed towards a possible resolution to the conflict we felt between simultaneously being a teacher and a researcher. In the end, when push came to shove, we agreed with Bauman (1996) that our teacher research philosophy placed teaching and students above all else. Since the realities of our teaching affected our decisions about classroom inquiry, we needed to find a way to adequately accomplish both at the same time.

Reporting our findings

The process of reporting our research findings actually began in the summer, mid-way through the intervention, between the spring and fall semesters. Our first task was processing the spring questionnaire data. Given its length and paper-based nature, this took longer than expected. A lack of familiarity with spreadsheet software slowed us down, as did general rustiness with procedures of basic statistical analysis. When finally completed, we had a large database of numbers, but what did it tell us? Long discussions about what our focus should be ensued. Should we look only at communicative competence? Student reactions to the various activities? Or should we examine how the intervention changed student behaviour? Each survey question seemed to pull us in a different direction. Our relative newness to classroom-based research had resulted in a lack of clarity that now left us feeling rather lost and frustrated. By the end of the summer, we did not feel much closer to the single clear narrative we were looking for.

As the school year ended the following spring, we were inundated with even more data and still no closer to understanding what our central focus would be. Again, the amount of work in front of us felt overwhelming. What was the point, after all, of spending hours on processing data without a clear plan for how it would be used? At that point life took over, and our attention was pulled in various other directions. The project entered a fallow period where nothing much happened.

A fortuitous break occurred a few months later, when a presentation proposal we had submitted to a large teacher conference in Japan was accepted. We were given a 25-minute slot to present our research findings. At first this seemed like a formidable task – how could we condense a year-long study into such a short time? Through accepting this challenge, however, we encountered an interesting and ultimately liberating paradox, that less truly was more. By having so little time, we were forced to look hard at our data and ask ourselves what really mattered. What were the most essential elements of our project? In the months leading up to the conference, we worked hard via regular Skype meetings at identifying only the key elements and putting aside the rest. Through this editing process we were finally able to settle on a single clear narrative. Imagining what our audience expected and wanted to hear helped us decide on what to cut and what to keep. The presentation was well received, and the positive feedback we got encouraged us to continue with the project.

Now that the conference was over, we had the basic blueprint for our research report. After identifying an international journal to submit to, we studied its submission guidelines carefully and worked steadily over the following months to tailor our manuscript to them. During this time we sought help from a more experienced researcher at a university outside Japan. She read an early draft of our paper and provided insightful feedback that helped us see how we could further clarify our research focus.

Again, as we found with the conference preparations, making the commitment to present our findings publicly helped unlock new levels of energy and motivation that produced deeper insights, such as the reminder that challenging teaching situations can often be the richest source of learning. This was especially true in our case, where the students we struggled with most ended up providing the most revealing data. Before the pre-A1 students actually heard themselves speak at the beginning and end of the year, it was difficult for them and us to see any improvement in their English. One wonders whether some of the poor behaviour and lack of effort that continued in the second semester might have improved if students had been given an opportunity to listen to before-and-after recordings of themselves at the end of the first semester. Furthermore, our attitudes towards the students might have improved if we had listened to and analysed recordings of their speaking earlier.

Another clear insight we had was that students and teachers need to see progress. However, simply listening to recordings alone might not be enough. Analysing the pre-A1 recording data showed us that a structured analysis of student output based on course objectives had potential as a tool for identifying specific areas of improvement irrespective of ability level. Realizing this possibility helped reduce some of the demotivation we felt in teaching our lowest level students and led to an idea for further research: if such a structured analysis could help us see progress, might it not benefit students as well? Using a simple bilingual checklist with which to comparatively analyse their performance over time could enable students to take ownership of their progress through self-evaluation. Furthermore, playing before-and-after recordings made by previous classes could be used to motivate students to make greater efforts to achieve a similar level of improvement as their near-peers. As Brown and Inouye (1978: 901) state, 'observing a model of comparable ability achieve success would create success expectations in observers and thus enhance their task motivation.'

Looking back, it is clear that the process of publicly sharing our research findings was instrumental in building our current understandings of the project. Reporting what we experienced elicited more questions which resulted in more answers which brought up further questions that led to deeper and deeper insights. Articulation was the key that unlocked deeper clarity and comprehension. In the end, it was not a process of figuring out everything first and then sharing; we had to discover our story through its telling. It was a simultaneous process.

Implications

While our action research project was undertaken in the unique context of our classrooms at a Japanese university, we believe the story of how this research was conducted can be relevant to the global English language teaching community. Going through the process of designing, implementing, and reporting on classroom research helped us understand that our concept of research is constantly evolving. We found that traditional definitions of research are often impractical when it comes to examining one's classroom, agreeing with Freeman (1998) that in order to make research a central part of teaching, we must redefine it. At times we felt tension between our roles as teachers and researchers, but as we came to understand, this is not necessarily a bad thing. Conflict in teacher research has beneficial aspects. It requires us to examine our purpose, question our motives, and refine our methods as the research unfolds (Bauman 1996).

Based on our experience, we would like to make several recommendations to novice teacher researchers. While some of these suggestions may appear obvious, they are also easy to forget for busy teachers. In hindsight, had we followed these simple steps, we would have saved a lot of time and effort.

Accept that action research is messy

First, it is helpful to accept the fact that action research is messy. As Burns (2010) notes, the nature of action research is such that the focus becomes clearer only when the research has begun; that it emerges as you proceed is quite common. In fact, an action research design that is too rigidly structured may prevent teacher researchers from gaining new insights – the kind that only come from making mistakes.

Do a literature review beforehand

Doing a literature review before beginning your research is a good way to begin and facilitate the focus-discovery process. As Nunan (1992) notes, identifying what others have said or discovered will help you acquire the necessary background information you will need to construct your research questions. In addition, you can gain ideas for research design, data collection, and data analysis (Burns 2010).

There's no such thing as collecting too much data

Equally important is the idea that you can never have too much data. Collecting extra data beyond what you think you might need will give you options when it comes time to report on your findings. It will also serve as a backup in case some of it becomes lost or corrupted. In our experience, some of our decisions regarding data collection were based on a perception that too much time would be needed. In the end, however, we realized that collecting more data would have saved us time. As Wallace (1998) says, one way of solving the problem of time is to involve your learners in the data collection process. Doing so will provide students with further learning opportunities while simultaneously providing data for your research. Our final year-end questionnaire was an example of this, where our students took part in a pedagogically sound exercise that also gave us the data we needed.

Clarify guidelines for data collection

In addition, negotiating guidelines for data collection and general project implementation can improve the overall data quality, ensure that its collection is tied to the focus of the project, and make processing more manageable. Whether you conduct research alone or collaboratively, being clear on how you intend to collect and utilize your data will make the research process smoother. As Farrell (2003: 18) asserts, 'a minimum set of guidelines needs to be negotiated to insure a deeper, critical level of reflection beyond mere descriptions of teaching.'

Report your findings

Next, commit to some way of making your research findings public. You could present at a conference, submit a paper for publication, or even just share your findings with colleagues at work. Doing so will help you identify and articulate a clear narrative which will, in turn, lead towards greater understandings. It will also increase the quality of your reflection on practice (Altrichter et al. 1993).

Get outside feedback

Finally, during the process of writing up your report or preparing your presentation, get another pair of eyes to look over what you have done. An outsider's point of view will help you identify unforeseen gaps or shortcomings. After all, things clear to you may not be clear to others. Also, getting input and advice from a more experienced published teacher researcher will increase your chances of getting your research published.

Final thoughts: on becoming a teacher researcher

> You may be able to get by, by putting little thought into your work, but if you want to be the best teacher that you possibly can, then there is in reality no alternative to reflective teaching.
>
> Grant and Zeichner (1984: 12)

Prior to submitting the final draft of our research report for publication, we took a moment to look over the paper one last time. As we looked for typos and made sure everything was just right, the contrast between the clean, organized, well-reasoned prose and our knowledge of what it took to reach this point felt rather shocking. Knowing what we had gone through over the past two years made it hard to believe this moment had actually arrived. Prior to this action research project, we had read books on how to conduct classroom-based research and dabbled in a few projects with other colleagues, but it was not until we finally embarked on an actual undertaking of our own that we realized how much more there was to learn.

Much of what we learnt now seems rather obvious in retrospect, such as the total non-linear messy nature of classroom-based research and the need to find one's research focus early on in the process. There were practical matters as well, such as the need to collect as much data as possible in a structured, coordinated manner and to trial online surveys before actually administering them. We were also reminded of the power of collaboration for enhancing the reflective nature of classroom inquiry. Through working together in a spirit of humility and honesty, we were able to more effectively challenge our beliefs in a constructive manner.

More than anything, however, was a reaffirmation of the importance of publicly sharing research findings. This was a critical step for us, one that opened the way towards current levels of understanding. Looking back, we were quite lucky. Were it not for that conference presentation opportunity, we may not have ever been able to submit our report for publication. Much of the learning we took from this project has come about through the telling of our story. In other words, it has been the process, not the final product, that has made the biggest difference. Bauman (1996: 35) puts it well:

> By struggling with ways to integrate inquiry into their work, teacher-researchers come to know themselves better as teachers and persons, learn to understand their students and families in ways heretofore unknown, increase their professional esteem and credibility, share their learnings with colleagues locally and beyond, and, most importantly, help their students develop intellectually, socially, and emotionally. And that is what a dynamic, reflective, action-oriented research pedagogy is all about anyway.

In conclusion, over the course of the year-long study and then the following year of working to share our findings, we learnt a lot about what it really means to be a teacher researcher. In this chapter we have aimed to provide an honest account of our research experience so that prospective teacher researchers can vicariously learn from our mistakes and consider how best to navigate through the difficulties inherent in simultaneously fulfilling teacher and researcher roles. We hope that by reading our account, teachers can clarify for themselves what it means to be a teacher who also does research.

Engagement priorities

1. According to Freeman (1998: 5), 'Teacher-research is the story of two nouns joined by a hyphen; being a teacher-researcher means working at

that hyphen.' Working at the hyphen brings together the two activities to emphasize their common focus. However, it also reshapes both activities.

How do you think teaching and research are reshaped by bringing them together in teacher research?

2. From Bauman (1996): some teachers argue that there are inherent conflicts between teacher and researcher: conflict of purpose and conflict of conduct. On the one hand, as a researcher, one is required to stand back and observe and let instructional experiences unfold without intervention of prompting and guiding students. On the other hand, in the teacher role, one is expected to assist students in their knowing and learning, even though that might alter the phenomenon being investigated. Other teachers have a different view of research and the role of teacher researcher. Rather than viewing them as competitive, they view them as compatible.

Which side of this debate do you favour and why?

3. In our action research project, we collected data from recordings that were also used for assessment purposes, took class notes that were also used for planning purposes, and administered a questionnaire that not only gathered student reactions to our intervention but also enabled them to self-evaluate their progress. What kind of data could you collect from your classes that simultaneously serves your research and pedagogical aims?
4. Burns (2010) mentions several ways that teachers conducting action research can narrow their focus, such as discussing ideas with colleagues or writing them out in a journal. What are some other possible ways of finding and narrowing your research focus?

References

Altrichter, H., Posch, P., and Somekh, B. (1993). *Teachers Investigate Their Work*. London: Routledge.
Andrade, M. and Williams, K. (2009). Foreign language learning anxiety in Japanese EFL classes: Physical, emotional, expressive and verbal reactions. *Sophia Junior College Faculty Journal*, 29: 1–24.
Bailey, A. A. (2004). Reforming English language teaching in Japanese universities: Creating a language community. *Ritsumeikan Journal of Educational Research*, 4: 94–112.
Bauman, J. F. (1996). Conflict or compatibility in classroom inquiry? One teacher's struggle to balance teaching and research. *Educational Researcher*, 25(7): 29–36.
Brown, I. and Inouye, D. K. (1978). Learned helpless through modeling: The role of perceived similarity in competence. *Journal of Personality and Social Psychology*, 36: 900–908.

Burns, A. (1999). *Collaborative Action Research for English Language Teachers*. Cambridge: Cambridge University Press.
Burns, A. (2010). *Doing Action Research in English Language Teaching: A Guide for Practitioners*. New York: Routledge.
Check, J. W. and Shutt, R. K. (2011). *Research Methods in Education*. Thousand Oaks, CA: Sage.
Farrell, T. (2003). Reflective teaching: The principles and practices. *English Teaching Forum*, 41(4): 14–21.
Freeman, D. (1998). *Doing Teacher-Research: From Inquiry to Understanding*. Boston: Heinle & Heinle.
Grant, C. A. and Zeichner, K. M. (1984). On becoming a reflective teacher. In C. A. Grant (ed.), *Preparing for Reflective Teaching*. Newton, MA: Allyn and Bacon, pp. 1–19.
Gregson, R. (2004). Teacher research: The benefits and pitfalls. *Australian Association for Research in Education*. Available at: http://www.aare.edu.au/04pap/gre04828.pdf [Accessed 16/11/13].
Hammond, C. (2007). Culturally responsive teaching in the Japanese classroom: A comparative analysis of cultural teaching and learning styles in Japan and the United States. *Journal of the Faculty of Economics, Kyoto Gakuin University*, 17: 41–50.
Harumi, S. (2001). The use of silence by Japanese EFL learners. In M. Swanson and D. McMurray (eds). *JALT 2001 Conference Proceedings*, 27–34.
Harumi, S. (2011). Classroom silence: Voices from Japanese EFL learners. *English Language Teaching Journal*, 65(3): 260–269.
Kelly, C. (1993). The hidden role of the university. In P. Wadden (ed.), *A Handbook for Teaching English at Japanese Colleges and Universities*. Oxford: Oxford University Press, pp. 172–192.
Kemp, J. B. (1995). Culture clash and teacher awareness. *The Language Teacher*, 19(8): 8–10.
King, J. (2013). Silence in the second language classrooms of Japanese universities. *Applied Linguistics*, 34(3): 325–343.
Lee, J. J. (2010). The uniqueness of EFL teachers: Perceptions of Japanese learners. *TESOL Journal*, 1(1): 23–48.
Lightbown, P. M. and Spada, N. (1999). *How Languages Are Learned*. Oxford: Oxford University Press.
Marchand, T. (2006). The immediate method: Immediate results? In K. Bradford-Watts, C. Ikeguchi, and M. Swanson (eds), *JALT 2005 Conference Proceedings*, 491–504.
Norris, R. W. (2004). Some thoughts on classroom management problems faced by foreign teachers at Japanese universities. *Bulletin of Fukuoka International University*, [Online Journal] 12. Available at: http://www2.gol.com/users/norris/articles/classman2.html. [Accessed: 16/11/13].
Nunan, D. (1992). *Research Methods in Language Learning*. Cambridge: Cambridge University Press.
Taylor, C., Beck, D. Hardy, D., Omura, K., Stout, M., and Talandis, G. (2012). Encouraging students to engage in learning outside the classroom. In K. Irie and A. Stewart (eds), *Learning Learning: Special issue. Proceedings of the JALT Learner Development SIG Realising Autonomy Conference*, 19(2): 31–45.
Wallace, M. J. (1998). *Action Research for Language Teachers*. Cambridge: Cambridge University Press.

3
Action Research as a Means of Stepping Out of the Teaching Comfort Zone

Megan Yucel and Vicki Bos

Introduction

Teachers' professional knowledge landscapes (Clandinin and Connelly 1996) are shaped by such factors as their own educational experiences and the contexts in which they teach, and in the case of English language teachers, these contexts may be incredibly diverse. As practitioners, teachers gain extensive practical knowledge through their teaching, but they may not always be given the time to do professional reading or attend conferences, let alone conduct research. Action research provides teachers with a means of gaining knowledge through reflective practice. It enables them to become researchers by exploring a classroom-based issue or problem in some depth. This exploration can challenge them to make changes and may lead to improvements in practice.

In this chapter, we will report on an action-research project conducted in an English language centre attached to an Australian university. The project was undertaken as part of English Australia's Action Research in ELICOS Programme, which aims to improve professional practice by equipping teachers with the skills required to explore and meet the challenges that they face in the Australian TESOL context. The chapter will describe how we, as participants in the programme, honed these skills through our exploration of the effects of teacher intervention on pronunciation outcomes. The participants in our project had been identified from diagnostic testing as being at risk of failing their speaking assessment due to poor pronunciation. Our intervention featured intensive pronunciation workshops and participation in a student choir. Our involvement in the programme prompted each of us to step out of our comfort zones in different ways, from doing research for the first time to exploring an unconventional method for pronunciation improvement. It is hoped that our experience could inspire other teachers in a variety of contexts to take on action research.

Teacher research

In a recent article, Penny Ur (2012) argues that there is a definite gap between the source of knowledge about teaching for teachers and for researchers. Teachers, as practitioners, reflect on their own experience or turn to colleagues for advice and ideas, whereas researchers go to the literature. She advocates more time for professional reading, conference attendance, and research to be built into teachers' job description as a way of bridging this gap. Action research is undoubtedly another way of narrowing the theory–practice divide, as it provides an alternative identity for teachers, teachers as researchers.

Action research is part of a broader movement which emphasizes reflective practice. Reflecting on practice, 'the idea that professionals carefully evaluate their own work, seeking to understand their motives and rationales as well as their practice, and then try to improve their work' (Bailey 2012: 23), is one way to develop as a professional. As we will explore later, reflective practice was a crucial part of our professional development in this action-research process. Bailey (2012) identifies some key advantages and disadvantages of reflective teaching. The disadvantages include its time-consuming nature, and the possibility of uncovering unwelcome information about one's teaching. The advantages include increased awareness, more sharing and collegiality, an improvement in teaching skills, less burnout, and more connections between theory and practice. We experienced these highs and lows in our own action-research journey, as will be seen in excerpts from our teacher reflection journals.

Pronunciation teaching

As reflective practitioners, we identified a need to address the issue of pronunciation intelligibility with a particular student cohort, which prompted us to explore the action research avenue in the context of pronunciation teaching. Dedicated pronunciation teaching has fallen in and out of favour throughout the history of English language learning and teaching. Kelly (1969) first used the metaphor of pronunciation as the Cinderella of language teaching, indicating its neglected status. However, in the years since Kelly's observation was made, the pendulum has swung back in favour of pronunciation teaching with the work of researchers such as Morley (1994) and pronunciation is again receiving the attention it deserves. Indeed, there is now a growing body of empirical evidence to support dedicated pronunciation teaching (e.g., Saito and Lyster 2012). Having identified our students' difficulties with communicative intelligibility, we wanted to experiment with the latest thinking in our classes.

Pronunciation teaching may have different purposes. Historically, accent reduction classes, which endeavour to make the learner sound more native-like, have long been marketed to L2 speakers of English, just as L1 speakers of English in countries such as Australia were once offered elocution lessons in order to sound more British. Researchers such as Jenkins (2007), with her English as a Lingua Franca (ELF), have done much to change the paradigm in the TESOL world and emphasis has now shifted to the importance of pronunciation for intelligibility and comprehensibility. For communication to take place, there is a fundamental need for one's pronunciation to be clear and intelligible. This was the desire of our student cohort; they wished to be understood.

Teachers may only have the opportunity to deal with pronunciation issues as part of an integrated programme, as most ESL courses lack a dedicated class for teaching pronunciation. Our course, for example, had a speaking component, but this focused on many different aspects of speaking, including presentation skills, thus allowing little actual time for pronunciation work. Therefore, a further consideration for language teachers is which aspect of pronunciation should be focused on in the limited time that is available, in order to achieve the best results. We wanted to collect data and make principled, informed decisions on the most effective way to go about this. Traditionally, EFL pronunciation textbooks such as *Ship or Sheep* (Baker 2006) focused on segmentals, such as minimal pairs. However, intelligibility is enhanced if suprasegmentals are also covered. As Brazil (1994) observed, the relationship between segmentals and supra segmentals seems to be symbiotic, with the work that learners do on one aspect helping their performance in the other. The Jenkins (2007) ELF framework reflects this stance by dictating a focus on consonants and consonant clusters, vowel length, and sentence stress in order to maximize intelligibility. Our own backgrounds in drama and singing prompted us also to consider vocal quality, including breath control, resonance, and how the voice is projected.

Music and language

Drawing on this shared interest in vocal training, we decided to explore the connection between language and music in the brain. In the growing field of research into this area, there are evident implications for language teaching. 'Singing appears to have a positive effect on language development, speech, and comprehension', writes Trollinger (2010: 21). Studies done on the use of music in the language classroom seem to indicate that this is indeed an observable phenomenon (Schwantes 2009), the neurological basis of which is most likely the overlapping areas of the brain in which language and music reception and production occur, and the way in which music triggers the reward/emotion systems in the brain (Blood and Zatorre 2001). This area of investigation is not necessarily without controversy, though. It has been argued by some researchers that music and language production are in fact autonomous systems (Peretz et al. 2004). It must be said that such studies are often done on dementia patients or aphasia sufferers, and focus a great deal on linguistic fluency in terms of *semantics* rather than *phonology*. When the physical process of language production in *phonological* terms is focused on, it is worth noting that in fact 'phonological generativity is seen as the major point of cognitive parallelism between (music and language)' (Brown et al. 2006: 11). Taking into account the positive effect of music on both the affective and phonological aspects of language production, it seemed to us, as researchers, that the use of singing could therefore assist students who have difficulties with their pronunciation. Consequently, this is what we hoped to put into practice by including the choral component in our course.

Context

The setting for this teacher research study was the Institute of Continuing & TESOL Education (ICTE-UQ), an English language centre at the University of Queensland (UQ). The researchers were both teachers on the English for Specific Purposes: Bridging English Programme (ESP: BEP), an English language pathway for direct entry to UQ undergraduate and postgraduate programmes for eligible students. ICTE-UQ offers this ten-week programme twice a year. It aims to teach not only the language knowledge and skills that students require, but also the academic culture and conventions of the institution that they are entering. Students undertake studies in English for Academic Purposes, with course components such as Academic Writing, Grammar for Academic English, and Communication in Academic Contexts. Students must achieve a pass in all four skills (speaking, listening, reading, and writing) in order to pass the ESP: BEP course and go on to their university studies. It is, therefore, a high-stakes course for students, as passing or failing has an impact on their future study and career prospects.

Our research focused on students who displayed a jagged profile in the results that they achieved in diagnostic testing conducted early in the course, with high scores in reading and writing, but poor performance in listening and speaking, particularly in pronunciation. Of a total student cohort on the ESP: BEP programme of approximately 200 students, 30 students were identified as being at risk of failing their final speaking test because of deficiencies in their pronunciation. We invited these students to participate in a special programme to assist them in improving their pronunciation. In terms of nationality, most students were Vietnamese, with the second largest group being Chinese speakers, and the remaining participants from Korea and Indonesia. Of the 30 students who began the programme, a highly-motivated core group of 24 students with varied pronunciation needs, in terms of the type and severity of the problems they were working to address, attended regularly for the entire seven weeks.

The issue we sought to address was essentially one of intelligibility of oral communication. As an innovative solution to improving our students' pronunciation, we decided to integrate intensive pronunciation workshops with choral singing. Drawing on the literature, we designed the speech production element of the course around recorded production tasks which ranged from imitative (listen and repeat) at the beginning of the course, through to rehearsed speech (a short prepared talk), and finally extemporaneous speech (a conversation) (Morley 1994). Music therapy theories also played a role in our programme development. As Schwantes (2009) points out, there is considerable evidence that the use of music in language therapy is an effective means of facilitating language production. This is due in part to the vocal mechanism (place and manner of articulation), in part to the connection between the musical ear and an ear for language, and in part to the affective factors associated with the use and production of music. With this in mind, we required our participants to join the ICTE Chorus, a student choir which is a long-standing and much-loved extra-curricular activity at ICTE, led by one of the researchers.

Insights

Through the process of this action research, we became acutely aware of our own teacher identities, particularly with regard to the meaning of the 'comfort zone' and how to develop professionally by moving out of what are seen as traditional teacher roles. In this section, we will begin by identifying how the role of the teacher is often conceptualized in language schools, and the ways in which our own participation in action research has interacted with this situational- and self-imposed comfort zone. We will then outline the key processes we underwent in moving from these prescribed roles to becoming teacher researchers, looking at the areas of reflection, collaboration, and empowerment.

Role of the teacher

The role of the teacher is most often characterized – by managers, students, and teachers themselves – as that of classroom practitioner. Many teachers find complete job satisfaction in this role and excel at it, but for those who wish to do research, there may be obstacles along the way. Managers (both administrative and academic) in language schools do not necessarily see teacher research as a necessary or worthwhile activity. If teacher research does go ahead, there can be a lack of logistical support and/or reluctance to implement recommended course, timetable or classroom practice changes when suggested by teachers as a result of their inquiry. For teachers wishing to learn from others who have conducted research, or to hear about current theories, sponsorship of teacher conference attendance may be limited or even non-existent (Ur 2012).

The effect of such workplace attitudes on teachers, whether expressed verbally or understood tacitly, is manifold. Teachers can internalize this view and feel unwilling or unable to undertake teaching research projects. There can be increased instances of teachers feeling undervalued, jaded, and lacking in professional development opportunities or career pathways. Finally, curricula, courses, and timetables are less likely to have teacher input in research-poor environments such as this, thus creating a gap between the designers of courses and the educators who deliver them (Lankshear and Knobel 2004).

All of this can lead to a form of identity crisis for teachers who would like to continue to develop professionally through keeping up to date with the latest language learning theories, and to implement recent pedagogical recommendations. In the field of teacher cognition, it is claimed that 'teachers are active, thinking decision-makers who make instructional choices by drawing on complex, practically-oriented, personalized, and context-sensitive networks of knowledge, thoughts, and beliefs' (Borg 2003: 81). What does this mean in practical terms, though, if these networks stagnate and are not given the opportunity to develop? When research is marginalized, how does a teacher take a step forward? Further, how can a teacher who does not benefit from evidence-based research – either conducted in their own classroom, or through reading and/or conference attendance – be expected to deliver best practice to their students?

In such circumstances, specialized research programmes can provide well-structured networks of assistance for teachers willing and able to participate in research projects. We, as the researchers of this project, were offered such an opportunity through the English Australia/Cambridge ESOL (now *Cambridge English*) Action Research programme. This programme is offered annually to ESL teachers around Australia who have identified problems or issues for their learners and would like to experiment with changes in methodology. The focus of the programme, and others like it, is evidence-based innovation (Burns 2010). Teachers are encouraged to investigate an issue methodically and approach solutions to their learners' difficulties in an innovative way, so as to determine whether there could be a more efficient and effective way of facilitating learning in their particular classroom or course environments. Despite the fact that the amount of professional time required to participate in this research project was considerable, the researchers felt that it would be a rewarding method of developing professionally. We were fortunate enough to be encouraged and supported by our employer, ICTE-UQ, to participate.

The questions raised above regarding teacher identity came to us gradually, as a result of going through the process of conducting our own action research.

It is significant, in retrospect, that until we were offered the opportunity to participate in this project, we, as teachers, had not really been aware of the idea of action research.

Stepping out of the comfort zone

Before examining the processes we, as teachers, went through in this research project, we might have argued that the 'comfort zone' concept was a misnomer. The term connotes a sphere of ease and security, which in turn implies a certain reluctance to progress or evolve in terms of classroom practice. In reality, teachers are constantly altering and improving classroom practice in response to feedback from students, due to their own experiences of the effectiveness of lessons or methods, and on the advice of their colleagues, among other things. This data collection and critical self-examination are an essential part of professional reflective teaching (Bailey 2012). However, it has subsequently become evident to us just how ensconced we had become in the so-called 'comfort zone', and just how far we really did need to step out of it in order to become teacher researchers.

Reflection

One way that teachers can reflect on their practice is through Narrative Inquiry. Using this qualitative research method, teachers can take a narrative approach to exploring their teaching context. In this sense, they can position themselves, their colleagues, and their students as characters in various settings such as the classroom or the staffroom at a particular time, what Clandinin and Connelly (2000) describe as a three-dimensional narrative space. With this in mind, we decided to keep journals throughout the course of the research project, which was immediately an experience out of the ordinary, as neither of us had voluntarily kept a journal before. We were aware of the value of journal-keeping, through our own independent reading of the literature surrounding reflective teaching practice. There are numerous examples of language learning diaries, such as Schmidt's study of his own attempts to learn Portuguese (Schmidt and Frota 1986), while works such as *Diary of a Language Teacher* (Appel 1995) show the power of teacher journals in bringing the classroom out into the public view. However, we had both considered it too time-consuming a process to go through for everyday teaching practice. Additionally, there is the aspect of self-consciousness that is inherent in reflective journal writing, which was something neither of us felt particularly comfortable or confident with. In fact, it was through the process of journal writing that it was revealed exactly how our involvement in the project did indeed take us out of what may be termed our comfort zone, as may be seen through the following extracts.

For Megan, a self-confessed 'non-singer', there was a critical moment during the project where she was forced to step out of the shadows and pick up the conductor's baton during Vicki's absence.

Megan
Week 3 Chorus

> I knew that Vicki was going to be away today but couldn't remember if we'd discussed what would happen in her absence. This afternoon in class I casually sidled up to a student who I knew was a regular and said 'So did Vicki say anything to you about Chorus today?' 'Oh yes,' she said brightly, 'Vicki said you'd be taking Chorus today.' 'Oh, good, I'm glad she arranged that with you,' I said through gritted teeth. Spent the next five minutes thinking 'Yikes, what am I going to do with them for an hour? I can't sing' and then the five minutes after that calming myself down and working out what I was actually going to do. So, I went down to the classroom, hoping that only a few people would turn up because our dear leader was away, and saw what seemed like hundreds of people streaming into the room. There was no escape.

This transformative experience was twofold. Not only did Megan as a researcher have to conduct a choir rehearsal without having experienced anything like it before, but then by using the journal as a recording tool for research purposes, she was able to describe exactly the thought processes she went through in making this professional development transition, and the steps she took in going about it.

Megan

> OK, so here's what I did. Relaxation and vocal warm-up? Check. Not that different from a drama one, so we did that and it was good ... Proposed that we practised the songs we knew so that Vicki would be impressed by our hard work next week. Asked the regulars to get into their groups for The Lion Sleeps Tonight and told the newcomers to join a group of their choosing. And away we went, after a quick run-through of all the parts ... I'd had a burst of inspiration before the rehearsal that I'd show them the songs on Youtube as I couldn't provide a model the way Vicki does, so we sat down and watched the song and sang along ... We then did the same thing for Hallelujah. What a magical song. Before I knew it, it was time to wind up, so I thanked them all for coming and promised that Vicki would be back to whip them all into shape next week! Hallelujah – I survived!!

This overcoming of discomfort with regard to singing publicly was a crucial part of Megan's research narrative, and one which demonstrates the dynamic, ever-changing nature of teacher identity.

Vicki's journal narrative similarly reflected the challenging yet stimulating and rewarding nature of conducting this action research project.

Vicki
Week 6 Workshop

> This action research caper is proving more exhausting and frustrating than we had anticipated. Today's workshop saw us flustered by technology failures and found us improvising to cover. I rather think we did extremely well with our improvisation, and were able to cover the materials, which we had anticipated would be self-access, in a plenary fashion. We also spent a considerable amount of time circulating amongst the students assisting with individual difficulties.

Journal reflections like this have value for a number of reasons. Through the process of reflection and self-evaluation, Vicki was able to examine her expectations, difficulties, and successes, while providing a written account of her own adaptability and that of her colleague. Furthermore, this entry in particular serves to show the amount of physical and emotional energy invested by teachers in action research. By expressing herself honestly, and stating that conducting action research is 'exhausting and frustrating', while documenting how the difficulties were overcome, Vicki was able to retain a sense of control over the demanding process. Finally, this entry stands as a record of issues arising from the research project, should further investigation or parallel research be conducted on this problem in the future.

The journals were crucial in revealing to us the ways in which we had conceptualized our students, our classrooms and our own roles in conducting research. This narrative of the research project, as told through the eyes of the teacher, has since informed our writing of articles and the presentation of professional development workshops to colleagues and to the broader TESOL community in Australia following the completion of the research itself.

Collaboration

The extent to which teachers operate as solitary practitioners varies widely according to the circumstances of their employment. However, in many schools and institutions there can be a highly individualistic culture among teachers, where ideas, resources, and methodologies are jealously guarded. Even in working environments where collaboration is encouraged, there can still be an element of detachment from colleagues in everyday teaching life. When considering the notion of the comfort zone, it is important to note that collaboration can make teachers feel professionally vulnerable. Sharing ideas, methods, and materials leaves teachers open to possible criticism by colleagues. Before conducting this particular action research project, both of us had considered ourselves people who worked more efficiently in an independent capacity. We had both had a great deal of experience of doing group projects at tertiary level, or working on committees in the workplace, and these were not situations in which we felt that our best work was being done.

Action research in general can change this tendency towards solo operation dramatically, through providing teachers with the goal of finding innovative and effective solutions to a particular issue. Kemmis and McTaggart (1988) characterize action research as a collaborative process carried out by those with a shared concern, and suggest that action research is a form of collective reflective enquiry.

The shared goal in our particular action research circumstance was that of improving students' pronunciation to the extent that they would be able to pass speaking exams in order to go to university. We had previously felt, as individual teachers, to be reasonably effective at modelling and drilling pronunciation in our own classes, but with the stakes so high, it was necessary to work closely together, without ego-driven sensitivity, to ensure that the methodologies used in the project were absolutely consistent. The success or otherwise of the programme, and the future careers of the students involved, depended on it.

Right from the beginning of the project, we found ourselves unconsciously shifting into first-person plural pronouns when talking about what we were doing. This is illustrated vividly in our reflection journals, which were supposed to be individual reflections on the progress of the programme, but often contained references to each other and to the duality of leadership that was occurring.

Megan

> We set a homework task this week which was a little different from the previous week's task. Students this week will be recording themselves giving a talk, so that we can give them feedback on more spontaneous speech (as opposed to reading a shopping list last week) and also on prosodic features, such as stress and intonation [emphasis added].

Vicki

> Our first choir rehearsal went very well in terms of attendance and enthusiasm from the group. The students seemed relaxed and happy ... although somewhat out-of-breath by the end of it all [emphasis added].

It was the first time that either of us had worked so closely with a colleague, and the naturalness with which it became 'our' project, 'our' class, and 'our' choir was not something that really struck us until after we had been through the entire process. At the time, although we had divided up our workload to some extent, we were so completely involved in working as a team to achieve our goals that to consider ourselves as separate teaching identities would have been counter-productive.

We also realized very early on that, in order for this project to be a worthwhile and successful experience, we would have to be prepared to listen to each other and accept suggestions without offence or ego. The spontaneous generation of ideas would have been severely hampered by extensive criticism, so we were also careful to ensure that we were striking a balance between making appropriate suggestions and letting each other's thoughts flow. Again, this instinctive desire to keep the collaborative relationship positive and fruitful was not something we considered consciously at the time, but it was reflected in the way we conceptualized our teaching relationship in our journals, as can be seen in the following extracts.

Megan

> Something I wanted to note was how helpful it is to talk to Vicki about our project. We always come up with ideas, solutions, and interesting comments about the project.

Vicki

> Megan was a great help in lending confidence to the group, and just having another teacher there was quite a valuable experience! Having an extra set of eyes and ears in the room was useful, too, and I'll be curious to see what Megan noticed in terms of what aspects of pronunciation we need to work on with this group.

Conducting action research stimulated a change in our notions of collaborative work, through providing us with a shared goal, and creating a need for positive movement in the same direction. Additionally, the process of meeting throughout the project with other Cambridge ESOL/English Australia action researchers and receiving feedback, suggestions, and encouragement cemented our own working relationship, and allowed us to experience points of view from language teachers across the country, as the following journal extract shows.

Megan

> The feedback from everybody at the action research workshop was interesting. It hit me afterwards that it was the first time we were presenting our project to outsiders. We knew what we were talking about when we discussed our project, but we realised that we had to make all aspects of it clear to an audience without 'insider' knowledge.

This prompted a shift in our solitary practitioner identities towards a greater awareness of the collective teaching experience within our institute, and in the wider profession as a whole.

Empowerment

The sheer amount of professional – and often personal – time required to conduct research, or even read up on the latest literature, means that it is often not a viable option for many teachers, despite the abundance of theoretical knowledge being published by researchers in the Second Language Acquisition field (Nassaji 2012; Ur 2012). This dichotomy was one of the issues we, as the researchers in this project, encountered in our own professional experience. As teachers, we were constantly doing professional reading and taking professional development courses, thereby enhancing our knowledge about teaching. However, there was something of a question mark over whether or not this was having a powerful effect on our teaching skills and repertoire.

As Johnson (2012) argues, by bridging the research–practice divide, action research can facilitate teacher empowerment. Knowledge of action research theory can help teachers to better understand classroom events, while, at the same time, the data collected can be used to 'understand or inform theories and research related to best practice' (Johnson 2012: 20). Having a systematic, strategic action research plan provides teacher researchers with the necessary structure, focus, and methodological tools.

Through conducting our research project, we found this indeed to be the case. As teacher researchers, we were empowered in two significant ways. The first of these was the nature of conducting research itself. The systematic setting of goals, reflecting on procedures, and recording of data gave us a degree of control over and insight into our methodological practices.

This sense of empowerment is illustrated in the contents of our reflection journals, in passages such as the following, where Megan comments on the way in which the students responded to the feedback she had worked so hard to give them.

Megan
Week 2 Workshop

> We gave back the feedback on the pronunciation test that the students had done in week 1. I thought that this task was a good way for students to really zero in on the sounds that were causing them problems. Later in the class, when we had split into two groups, they really wanted help in forming those sounds, so I was able to give them individual attention to assist them. Lots of demonstrations and talking about what the different speech organs were doing.

In this entry, Megan records class procedures and strategies implemented to address individual students' difficulties. The implication is that the students responded well to her feedback, and made every effort to improve based on her recommendations and individual attention. Thus, the research process provided Megan with an opportunity to assess the efficacy of her approach, not simply at the time, but for posterity through her journal reflection.

The research process also ensured a certain vigilance on our part, focusing on the rigour of our methods in order to achieve the desired outcome of spoken comprehensibility in our students. This entry from Vicki demonstrates the degree to which action researchers need to methodically devote attention to every detail of their project, keeping their goals clearly in mind.

Vicki
Week 5 Chorus

> I did notice today that we're losing a bit of the linguistic clarity we worked on in the last couple of weeks. Next week, I'd like to really go over all the words to all the songs again, just to make sure the students are saying them clearly and intelligibly.

A further way in which action research empowers teachers is through the results of the research, which, in this case, provided us with evidence for our claims about the efficacy of our teaching methods. The results of our research were extremely positive, in that the participants involved all passed their final speaking assessment, and felt as if they were more confident, effective oral communicators in English, having had the experience of being part of a choir.

One of the key ideas which appeared repeatedly in participants' comments was the importance of the pronunciation intervention programme in terms of awareness-raising. It is widely recognized that awareness-raising is an important tool in teaching pronunciation (Burgess and Spencer 2000). We, as teacher researchers, felt a high level of professional satisfaction that our methods, such as considerable amounts of teacher feedback, intensive work on the different places of articulation, focus on effective breathing techniques and vocal warm-ups, had produced an awareness in these students of the physical nature of language production.

Action research can also empower teachers in ways which had not been anticipated. The most surprising insight for us, as researchers, was the effect of confidence, relaxation, and enjoyment on the students' communicative abilities and motivation. Affective factors contribute significantly to willingness and ability to take risks in both speech production (mechanical sounds) and speech performance (prosodic features). This in turn benefited the students' oral proficiency assessment results, as those students who still received relatively low grades for pronunciation at the end of the course found their fluency results had improved dramatically. Before embarking on this research project, we had not really expected affective factors to play such a large role in addressing the issue of pronunciation.

Indeed, although we had hypothesized that choral singing in particular would have an effect on pronunciation, we had not previously obtained any quantifiable evidence of our own to demonstrate that this was so. As can be seen from this throwaway comment about a placebo effect in Vicki's reflection journal from early on in the process, we were not sure what our results would be and were as yet unaware of the crucial role that this enthusiasm and positivity would play.

Vicki

> First rehearsal today for our participants. Great turnout, and most were highly enthusiastic and positive about the potential effects of the choir on their pronunciation. (If nothing else, it might work as a placebo!)

Throughout the project, both of us continued to record observations about the affective aspect of the programme, perhaps instinctively understanding the significant way in which it would contribute to the overall improvement in the students' communicative effectiveness.

Vicki
Week 5

> What a high!
> Ahem, that is to say, I really enjoyed today's rehearsal, and I feel as if we're starting to sound better and better musically. We had about 50 people at choir today, and it sounded glorious. I was worried that the PAP participants

would not enjoy being 'forced' to attend choir, but not only have they embraced it wholeheartedly, they've brought along their friends and classmates to join in. Talk about positive affirmation!

Megan
Week 8

> I'm feeling optimistic about the positive effect PAP has had on our students. I can really see an affective change – they're really positive and keen to work on their pronunciation. I just hope that translates to an improvement in their marks in the Week 10 test.

Vicki
Week 8

> I don't think I am imagining it – I really think the students' pronunciation is starting to improve dramatically. The imitative and rehearsed speech aspects which were covered today are starting to sound more natural, and sounds which some students previously had trouble distinguishing between in earlier recordings are starting to become more distinct.

As the improvement of the students became noticeable, the effect on us, as teacher researchers, was to provide an affirmation of our choice of intervention techniques, such as we had not previously experienced in our everyday teaching lives. The rigorous following of research procedures ensured that we were able to check our intuitive feelings about how the research was progressing with the facts presented by the data. Discovering that our experiences and the direction of our own research were supported by the evidence lent us a confidence as teacher researchers that we had not necessarily previously felt when we were hypothesizing about the pronunciation problem-solution paradigm in the first place.

Implications

There are a number of lessons which emerged from going through the process of conducting this action research project. These can be categorized broadly into two groups: 1) finding solutions to teaching/learning issues and 2) re-inventing teacher identity through stepping out of the comfort zone.

Teachers wishing to find innovative and practical solutions to problems, difficulties, or questions arising in the classroom can benefit greatly from pursuing an action research project. Our action research enabled us to tackle a teaching problem that we had identified in a systematic way, providing us, our teaching colleagues, and our directors with a rich data resource and evidence upon which to base approaches to course design. As we learnt through our participation in action research, the support of English language teaching bodies, schools, managers, and colleagues is crucial to the successful and overall rewarding completion of what is a time-consuming and challenging task. This support needs to take the form of logistical arrangements such as rooms and facilities, pedagogical considerations such as being timetabled onto the course which is being researched, and finally emotional and psychological encouragement. When these conditions are met, action research provides teachers with a method for taking control of issues in the classroom, and necessitates their pro-active engagement with the teaching/learning paradigm.

Indeed, the programme acted as a kind of catalyst in our institution, prompting managers and teachers alike to consider and investigate ways in which action research could be conducted in a number of fields school-wide. A number of our teaching colleagues were stimulated by observing the potential for growth, development, and improvement of practices which characterized our action research journey. Similarly, managers have become aware, through our project and those that have followed, of both the desire of teachers to become teacher researchers, and the need for logistical management support of those that do. Formal and informal action research projects have thus become an integral part of the teaching culture in our institution, resulting in the continuing development of networks of knowledge and experience, the fostering of dynamic, evolving teacher identities among our colleagues, and the finding of innovative solutions to student problems.

It must be said, however, that the most important part of our participation in this research project was the way in which we, as teacher researchers, developed our professional identities through this process, and the implication this has for teachers who may be thinking of taking their first tentative steps out of their own comfort zone. This reflective, collaborative and empowering journey imbued us, as teacher researchers, with a great sense of accomplishment, and altered the ways in which we perceive our roles and practices both in and out of the classroom. The material rewards of conducting research, however, have been only half the story. Conducting action research is a transformative experience. Investigating systematically, working closely with colleagues, reflecting on practice, coping with setbacks, achieving results, and ultimately finding yourself as a teacher researcher attempting things you had never attempted as a teacher are all key elements of your evolving teacher identity through this process.

Conclusion

Overall, as a way of developing professionally, this action research project proved incredibly effective. For the researchers, the benefits included an increased awareness of best practice in terms of pronunciation instruction, insights into personal teaching preferences, and directions for future research. These positive experiences have only strengthened our view of the need to broaden the perception of teachers as both classroom practitioners and researchers in workplaces. However, one of the most positive results of teachers continuing to engage in this sort of action research is the effecting of this slow progressive change.

Engagement priorities

1. Consider the source(s) of your professional knowledge base as an English language teacher, such as professional reading, your own educational experiences, observation of colleagues, and so on. Is there a gap between research and practice in the field of TESOL, as Ur (2012) argues? If so, how can it best be bridged?
2. The chapter reports on the beneficial effects of integrating singing into pronunciation-focused lessons. Is there an aspect of pronunciation learning and teaching that you would like to investigate in your own teaching context?
3. As reflective professionals, teachers may sometimes be encouraged to keep a journal of their experiences. Consider what kind of information could be recorded in such a teacher journal. How could it be used to benefit both teachers and students?
4. In describing the transition that the researchers experienced in moving from a traditional teacher role to a teacher researcher role, the chapter mentions three key processes that emerged from the journal data: reflection, collaboration, and empowerment. Looking back on your teaching career, can you think of instances where you had the opportunity to be reflective or collaborative, or you felt empowered as a teacher?

This chapter reports on research supported by Cambridge English Language Assessment, University of Cambridge.

References

Appel, J. (1995). *Diary of a Language Teacher.* Oxford: Heinemann.
Bailey, K. M. (2012). Reflective pedagogy. In A. Burns and J. C. Richards (eds), *Pedagogy and Practice in Second Language Teaching* (pp. 23–29). Cambridge: Cambridge University Press.
Baker, A. (2006). *Ship or Sheep?: An Intermediate Pronunciation Course.* Cambridge: Cambridge University Press.
Blood, A. J. and Zatorre, R. J. (2001). Intensely pleasurable responses to music correlate with activity in brain regions implicated in reward and emotion. *Proceedings of the National Academy of Sciences of the United States of America, 98*(20), 11818–11823.
Borg, S. (2003). Teacher cognition in language teaching: A review of research on what language teachers think, know, believe, and do. *Language Teaching, 36*, 81–109.
Brazil, D. (1994). *Pronunciation for Advanced Learners of English.* Cambridge: Cambridge University Press.

Brown, S., Martinez, M. J., and Parsons, L. M. (2006). Music and language side by side in the brain: A PET study of the generation of melodies and sentences. *European Journal of Neuroscience, 23,* 2791–2803.

Burgess, J. and Spencer, S. (2000, June). Phonology and pronunciation in integrated language teaching and teacher education. *System, 28*(2), 191–215.

Burns, A. (2010). *Doing Action Research in English Language Teaching: A Guide for Practitioners.* New York: Routledge.

Clandinin, D. J. and Connelly, F. M. (1996). Teachers' professional knowledge landscapes. *Educational Researcher, 25* (3), 2–14.

Clandinin, D. J. and Connelly, F. M. (2000). *Narrative Inquiry: Experience and Story in Qualitative Research.* San Francisco: Jossey-Bass.

Jenkins, J. (2007). *English as a Lingua Franca: Attitudes and Identity.* Oxford: Oxford University Press.

Johnson, A.P. (2012) *A Short Guide to Action Research.* New Jersey: Pearson Education.

Kelly, L. (1969). *Twenty-five Centuries of Language Teaching.* Rowley, MA: Newbury House.

Kemmis, S. and McTaggart, R. (1988). *The Action Research Planner.* Melbourne: Deakin University.

Lankshear, C. and Knobel, M. (2004). *Teacher Research: From Design to Implementation.* Maidenhead: Open University Press.

Morley, J. (1994). *Pronunciation Pedagogy and Theory: New Views, New Directions.* (ed. J. Morley) Alexandria, VA: TESOL.

Nassaji, H. (2012). The relationship between SLA research and language pedagogy: Teachers' perspectives. *Language Teaching Research, 16*(3), 337–365.

Peretz, I., Gagnon, L., Herbert, S., and Macoir, J. (2004). Singing in the brain: Insights from cognitive neuropsychology. *Music Perception: An Interdisciplinary Journal, 21*(3), 373–390.

Saito, K. and Lyster, R. (2012). Effects of form-focused instruction and corrective feedback on L2 pronunciation development of/ɹ/by Japanese learners of English. *Language Learning, 62*(2), 595–633.

Schmidt, R. W. and Frota, S. N. (1986). Developing basic conversational ability in second language: A case study of an adult learner of Portuguese. In R. R. Day (ed.), *Talking to Learn: Conversation in Second Language Acquisition* (pp. 237–326). Rowley, MA: Newbury House.

Schwantes, M. (2009). The use of music therapy with children who speak English as a second language: An exploratory study. *Music Therapy Perspectives, 27*(2), 80–87.

Trollinger, V. L. (2010). The brain in singing and language. *General Music Today, 23*(2), 20–23.

Ur, P. (2012, October 17). How useful is TESOL academic research? *Guardian Weekly.*

4
Learning to Do Teacher Research Independently: Challenges and Solutions

Jianmei Xie

Introduction

Much has been written about the importance of teacher research (e.g. Cochran-Smith and Lytle 1999), how to do it (e.g. Burns 2010) and teachers' engagement in it (e.g. Borg 2013). There are, however, relatively fewer accounts of teachers learning to do teacher research; those which are available investigate the learning process from the researcher's (outsider's) perspective (e.g. Kiely 2006) or take place in the context of collaborative or large-scale funded projects (e.g. Liu and He 2008; Zheng and Hu 2004). Teachers may very often, though, learn about teacher research independently and it is this process that I will examine in this chapter, drawing on my own learning experience. The perspective I adopt is a reflective one (Schön 1983) – I retrace and reconstruct my experience of becoming a teacher researcher in order to identify and to understand the processes I went through. In doing so, I examine both factors that facilitated my learning as well as the challenges I faced and the ways I responded to them.

Context

I was trained to be a teacher of English and was then employed to teach English at a university in China. The faculty I was based in offered courses to adult learners (e.g. working professionals, undergraduates and student teachers). The purpose of these courses was to enable learners to attain diplomas, certificates, and degrees via examinations at regional, provincial and national levels. Teaching in the faculty, therefore, was exam-oriented.

My experience of learning to be a teacher researcher occurred in the first two years (2002–2004) of my professional career. The process of inquiry was prompted by a teaching crisis: my communicative teaching methodology and style were criticized by some students for not being sufficiently examination-oriented (exams were accuracy-focused) and were perceived by a few colleagues as unconventional. This crisis motivated me to discover what the 'right' teaching methodology might be. I decided to explore my colleagues' language teaching methodologies: as I discuss below, I wrote a research proposal, reviewed some literature, chose research methods, constructed questionnaire and interview questions, looked for and interviewed the participants, and analysed all the data independently. In retrospect, I can see that my orientation to research was somewhat academic in that I was studying others rather than focusing on myself and using fairly conventional frameworks to do so. However, the inquiry I conducted *was* motivated by a desire to better understand how my own teaching related to that of my colleagues and to consider alternative ways of working with my students. In that sense I feel I was engaged in a process of teacher research.

The results of my investigation showed that my colleagues (those I worked with in the past rather than now) were very interested in my topic and held a large number of ideas and opinions about different methods of language teaching. Most of them believed that communicative language teaching was a more appropriate method than the grammar-translation approach for teaching English. However, teachers revealed that it was the latter method that they often had to follow in their teaching because of the pressure of examinations. I found this quite interesting: my methodology was seen to be effective but not, my colleagues felt, appropriate to the context we worked in. They did not disagree with my approach to teaching English but their beliefs about L2 teaching were subservient to the more highly rated need of helping students pass the form-focused examinations.

One feature of the above research experience which was significant for me was that I went through it largely independently; I was referred to colleagues who were believed to have a good knowledge of research and received some guidance at the 'proposal' stage, but overall I had to make sense of the process alone. I do not know how common this is in L2 teaching contexts around the world, but there is increasing evidence (including elsewhere in this volume) that teacher learning is facilitated through opportunities for dialogue, sharing, interaction, and support. Such opportunities were seriously lacking for me during this initial foray into research into the teaching of English.

Insights

Having summarized my story, I will now examine aspects of it in more detail with specific attention to factors that facilitated and hindered my progress as a novice teacher researcher.

Responding to a crisis

When my value as a teacher was questioned by students and colleagues, I suddenly became vulnerable. Some students refused to attend lessons and others showed clear signs of not wanting to participate in class. I was also concerned about the effect this would have on students' formal evaluations of my teaching performance. This was quite serious given that low student evaluations had financial consequences for teachers in the university I worked for at that time.

I was thus anxious about students' opinions of me, my position, and my career, and so my immediate motive was to resolve the teaching crisis. It was this anxiety and pressure that drove me to become a desperate enquirer and to discover what was 'wrong' with my teaching. With this burning desire for solutions and positive evaluations of my work, I wanted to examine this problem in an objective, thorough, and convincing way, and if possible, to persuade my colleagues that my teaching methods were not wrong, and to obtain their support.

However, I was not sure where to start. On the one hand, I needed to keep on teaching and to try my best to prevent more students boycotting my lessons. On the other hand, I was not in a position to take a full-time research methods training course to assist me with my inquiry. What I really needed was someone to consult, someone whom I trusted.

I turned to Diana, a senior teacher who had previously observed my lessons and supported my teaching style. Diana assured me of the correctness and appropriacy of my teaching methodology; at the same time, she acknowledged her own 'inadequate' knowledge of research on teaching and referred me to another teacher, Daniel, who she considered a more seasoned guide. Unfortunately, when I contacted Daniel, he seemed to be more interested in sharing his philosophy of teaching than advising on how I could use research to investigate my problem. I returned to Diana and she introduced me to a western colleague, Matthew, who had a doctorate and worked in a different faculty at my university.

To my surprise, Matthew suggested that I begin by writing a research proposal, although I had limited knowledge about what it was, what its relationship with my teaching was, and what I should do to complete such a proposal. I then searched materials at the university library and found a useful and practical English book: *Practical Research: Planning and Design* (7th Edition), written by Leedy and Ormrod. As contract-staff, I was entitled to borrow only a limited number of books and only on short-loan; I wanted to have my own copy of this book but I hesitated as I was unsure about whether the investment could be justified (the book would have to be ordered from America and it would cost about half my monthly salary). I consulted a friend from another university and their advice was that if the book was important, then I should purchase it, so I did. Once it arrived, I began to study it seriously, starting from the section on writing a research proposal.

I shared my proposal with Matthew and he asked me many questions regarding, for example, the background to my research problem and the research methods I was planning to use. I was again perplexed by Matthew's questions, for I did not know that I needed to go into so much detail at that stage. I had to continue reading more material about research techniques. I remember feeling uncertain about whether I should use questionnaires because I doubted the value that numerical results would have in allowing me to solve my problems.

Therefore, I was still unsure how my study should proceed: in a second draft of my proposal, I inserted some questions for Matthew. One such question appeared in the methodology section, and is shown in the following extract from the second draft:

> The subjects for this study will be all 33 reading teachers engaged in teaching the English Intensive Reading course ... from the period of September 2002 to June 2004. (Jianmei annotated: It might not be 33 teachers since a few of them are gone; another problem is not all the subjects taught from Sep,2002 to Jun 2004, some of them only taught one term or two, some changed courses and so on, so I am not sure how I should express myself clearly here.)

This extract indicates, as I note elsewhere here, that my concerns in this early stage of becoming a teacher researcher were overly technical (i.e. I was worrying excessively about the exact number of teachers that would take part in the study). Matthew then lent me a copy of an MA dissertation by his Chinese friend (who had studied in the United States) in order to help me to see what a research paper looked like and how I could draft one myself. Again, with hindsight I see that using an MA thesis as a reference point may have simply increased my concern with the technicalities of doing research beyond a level that was necessary for my work as a teacher researcher.

When the proposal was ready, I began to design a questionnaire and seek teacher participants. For some unknown reason, however, I received less guidance from Matthew (and others) from there onwards. I continued to encounter many challenges, including the long process of recruiting individual teacher participants, my puzzles about suitable techniques for analysing the questionnaire data, and the painstaking procedures of dealing with the interview data. Once again, I recognize with hindsight that although I was a teacher and I was doing research stimulated by the need to examine (or at least to validate) my own teaching, my approach was shaped by the academic notions of research that were predominant (and still dominate, though less so) in the Chinese tertiary ELT context.

As noted above, though, the outcome of the study was that I felt much better about my work because I discovered that my approach to teaching was valued by my colleagues (even though they did not practise it themselves). The experience, for the first time, of using research to explore professional problems, though challenging, was ultimately a positive one for me; it gave me the confidence to persist in seeking ways of winning over my students and ultimately allowed me to save my reputation as a teacher. Becoming a teacher researcher provided relief from my anxiety and restored my self-esteem and self-confidence as a novice language teacher. Rather than abandoning my methodological principles, I explored how I could apply them in ways that students would accept and respect. To do so, I had to become more sensitive to my students' needs than I had been in the past – that was another important lesson I learnt from my initial experience of teacher research.

Reflections on the process

Teacher learning occurs through both 'personal and professional socialization of individuals into teaching' and 'formally organized pre- and in-service teacher training and professional development' (Freeman 2001: 608). I interpret this distinction simply as informal and formal learning. Although I drew on formal knowledge (e.g. through the research methods textbook I purchased), I would describe my learning process as a more informal one. I learnt to do research through self-study and largely alone.

Considering the purpose of my learning, it was, as noted earlier, clearly professional; I did not engage in research for academic purposes (e.g. to obtain a degree or to publish a paper) but to address a very real and immediate problem in my own teaching. In this sense I am happy to characterize my inquiry as teacher research. Ur, in distinguishing academic from professional inquiry, notes that in the latter the researcher 'is interested in finding out what works' and 'thinks in order to improve action' (1992: 57). This reflects my experience, for even though I retained the essential features of my communicative approach to teaching, I modified the manner in which I demonstrated it to (or enforced it on) my students. I was also less aggressive in advocating my teaching philosophy to my students as I realized that this may have been one cause of students' resistance. My inquiry, then, did change the way I thought about my work.

As to the difficulties this learning process presented, I dealt with several major challenges. First, I was unfortunate in my attempts to find a mentor. Maneekhao and Tood (2001) found that mentoring played a positive role in assisting a novice teacher researcher on a formal and institutional training programme in Thailand. Compared to Maneekhao (an ELT university teacher) who had a research mentor to guide her through her first action research study, I had to seek out my own mentors and was not particularly successful in identifying any who could provide sustained guidance. In some senses, perhaps, one mentor's suggestion that I write a full research proposal may not have been wholly helpful given my limited understandings of research and the professional goals of my inquiry; at the same time, having to write the proposal and to show it to the mentor did force me to think deeply about what I wanted to do. My experience raises interesting questions about the attributes that mentors of teacher researchers need; experience and knowledge of (a particular kind of) academic research (which Matthew clearly had) may not suffice.

A second challenge was that I had limited knowledge of and systematic training in doing research, although I see now that it is unrealistic to expect teachers generally to have such training, especially early in their careers. To address the knowledge and skills gaps I felt I had, I trained myself by reading intensively and learning informally from friends and colleagues. Teacher researchers cannot operate without a basic set of knowledge of skills; interesting questions here relate to what kinds of knowledge and skills are most important and how teachers can be assisted in developing them.

At the time I felt that access to resources (a common problem for teacher researchers noted by Borg 2003), particularly a lack of funding, was a major obstacle. Reflecting on that issue now, though, I am puzzled by my decision to spend so much money on one book about research methods when several similar resources would have been available in the library. It was perhaps a combination of over-eagerness and lack of knowledge on my part that led me both to over-complicate matters somewhat and to overlook the resources that were available. It is possible to do teacher research without funding, though of course if it is available, it can certainly facilitate the process.

Two further challenges were lack of community support (another important condition for teacher research noted by Borg 2006) and pressure from the broad educational system. I was not only a novice teacher but also a solitary novice teacher researcher. I felt uncomfortable about my isolation because I seemed to be doing something incompatible with the dominant working culture – at the time, the emphasis within the faculty was on teaching and examinations rather than on teacher development, and my activities were thus at odds with predominant practices and policies. This is an issue that must be considered by anyone who wishes to promote teacher research – the extent to which the characteristics of the wider context, such as the school system, are compatible with the ideas and practices that underpin teacher research as a form of professional development. High levels of incompatibility are likely to mean that teacher research will be severely restricted.

Despite these challenges, though, I feel that the outcomes for me were positive and that I certainly learnt much from the experience. Two factors in particular facilitated the progress that I made: personal characteristics and support from others.

In terms of personal characteristics, I had a great enthusiasm for teaching and took the responsibility for the quality of my teaching and of students' learning very seriously. Thus, once something had 'gone wrong' in my teaching – the discrepancy between my own philosophy of teaching and that of the workplace – I made a determined effort to put it right. My teacher image and identity (i.e. as an effective teacher of English) drove me forward; I felt the need to prove that I was a qualified, professional, and capable teacher to the whole teaching community – my students, my colleagues, the administrators, and the department.

I was also a keen learner, willing to spend time exploring something unknown in relation to my profession, and I tended to make good use of resources already available for me, such as books on doing research (though, as noted above, my initial fixation on one particular book may have blinded me to additional resources that were available).

With reference to support from others, I have already noted the challenges I faced in identifying a mentor who could provide sustained and appropriate support. It would be wrong, though, to dismiss the support I did receive at various points from different individuals. These individuals fell into two groups: one included experienced teachers who had a rich knowledge of ELT (and ideally, had some knowledge of my teaching performance); the second group were individuals who had experience and knowledge of research. Additionally, informal advice provided by friends and colleagues contributed in different ways and sometimes just the fact that they listened to me was important. I must not forget, too, the colleagues who participated in the study. Without their generous contributions my work would not have been possible. So, overall, while my experience of learning to be a researcher was not highly social, various interactions along the way contributed significantly to my work.

Implications

My experiences highlight factors that impacted on my early attempts to become a teacher researcher and which are of relevance to those responsible in the workplace for supporting teachers' growth as researchers. Individual teachers who, like myself, want to (or have to, due to lack of support) embark independently on the process of becoming a teacher researcher may also find aspects of my story instructive.

My approach to learning to do research was adventurous and independent. I did feel at many points that I was venturing out into the unknown and was very uncertain about the direction I was going in. At the time this troubled me but today I recognize this as part of what it means to become a teacher researcher; clearly, appropriate guidance can minimize inappropriate decisions, but to a certain extent experimentation, learning to cope with uncertainty, and learning through trial and error are central processes teachers need to engage with if they are to adopt the stance of a teacher researcher. This is an important point for those who support teacher research; teachers need the space to work out for themselves how to go about investigating the issues that are of concern to them; too much external control and direction may lead to research which is technically better but which contributes less effectively to the teacher's development as a reflective practitioner.

The experience I have narrated here was shaped by conventional notions of research and I approached my project in a rather textbook-like fashion. This approach worked for me but I do not want to suggest that this is the optimal approach for novice teacher researchers everywhere. Just as different ways of learning are more or less effective for different learners, so too it is likely that individual teachers will respond in different ways to learning to be teacher researchers. For some, a more formal, structured approach will work well; others may prefer more open-ended and emergent ways of learning to carry out research in their classrooms; and while some teachers may value collaborative forms of learning, for others individual learning will appeal more. These too are important points for those who support teacher research to reflect on.

I have noted in various places here that I approached teacher research rather conventionally and in some respects I may have over-formalized the process. I recognize now that teacher research need not be defined by the parameters that apply to funded research done for academic purposes. In the latter there is an obvious need for a detailed proposal to be written as this is the mechanism through which decisions about funding are made; for teacher research, though, a detailed formal written proposal can be an unnecessary obstacle; such documents assume an existing level of technical expertise and familiarity with the literature which full-time teachers will not have. One key to promoting teacher research, then, is making the process more accessible to teachers; this does not mean reducing attention to quality, but it can mean thinking carefully about the extent to which formal structures such as research proposals are really necessary. I did not know better at the time and followed the advice of a mentor who perhaps did not fully appreciate the special nature of teacher research.

A further point that is worth noting here is that it should not be assumed that teacher research is necessarily the most appropriate strategy for teachers everywhere and at different stages of their career to adopt in response to pedagogical challenges that arise. Teacher research is undoubtedly a powerful strategy for professional development. However, others exist and in many situations these will be more appropriate. For example, teachers who are new to the idea of reflective practice will benefit from less formal and more collaborative approaches to professional development such as teacher support groups (Richards and Farrell 2005); teacher research may then become appropriate at a later stage. Reflecting on my case, teacher research seemed an appropriate strategy for me to adopt in exploring my teaching problem, but I could have (if I had been aware of alternatives) explored this problem in other ways. The point I want to make is that it is important to think about the appropriateness of teacher research for particular contexts rather than assuming it will always be the best option.

My experience also highlights the need for teacher research to be driven by a concrete need that is rooted in the classroom. Teachers thus need to identify, alone or with support, the need that will provide the motivation for their inquiry. A clear practical focus makes it more likely that teacher inquiry will impact on what happens in the classroom. Without such a focus it is difficult to discern any meaningful purpose in teacher research.

The final implication of my experience I will note here relates to the role that institutions and colleagues can play in creating a supportive environment for teacher research. My apprenticeship as a teacher researcher was a rather lonely one and I did not feel supported by the department I worked in. Teacher research is more likely to thrive, though, when teachers are able to work together, are encouraged to do so, and receive appropriate support for their inquiries (Borg and Liu 2013).

Conclusion

This chapter has described my experience as a novice teacher of English learning to do research in an examination-oriented tertiary education context in China. Despite various obstacles, related both to personal factors and others external to me, I was able to examine a professional issue that threatened my confidence as a teacher and, through my inquiry, to reaffirm my identity as an effective practitioner. Reflecting on my experience has highlighted factors, personal and interpersonal, that contributed to what I achieved and has also allowed me to reflect on some of the limitations in the rather formal approach to teacher research that I took. Thus, while I would restate the importance of the adventurous spirit with which I embarked on my research project, I also recognize now the need for teacher research to be made appealing and motivating and not just technically correct. I hope that readers in ELT contexts similar or different from my own will find something interesting in this chapter that can be useful for their own work in doing or facilitating teacher research.

Engagement priorities

Recommendations for encouraging teacher research are plentiful (e.g. Borg 2013) but these often focus on formal strategies such as courses and less attention has been paid to teachers who engage in research in the independent and isolated way I did. Questions that can be asked in this respect are:

- What factors motivate teachers to engage, independently, in teacher research and to sustain their motivation? Are particular kinds of personal characteristics influential in such situations?
- Teachers very often have negative feelings about research and this means that they lack the motivation to engage in teacher research. What strategies

are useful in changing such negative attitudes and motivating teachers to engage?
- Even where teachers engage in teacher research independently, support from others can play an important role. What different kinds of support do teachers find most useful, at what stages of the teacher research process, and from whom?
- How can teachers assess the value of changes they make to their teaching during or as a result of teacher research and what criteria can be used in making such judgements?
- To what extent should teachers persist with teacher research when they do so in isolation of colleagues and their institutions more generally? Do the benefits to teachers in such situations outweigh the disadvantages they experience by being different?

References

Borg, S. (2003). Research education as an objective for teacher learning. In B. Beaven and S. Borg (eds), *The Role of Research in Teacher Education*. Whitstable, Kent: IATEFL, pp. 41–48.

Borg, S. (2006). Conditions for teacher research. *English Teaching Forum, 44*(4): 22–27.

Burns, A. (2010). *Doing Action Research in English Language Teaching. A Guide for Practitioners*. New York: Routledge.

Borg, S. (2013). *Teacher Research in Language Teaching: A Critical Analysis*. Cambridge: Cambridge University Press.

Borg, S. and Liu, Y. (2013). Chinese college English teachers' research engagement. *TESOL Quarterly, 47*(2): 270–299.

Cochran-Smith, M. and Lytle, S. L. (1999). The teacher research movement: A decade later. *Educational Researcher, 28*(7): 15–25.

Freeman, D. (2001). Teacher learning and student learning in TESOL. *TESOL Quarterly, 35*(4): 608–609.

Kiely, R. (2006). Teachers into researchers: Learning to research in TESOL. In S. Borg (ed.), *Language Teacher Research in Europe*. Alexandria, VA: TESOL, pp. 67–80.

Liu, X. and He, H. (2008). *Jiaoshi Zheyang Zuo Yanjiu (*教师这样做研究*)*. Chengdu: Sichuan Publishing Group & Sichuan Education Press.

Maneekhao, K. and Tood, R. W. (2001). Two kinds of becoming: The researcher's tale and the mentor's tale. In J. Edge (ed.). *Action Research*. Alexandria, VA: Teachers of English to Speakers of Other Languages, pp. 57–68.

Richards, J. C. and Farrell, T. S. C. (2005). *Professional Development for Language Teachers*. Cambridge: Cambridge University Press.

Schön, D. A. (1983). *The Reflective Practitioner: How Professionals Think in Action*. London: Avebury.

Ur, P. (1992). Teacher learning. *ELT Journal, 46*(11): 56–61.

Zheng, H. and Hu, X. (eds). (2004). *A Teacher and Researcher (*教师成为研究者*)*. Shanghai: Shanghai Educational Publishing House.

5
Teacher Research in Video-Based Online Classrooms

Paula Charbonneau-Gowdy

Introduction

A few years ago, a professor of mine, a well-regarded lecturer and researcher in Second Language Education at a leading Canadian research university, remarked in somewhat disparaging terms that classrooms are 'messy places'. She shared how she yearned to take her research back to the laboratory where she could control more of what was going on in the context of her research. Yet since that remark, the interest in and complexities of conducting classroom-based research have grown exponentially – and so has the need to investigate and report on them. If we are to heed the advice of Ursula Franklin, the highly respected physicist researcher and public intellectual, it is precisely through looking at 'ordinary' places and through 'different' eyes, as opposed to solitary inquiry, wherein great contributions of knowledge lie (Franklin 2014). Indeed, examining ordinary classrooms is often considered essential by those in education concerned about making advances in our knowledge of how best to apply efforts in the interests of learners and their learning. More recently and increasingly, technological developments are driving formal learning contexts from traditional classrooms to online spaces. This trajectory has opened up a whole new set of unique challenges both to teachers and also to those who seek through research to understand learning contexts. In this chapter, I share some of the insights I have discovered as a teacher researching my own classroom in an online distance-learning programme.

Traditionally, and indeed only until just over a decade ago, research was reserved for professional researchers in education; they, too, set the agenda by defining what issues merited study and how such study should be conducted. But just as the printing press slipped the proverbial rug out from under the secluded monks in earlier times in terms of who controlled access to information and knowledge, so too a change, arguably equally as profound, seems to be occurring in the field of educational research. For a growing number of educators like myself, who are concerned about understanding our classroom practices more deeply, technology is not only supporting this drive to know but has opened the doors of classrooms in terms of who can conduct research. The availability of information and literature that abounds online is also making it easier for teachers to research their classroom practices. With this change, new voices are being heard, and importantly, different interests are being served. These voices are helping to structure a dialogue that is promising to, and indeed is already beginning to, drastically alter the course of research in education, and education itself, as we know it today.

My own journey into classroom-based research began 12 years ago, after more than 20 years of teaching. I started researching what was happening in my English as a Second Language (ESL) classroom because the burning issues I was facing at the time were not being adequately addressed by others. In other words, the wisdom of the 'experts' in educational research, the traditionally accepted sources for answers to pedagogical questions, was either inaccessible to me or was not providing appropriate answers and strategies I felt I needed to ensure that the learners in my classes were indeed reaching their potential. More importantly, my classroom at the time was a video-based synchronous online environment, and the answers I was seeking for that particular kind of classroom context were mostly non-existent, and in some respects, are still limited today.

Recent work in the area of distance learning has offered a sociocultural framework (Wertsch 1998) for researching that could be applied to video-based classroom settings such as those I work in. Blake's work in virtual classroom learning focuses on 'the ability of students to create communicative meaning' (2009: 822) in a classroom that is learner-centred and where teachers take on the role of guide. Although Blake is referring to a language classroom, his emphasis on looking at classrooms through the lens of student agency is certainly applicable to a wide range of other subject areas of teaching. He warns against research that is directed towards finding whether technology works instead of the more valuable knowledge we need, in keeping with a sociocultural perspective – how it works and its implications for the new roles that teachers and students assume. Goodfellow and Lamy (2009) also look at virtual classroom contexts and take a somewhat related perspective in integrating the notion that as learning goes online, students will increasingly be faced with negotiating culture along with meaning. In this increasingly globalized world, virtual classrooms will need to be examined for ways that culture and identity are negotiated and intersect online, especially as these classrooms are often multicultural. Norton's (2010) notion of investment is also useful in relation to the context of online learning. The former construct departs from traditional conceptions of motivation and instead suggests that, depending on the context, as learners invest in learning and in developing their skills, they also influence their sense of self, their identities, and their opportunities for the future. Together the constructs discussed above reflected the kinds of concerns I had when I first began my teaching online and made up a framework for my research efforts in the virtual classroom.

In the next sections, my aim is to take the reader on the journey of my research, specifically of a video-based online classroom used for distance language learning (Charbonneau-Gowdy 2008; Charbonneau-Gowdy and Cechova 2009). In doing so, my efforts in describing the story of the research process I followed are intended to add to the ongoing dialogue about virtual classrooms that I strongly hold needs to be encouraged and fostered. The necessity to have those conversations and to add to them becomes all the more pressing as the influence of social networking technologies crosses the line into formal learning settings and the existence and role of institutions of learning are being challenged like never before (Nielson 2011). Through uncovering my own particular trajectory of doing classroom-based research in a virtual space, wrought with pitfalls, challenges and lessons learnt, I also aspire to encourage those whose own unique set of issues in their teaching practices are not being answered, to consider teacher research themselves.

Context

Prior to the beginning of my online classroom teaching where I decided to conduct research, I had been involved in a NATO language immersion programme in Canada. Groups of military personnel primarily from Central and Eastern Europe came to study either English or French in a programme lasting five months. Because of this experience, I understood that most of these individuals were highly motivated, hard-working, and intelligent officers and yet many were not engaging in opportunities to use their new language. In other words many of these individuals were not putting into practice the learning that they were 'acquiring' in the classroom. Essentially, they were at risk of not maintaining and developing their skills in the target language. I recognized that my job as their teacher was to teach the assigned programme and prepare them to pass their tests at the end of the course. Yet, I also knew that it was important to understand their everyday challenges as they did so. In my first attempt at classroom research in the traditional setting of the immersion course, I discovered that many had identity issues both inside and outside the classroom that created tensions and barriers to their investing in using the language.

After several years of teaching in the traditional classroom setting in the NATO programme, it became obvious to me that many of the learners I taught would return home after the immersion programme with few opportunities to practise their newly acquired languages. With the help of contacts in Europe and former students, I subsequently sought ways to teach online to groups of students in the countries that were represented in the programme. This situation eventually led to my conducting classes from Canada with military personnel overseas in videoconferencing-based classrooms. The tensions and challenges that the first groups of students had in traditional classrooms I taught were also evident to those whom I met online. Although the literature available at the time helped in trying to understand the identity and agency issues I had encountered in learners in the traditional classrooms (Norton 2000; Norton Pierce 1995; Norton and Toohey 2001), I discovered that ways to respond to those issues in the virtual site were not being addressed by those who were discussing educational issues in my field in the research or in the teaching materials that were being supplied to me.

My inclination was to find my own answers. My questions centred around learning and why it was not happening for many of these unique students as they struggled to learn, in this unique programme, at a unique time in history given their unique backgrounds from former Eastern-bloc countries, in a unique online setting. How could I apply to my own teaching situation the results of emerging studies, and the information that was available to me as a teacher on the use of technology? Much of this material and research was focused on usability, i.e. measuring or assessing the quality of the technical features of the technology and learners' satisfaction with the tools. On the other hand, I was looking at ways to understand the influence of the tools and the discussions they supported on the identities of the learners in my groups and on their engagement or investment in learning.

With a dearth of information to help me look at the online spaces with these issues in mind, I was forced to look more deeply at what was happening in the context of my teaching and to try to understand through 'different eyes'. My interests revolved around my students taking part in discussion sessions at a distance, using video-based technology, which was state-of-the-art at that time. In a six-week distance-learning EFL programme, I taught two separate groups of individuals – university students in the Czech Republic and military officers in Romania. As I interacted online with these individuals, issues surfaced that led me to question the nature of our sessions and what influence they were having on the learners and their learning. I began to reflect on the steps I needed to take to find answers to the questions I had. My hope was that the answers I found would ultimately allow me to understand how to enable learners to reach their individual potentials and to meet their learning goals.

The researcher strategies I adopted (as I discuss further below) were qualitative, open-ended, dynamic, and participatory. To help me understand my learners and their learning I collected data through interviews, emails, photographs, recordings of our online classes and examples of learners' work.

On a pedagogical level, using teacher research to understand learning and how it is best accomplished has enabled me to better support the learners with whom I work. I see evidence of the value of my improved pedagogical practices, for example, in the increased engagement of learners in my classroom teaching. Other signs come from the proud remarks of many about their progress in learning or from the expressions of former struggling learners when their efforts are reflected in positive assessments. These signs speak to me of empowered learners whose language identities have changed. I understand that empowered language learning identities lie beneath the confidence and self-directedness I witness in the classroom, and importantly, beyond, once many of these learners leave the formal classroom context we have shared. I take this self-directedness as an indication of the potential for future, continuous life-long learning and skill development. The findings clearly indicated that many of the individuals in the first group I researched online had changed in these ways. Through their words and actions I understood how they viewed themselves differently as learners, how they felt empowered with their new level of language both in their work and in their lives. I also understood from the research that, supported by the transformations of their identities and language abilities, they saw new opportunities to take part in the global dialogue using technology for communicating.

On a personal level, conducting classroom-based research gave me confidence as a teacher practitioner to realize that I can take steps to change what I see needs to be improved, rather than to accept blindly or unquestionably what I am often asked to do. Having a critical awareness of my teaching and my potential to find alternative ways of doing has led me to seek out and test new innovations in new cultural contexts. I have learnt to listen more intently to and share more actively with others, including learners. These skills – critical thinking, innovation and social competency – are deemed most crucial in the 21st century and are proving valuable to me in all parts of my life, not only in my teaching practices.

Having outlined the context in which I have engaged in teacher research, I now discuss key insights which have emerged from my reflections on the processes I went through.

Insights

Uncovering 'different' answers to 'different' questions

Incited by my professional curiosity, the decision to research my online classroom context began first and foremost with questions. I could have continued to conduct the discussion sessions that were planned and seen the online experience as simply an interesting experience in the use of technology. But I wanted to know more about what was happening below the surface of these discussions and what part technology was playing in them. My curiosity drove me to look for ways to understand the issues I was witnessing and to frame these issues in questions that reflected the 'new' online setting. The studies involving technology available to me at the time, with a few exceptions (Warschauer 2002, 2003), seemed mainly preoccupied with the technical and accessibility questions related to the use of technology. I was not content, however, only to know, for example, whether the learners I was meeting each day in the virtual classroom were happy or not with this innovative way of classroom teaching. If that were the case, I realized that I could simply develop a questionnaire and tabulate and analyse the numerical results based on my students' responses. My questions, on the other hand, were more centred on the ways these sessions were influencing any changes in students, that is, in terms of their identities as learners and the process of their learning.

Destabilizing my own perspectives

This exercise of formulating questions and choosing a research design forced me to re-examine my beliefs and understandings at a level to which I was previously oblivious. In my daily routine as a teacher, my views of the nature of human beings and reality (ontology), my ways of knowing or my connection to the known (epistemology), what I viewed as moral (ethics) and how I practised gaining knowledge about the world (methodology) were buried beneath my busy timetable, concerns for lesson preparation, administrative demands, and actual teaching. Having to pause and stand outside my actions and thoughts and make declarations about how those stances fit with research paradigms is not an easy task. What is even more challenging is to come to grips with the fact that the principles behind those thoughts and actions, like identities, are complex and constantly changing.

Even at early stages of the research process, I began to question some long-held assumptions and presumptions. The fact that I was researching within a virtual classroom setting that resembled in many ways a traditional one, yet in other ways was very different, added to the complexity of re-examining my views. For example, I was re-assessing my role as a teacher as holder of all knowledge. I asked myself how I could assume that hierarchal role when much of the online discussions were revolving around what the learners knew and/or around information that was available online. Moreover, even if I had wanted to assume a more controlling role, the very nature of the classroom interface online prevented me from doing so.

This process of re-assessing my views in the context of the research I had undertaken was a destabilizing one. On the other hand, I believe it led to a bold turning point in my professional development. In my teaching online and increasingly in every context I teach, I have become more aware of my actions and that with the learners in my classrooms, I am creating reality rather than representing some objective interpretation of what reality should be.

Choosing an appropriate research design

Exploring my options for uncovering differences among and understanding changes in learners and their learning required a more in-depth look at what was occurring in the online classroom than numbers-driven research approaches could offer. Looking below the level of what is immediately visible required research tools that were available to me in a qualitative research paradigm. I was familiar with these tools from my reading of the work of Denzin and Lincoln (2000) that I had used initially when conducting more traditional classroom research earlier in my career. The tools I chose consisted of interviewing and observation as well as exploring through written documents the multiple layers of contexts that seemed to be influencing what was happening in the online sessions.

My challenge was how to use these tools in the technology-based context in which I was teaching. For example, in the virtual classroom, I quickly discovered there were not the same opportunities for observing learners as in a traditional setting – those incidental meetings (Kearns 2012) that help teachers get to know learners and assess the progress they make. Observations of learners' interactions between classes or in casual conversations at the end of a lesson were important data sources in my prior traditional classroom research.

Knowing the multi-layered contexts of classroom research

Another challenge that confronted me in the virtual classroom was how I would come to know the contexts the learners lived in as individuals given the physical distance that existed between us. This point is a crucial one for qualitative researchers. According to Maguire (1994), uncovering the 'multi-layered contexts' of learning is essential in the initial stages of any classroom-based research. Without an in-depth knowledge of the ideological, political, pedagogical, historical, personal, socio-economic and cultural webs that classroom learners are spun in, we have little hope of clearly understanding the issues that confront them as they strive to learn. Maguire has shown that within these interconnected contexts lie embedded relations of power, or the fallout from them. Power relations within various learning contexts play an integral part in the opportunities that learners have for learning. These power relations have the potential to influence the research process as well. For example, I wondered how the participants in the virtual classroom from former Eastern-bloc countries would view me as a privileged North American educator and respond to my research efforts. Would they shy away from sharing their perspectives of their learning online and the kinds of experiences they were having in the online classroom? Were there contextual issues – cultural, personal, pedagogical – that would prevent them from engaging in the online learning sessions? And if so, would I be able to identify the issues given that I was thousands of kilometres away living in a very different cultural context? Were there unique ethical considerations for me to consider due to these power differences and especially because of the kinds of video and audio information that I would have access to from these individuals?

A collaborative process

Many of the research challenges that arose were addressed collaboratively. This collaboration was shown in the participants' cooperation, indeed diligence in ensuring that their contexts and perspectives were clear to me and even by offering their support when the limitations of the technology caused problems in conducting the sessions. This collaboration partly reflected the decision I had made to conduct Participatory Action Research (PAR), a research approach that lies within the qualitative research paradigm. Essentially, PAR implies a collective effort on the part of a group of individuals to take steps to create changes to an existing unsatisfactory situation. In the case of the distance-learning classroom, from the learners' perspective our cooperative efforts would result in access to much-needed opportunities for formal learning. Indeed, the participants were instrumental in helping me gain access to their military decision makers who could allow me to conduct the teacher research. For my part, the research-grounded online sessions would help me understand whether this form of teaching could be a viable option for the face-to-face students I was still teaching in Canada once they returned home.

With our shared desire to succeed in this initiative, the learners also cooperated in constructing pragmatic solutions to the challenges that arose due to the use of technology in the research process. For example, some made time after sessions to talk to me individually online. Through email and pre-session meetings, online teachers in Europe reported on after-class discussions that transpired when the technology had been turned off. In other words, affordances of the technology, while sometimes limiting, were also supportive in the research process. For instance, many participants wrote their thoughts and preoccupations with the sessions in daily emails. Some sent personal and professional photos, suggested sources and links to information of a political, historical, geographical nature in order for me to learn more about their countries and the multiple contexts that influenced their lives. Others sought IT solutions at their end if there were problems with the video or audio transmission in the videoconferencing rooms. Many were technically savvy and could help others in the class when there were technical issues. Ultimately, I realized that the collaboration of these learners in the research process was closely tied to the success of the research and the richness of the data that surfaced. This collaboration confirmed for me that the choice of PAR was a good one.

Collecting and analysing data

While there were challenges in the virtual classrooms setting that I initially encountered in researching the questions I had, there were also advantages. These advantages not only influenced the data collection but, I believe, allowed for a deeper analysis of the findings. I discovered, for example, that the nature of the digital interface resulted in a feeling of being closer physically and for some reason, emotionally as well, to the learners and me to them, in the classroom scenario. In online interviews I conducted, they seemed to create unexpected bonds of trust and a sharing of confidence much more readily than I was accustomed to. This closeness surprised me and at the same time allowed me entry into their lives and their understandings that I know, from over 30 years of teaching practices in traditional classrooms, would not have been possible. Also, the seamlessness of watching, listening to and reviewing videotaped versions of the online classroom proceedings as well as the individual and group face-to-face interviews offered further advantages at the analysis stage. In the time since the initial virtual classroom research, advances in technology are now helping to simplify the analysis process.[1]

Reporting results

Although I do not have space to elaborate on this issue here, I do want to note that another advantage of researching in virtual classrooms is the exciting opportunities that arise for teachers to share their knowledge and experience. Kress (2003) predicted that the Internet will be responsible for a major shift – a 'revolution', in the way we use language to communicate. That images will replace the written text in this new paradigm is certainly holding true. This paradigm shift suggests new innovative ways through which teacher researchers can share the unique image-based data they have collected in the virtual classrooms – ways that still seem to be eluding much of the current research reporting. The Internet offers a new forum for teachers and their representations, albeit with unique ethical considerations, that will ensure their voices are heard.

Implications

The understandings that emerge from the analysis of my experiences as a teacher researcher have had implications for my own professional and personal development. Indeed, Rathgen (2006) found that the lessons that emerge from teacher research become embedded in teachers' practices simply because the understandings are context-specific. The initial and subsequent groups of learners that have taken part in my teaching in similar distance-learning sessions have also benefited. But I would argue that the value of the insights gained from virtual classroom research goes beyond those involved. They may have relevance for teaching and teachers, for teacher trainers and for institutions elsewhere – particularly those contemplating research in digital spaces.

With regard to EFL teaching and teachers, the high-stakes that are attached to communication in this field are not limited to language development but extend more importantly perhaps to allowing learners to participate in a global community. In this 21st century reality, it seems more essential than ever to look carefully at the context-based nature of our practices beyond traditional classrooms to virtual classrooms as well. The valuable affordances that these technology-based spaces offer that can help support our understanding of the sociocultural perspectives of our language teaching are too attractive and too important to ignore.

The need to recognize the powerful part that technology can play in understanding teaching and learning practices is a wake-up call. This call needs to be harkened especially and more actively by teacher trainers. Discussions on the topic of technology must be more than just an add-on to the core teaching practices they model, more than a list of best websites or tools in EFL teaching. Researching in digital spaces can provide a variety of unique perspectives on teaching and learning, some of which I have highlighted in the limited space in this chapter. As a growing group of others in the field of ICT education opens the gate to questions about online practices, teacher training programmes should see the promotion of the process of researching such practices as one of their key mandates.

In the case of institutions, there is significant scientific support to suggest that the investment in technology in formal classroom learning has often reaped poor returns (Cuban 2001; Warschauer 2011). While the reasons for this may be multiple and complex, solutions seem to point clearly to teachers. The remark I read recently in the media that 'after 30 years of scientific research in education, the only thing that can be said with certainty from research is that teachers are key to students' successful learning' seems particularly relevant when it comes to the use of technology. Decisions regarding technology will need to involve teachers. For teachers to be implicated closely in that process will require stronger support from institutions for more enriched and long-term professional development, especially in the area of technology. This support will need to include active encouragement to gain knowledge and understanding through the research of teachers' digital teaching practices. Such a solution can ultimately ensure that teachers' own voices and those of learners will be clearly heard as the pressure and demands to adopt new technologies in classrooms emerge.

Conclusion

In this chapter, I have outlined some of the understandings I have arrived at in my own attempts at teacher research. These understandings consist of directions and tools for teachers to consider on their own research journeys. Choosing an appropriate research approach to uncover deeper knowledge is one suggestion. Understanding the unique and multi-layered contexts implicated in each of these virtual spaces is another. The global consequences of gaining a deeper understanding in light of how much more we need to know about language learning and the fact that many of these virtual classroom spaces are multicultural cannot be underestimated. Researching by its very nature can be destabilizing. Teachers who are bravely considering teacher research in video-based synchronous spaces will discover environments where new rules about learning and teaching are being negotiated. Teacher researchers will often be obliged to re-examine their views and adapt to a more collaborative and ethically challenging context.

Teachers, for the most part, are by nature quite bold individuals. In most countries of the world, the qualities of the boldest among them are hidden behind doors or live in the memories of the fortunate learners who pass in and out of their classrooms. The rewards for exercising their boldness and strengths can be measured in minds that have changed, and identities that have been empowered. As increasing numbers take on classroom research, they are beginning to open the doors to the valuable insights they have that can add to the dialogue on learning. In taking on this new role, it is within their power, especially in virtual classrooms where anything is still possible, to lead the changes in education that many are seeking globally. With direction and encouragement, I believe there is still time for teacher research to move the dialogue, as John (2005) has called for, from seeing education as a means to serve the economy through the production of human capital to another perspective where education is viewed as playing an essential part in developing the potential of individuals.

Engagement priorities

In this chapter, I have alluded to the important and unique issues that can arise in researching virtual classroom spaces, especially in light of the affordances that technology offers with regard to collecting data and reporting findings. Following from my account, here are some issues that merit ongoing attention:

- What kinds of unique challenges are created in online language learning contexts and what kinds of research and conceptual frameworks are best suited to examining these in ways which are socioculturally sensitive?

- What strategies can teacher researchers adopt to secure the investment of learners in the research process and to make it a truly participatory one?
- What kinds of ethical issues might be specific to teacher research in online contexts (see Evans and Jakupec 1996) and how might these be addressed?
- What kinds of alternatives to conventional forms of dissemination are available for teacher researchers and their learners to share the processes and findings of inquiry conducted in online contexts?

Note

1. See John (2005) and Silverman (2003) for examples and explanations of the kinds of data analysis tools referred to here.

References

Blake, R. J. (2009). The use of technology for second language distance learning. *The Modern Language Journal*, 93: 822–835.

Cuban, L. (2001). *Oversold and Underused: Computers in Classrooms*. 1980–2000. Cambridge: Harvard University Press.

Charbonneau-Gowdy, P. (2008). *Speaking to Learn: Accessing Language, Identity and Power Through Web Conferencing*. Saarbrucken: VDM Verlag Dr. Muller.

Charbonneau-Gowdy, P. and Cechova, I. (2009). Moving from analogue to high definition e-tools to support empowering social learning approaches. *Electronic Journal of eLearning*, 7(3): 225–238.

Denzin, N. K. and Lincoln, Y. S. (2000). *Handbook of Qualitative Research*. Thousand Oaks, CA: Sage Publications.

Evans, T. and Jakupec, V. (1996). Research ethics in open and distance education: Context, principles and issues. *Distance Education*, 17(1): 72–94.

Franklin, U. M. (2014). *Ursula Franklin Speaks: Thoughts and Afterthoughts. 1986–2012*. In collaboration with S. J. Freeman (ed.). Montreal, QC: McGill-Queen's University Press.

Goodfellow, R. and Lamy, M.-N. (2009). Directions for research in online learning cultures. In R. Goodfellow and M.-N. Lamy (eds), *Learning Cultures in Online Education*. London: Continuum Books (Continuum Studies in Education), pp. 170–183.

John, P. (2005). The sacred and the profane. Subject subculture, pedagogical practice and teachers' perceptions of the classroom uses of ICT. *Educational Review*, 57(4): 471–490.

Kearns, L. (2012). Student assessment in online learning: Challenges and effective practices. *Journal of Online Learning and Teaching*, 8(3): 198–208.

Kress, G. R. (2003). *Literacy in the New Media Age*. New York: Routledge.

Maguire, M. H. (1994). Cultural stances informing storytelling among bilingual children in Quebec. *Comparative Education Review*, 38(1): 115–144.

Nielson, K. B. (2011). Self-study with language learning software in the workplace: What happens? Language Learning and Technology, 15(3):110–129.

Norton, B. (2000). *Identity and Language Learning: Gender, Ethnicity and Educational change*. London: Longman/Pearson Education.

Norton, B. (2010). Language and identity. In N. Hornberger and S. McKay (eds), *Sociolinguistics and Language Education*. Bristol, UK: Multilingual Mattersm, pp. 349–369.

Norton, B. and Toohey, K. (2001). Changing perspectives on good language learners. *TESOL Quarterly*, 35(2): 307–323.

Norton Pierce, B. (1995). Social identity, investment, and language learning. *TESOL Quarterly*, 29: 9–18.
Rathgen, E. (2006). In the voice of teachers: The promise and challenge of participating in classroom-based research for teachers' professional learning. *Teaching and Teacher Education*, 22: 580–591.
Silverman, D. (2003). Analyzing text and talk. In N. K. Denzin and Y. S. Lincoln (eds), *Collecting and Interpreting Qualitative Materials*. Thousand Oaks, CA: Sage Publications, pp. 340–362.
Warschauer, M. (2002). A Developmental perspective on technology in language education. *TESOL Quarterly*, 36(3): 453–475.
Warschauer, M. (2003). *Technology and Social Inclusion: Rethinking the Digital Divide*. Cambridge, MA: The MIT Press.
Warschauer, M. (2011). *Learning in the Cloud: How (and Why) to Transform Schools with Digital Media*. New York: Teachers College Press.
Wertsch, J. V. (1998). *Mind as Action*. New York: Oxford University Press.

6
Border Crossings: Researching across Contexts for Teacher Professional Development

Patsy Vinogradov

Introduction

One border crossing

For an adult educator, there is perhaps no educational context more uncomfortable and puzzling than one filled with young children. Everything about an early childhood classroom is unlike one meant for adult learners: the tiny desks and chairs, the relentless colours and images on the walls, the festive songs and clapping, the carpet squares to sit on, and the strict, well-taught routines for everything from sharpening one's pencil to moving from one room to another. It is a foreign space for a teacher of adults. In a collaborative project to explore early literacy instruction, a handful of adult English language educators and I chose to venture into this new environment. To walk past the macaroni art on the walls and to enter a kindergarten classroom was a professional border crossing for us. Yet, it proved to be a crossing full of intellectual challenge and changing perspectives, and the teachers who joined me to research early literacy across these contexts can attest to both their initial discomfort and, in the end, to their gratitude for the experience.

In 2012, Tarone compared the work of applied linguists to that of *Médecins sans Frontières* (MSF), or in English, *Doctors without Borders*. She appreciates the MSF not only for their life-saving work, but for their work 'crossing borders', branching out beyond their professional territories. She claims much can be gained by both parties, by the doctors crossing the borders and by those in need on the other side receiving their aid. She suggests that it is admirable when professionals in our field of English language teaching do the same, when they too 'cross borders and move into and out of different communities' (Tarone 2012: 3). Applied linguists can take their community's set of tools for investigation and move into other spaces and borrow from other disciplines. 'And in doing this', writes Tarone, 'they LEARN themselves, learn facts, processes, new viewpoints, and explanations for the way humans use and process multiple languages that would have been utterly inaccessible to them if they'd stayed "inside the borders"' (2012: 4, emphasis in original). In this chapter, I continue this volume's stance that engagement in teacher research is a valuable professional development tool, and I add that researching intentionally across contexts can be particularly worthwhile, even transformational.

To improve our classroom practice, we can reach out to related, but different contexts. Moving out of our 'comfort zone' allows for new ways of thinking. It is challenging work to conduct teacher research, and to do so in an unfamiliar educational context adds another layer of complexity. In professional development (PD) of this sort, teachers are asked to be investigators and thinkers. Roskos and Bain propose that, when teacher PD is intellectually challenging, it can move teachers toward a 'pedagogy of thoughtfulness', one that values inquiry and is student-centred (1998: 91). They write that 'if instruction is to keep pace with new advances in learning theory, technology, and communications, then professional development activity must shift its emphasis from narrowly construed techniques to the expansion of teachers' thinking and intellect' (Roskos and Bain 1998: 92). In such endeavours, teachers are viewed as scholars, learners, and inquirers (Cochran-Smith and Lytle 2009).

In the study used to illustrate this chapter, my colleagues and I crossed a major border in the field: we crossed from adult ESL education into kindergarten to research early literacy instruction with the purpose of enhancing our work with adults. We teach low-literate adult ESL learners, those new to both English and print literacy. As well-trained adult ESL teachers, we came to understand that our preparation had assumed literacy in our learners; therefore, little, if any, attention was given to how to teach reading to someone who had never encountered print before. Yet, many immigrants and refugees across the globe have not had the opportunity to go to school, or they come from oral cultures whose languages do not have a written script. In our conversations together, we shared our struggles in teaching early print literacy. In beginning our project, we asked a simple question, *Who knows more about this than we do?* One answer was obvious: teachers of young learners. With that recognition, our cross-context research project unfolded.

Professional development: a critical need for adult basic educators

When adult immigrants and refugees in the United States seek English as a second language (ESL) instruction, they often turn to the public adult basic education (ABE[1]) system. English instruction for adult immigrants in ABE is a hodgepodge of well-meaning organizations and schools, varying greatly from place to place (Crandall 1993). Some programmes are highly professional with well-developed curricula, excellent facilities, set standards of effective practice, and appropriately credentialed teachers. Other programmes, however, rely entirely on volunteers and may meet in church basements, apartment complexes where students live, public libraries, or wherever space is available (Vinogradov and Liden 2009). As adult literacy scholar Heide Wrigley writes, 'The United States is a long way from having a coherent system of immigrant education and workforce training' (Wrigley 2008: 170). By glancing even briefly at the patchwork of adult ESL programmes across the United States, it is clear that quality programming is irregular at best, and that teachers are frequently not adequately trained to do the work they are doing (Crandall 1993; Smith and Hofer 2003; Wrigley 2008). These facts do not discount individual teachers who very often successfully create productive, responsive learning environments.

Taken together with the reality of limited pre-service preparation, professional development for in-service adult ESL teachers becomes even more critical (Smith and Gillespie 2007). Published survey research on ABE professionals at state and regional levels shows that most teachers have teaching licences and bachelor's degrees, but most do *not* have training specifically in teaching adults, nor in teaching ESL (Marchwick 2010; Smith et al. 2003; Wilson and Corbett 2001). Their qualifications and work experience vary from Master's degrees in ESL, to teaching middle school science, to a few hours of volunteer-training through local literacy councils, to no formal training whatsoever. The vast majority of adult ESL teachers works part-time, and many teachers patch together various part-time positions to make a living (Auerbach 1992; Crandall 1993; Johnson et al. 2010; Smith et al. 2003).

The role of professional development in adult ESL fills a critical need, but providing high-quality PD in this dynamic and non-uniform field is a difficult endeavour. As adult ESL programming is often encompassed by larger programmes for adult basic education, the PD discussion here draws from work enhancing teacher quality of adult basic educators in general as well as specifically for adult ESL instructors. Cristine Smith, an adult basic education scholar in the United States, describes this acute dilemma in this manner: 'While research results support the need for in-depth PD and professional learning opportunities to improve teacher quality, the adult learning and literacy field is structured in and funded in such a way that we do not currently offer the kinds of PD most likely to improve teacher effectiveness' (Smith 2010: 68). Smith is referring to a fundamental shift in improving teacher quality that began in K–12[2] schools and is now taking hold in adult education as well: a shift from traditional workshops and conferences to more job-embedded, longer term, intellectually nourishing professional learning.

Teacher research as PD in adult ESL education

Educational researchers in K–12 settings have long grappled with teacher effectiveness and how teachers grow and change (Borko 2004; Darling-Hammond and Young 2002; Little 1987). Part of this research has focused on professional development; it is widely accepted that in-service PD for educators should be grounded in educators' actual teaching contexts, should take place over time, and should encourage peers to collaborate (Desimone 2009; Shulman and Shulman 2004). Webster-Wright (2009) articulates a distinction between traditional professional *development* and professional *learning*.[3] Webster-Wright contends that while professional *development* includes activities such as workshops and conference sessions that are largely removed from teachers' daily work, professional *learning* includes learning from experience, learning from reflective action, and learning mediated by context (2009). Professional *learning* takes PD out of the workshop and conference model and moves it into teams of teachers working toward common goals, where collaboration and shared interests are vital (Wenger 1998). Such professional learning is now a growing facet of ABE PD efforts as well. In a seminal article on the topic as it pertains to adult ESL, Crandall describes various models of PD for *TESOL Quarterly* and writes, 'the most exciting professional development programs and those which are likely to have the greatest impact on teachers, programs, and learners are those involving some kind of action research, reflective practice, or inquiry-based professional development' (Crandall 1993).

Although job-embedded professional learning may be most effective, workshops and conferences are still much more commonly attended by adult educators (Smith and Hofer 2003). A groundbreaking study of adult basic educators in 1998–2000 by NCSALL (National Center for the Study of Adult Learning and Literacy) focused specifically on professional development for ABE teachers (Smith et al. 2003). One hundred and six teachers in New England completed an extensive survey, and then 18 focal participants were identified. Researchers interviewed these 18 teachers and their programme directors and also visited their classes. They found that workshops and conferences were by far the most common form of PD in ABE, with 75% of respondents having attended this type of PD activity in the last 12 months. Most teachers had attended a single-session workshop or a state annual conference. Far fewer (36%) had attended a study circle, had participated in peer coaching (35%), or had participated in practitioner research (26%). Researchers found that, while most teachers had participated in some kind of PD in the last year, overall participation in PD was limited; main barriers included lack of funding, part-time status, lack of time, and lack of motivation by the ABE practitioners themselves. It should be noted that this study was limited to New England, only 18 focal participants, and relied on teachers to self-report their experiences. Smith and her colleagues' findings echo those of Wilson and Corbett (2001). In their large research study on adult educators' participation in PD, Wilson and Corbett interviewed 60 adult education administrators and practitioners from ten states. This inquiry also identified lack of time and financial constraints as key barriers to PD participation, stemming from the fact that so many adult educators are employed part-time and are not funded to attend PD. In addition, the study identified distance to PD activities, an absence of information about events, and a mismatch between the practitioners' needs and the goals of the PD as reasons teachers did not attend (Wilson and Corbett 2001).

What can be made of the mismatch between teachers' needs and the PD available to them? Adult educators are also adult learners, and, as such, they are similar to the learners they teach. If the PD available is not immediately relevant, it will have little effect. Teachers too have unique preferences as learners, and many factors will affect how they grow and develop (Smith and Hofer 2002). Such findings are consistent with Desimone's (2009) work in effective teacher professional development. Desimone identifies certain elements that must be in place in order for PD to truly impact teacher quality, which include the following: a) content focus, b) active learning, c) coherence, d) duration, and e) collective participation (Desimone 2009). *Content focus* refers to a specific subject matter content chosen and how students learn that content. *Active learning* involves an emphasis on student work and thinking, and encourages analysis, reflection, practice, and observation as means to professional growth. *Coherence* is the extent to which teacher learning is aligned with teachers' knowledge and beliefs, and also refers to how consistent the content of PD is with policies at the state, district, and school level. *Duration* refers to the time over which the PD activity is spread, and it assures that conversations with colleagues are not simply started, but continue over time. *Collective participation* is the final element of effective professional development and refers to the coming together of like-minded colleagues to grow professionally.

When teachers are able to gather with similar colleagues of similar teaching contexts, they can share resources, discuss research that applies to their settings, share successes and challenges, and find professional support. Teacher research, particularly collaborative teacher research, meets all of these recommendations for effective professional development. In researching collaboratively across contexts, teachers can further engage in an intellectually challenging, self-directed, meaningful, and potentially highly impactful project.

Context

Teachers researching together across contexts: adult ESL educators go back to kindergarten

In deciding to explore early literacy, we asked the simple question mentioned in the *Introduction* of this chapter: *Who knows more about this than we do?* Those who teach adult English speakers with low literacy were one possibility, but several obstacles kept us from pursuing this route. Adults born in the United States who have not attained *any* alphabetic print literacy (as is the case with our low-literate adult ESL learners) are rare. While adult basic education programmes have many adults pursuing high school completion, basic skills, or work readiness coursework, they are still generally much more literate than the adult ESL students we serve. Those L1 English-speaking students, who are truly struggling readers and at the beginning stages of literacy, often have learning disabilities, brain injury, or other conditions that have impeded their progress with reading. They are generally not lacking literacy for lack of exposure to print or educational services, as is the case of our adult ESL low-literate learners, making such a comparison problematic. To delve deeply into instruction of early literacy for learners who have more comparable literacy instructional needs, we looked to professionals who work with learners with similar levels of exposure to print and similar reasons for not reading well yet. Our adult low-literate ESL learners and K-2 learners are not expected to have read until recently, when they enter their first classrooms. And only now are they being introduced to the alphabetic principle and the many factors that make reading possible. These two groups of educators, low-literate adult ESL teachers and K-2 instructors, are doing extremely similar work, although arguably with quite different students.

Although they both teach reading, develop language, and, in the case of adult learners with limited education, socialize their learners to formal schooling, adult ESL educators and early elementary teachers have virtually no professional contact with each other. The amount of overlap is impressive, and yet this is a fierce and even well-guarded border. Some adult educators have told me directly that there is little to be gained from visiting classes for young children, that our contexts for teaching and learning are *so* different that it is futile to attempt to connect them. Others see the potential value, but the border is guarded by restraints in adult education such as the part-time nature of teachers, lack of support for PD activities and for teachers as researchers, and additionally, at times, little tolerance for change.

Nevertheless, a band of brave adult ESL teachers had formed as this project began. We were determined to learn more about teaching early literacy. My role was one of participant, facilitator, and also researcher. I was eager to learn about literacy instruction, but I also facilitated our meetings, and observed and documented the teachers' participation and learning throughout our research together. Data sources included transcriptions of our PD meetings, teachers' written conversations and other postings on a private website for our group, interviews before and after the research, and observations of the teachers' adult ESL classrooms before, during, and after our inquiry.

A study circle format was used to structure our collaborative teacher research project. Study circles offer teachers a place to explore important issues together over time. This type of collaborative inquiry, as defined by Kasl and Yorks, is 'a systematic process in which participants organize themselves into small groups to explore a question that all members find compelling' (Kasl and Yorks 2010: 315). A study circle brings practitioners together and is one way of creating the conditions for what Lave and Wenger call a community of practice (1991). Communities of practice are groups of people who share an acute interest for an activity and who interact regularly to improve their own performance (Lave and Wenger 1991).

Four participants and I entered an elementary school in search of new ways to enrich low-literate, low-beginning adult ESL classrooms. Moving past hallway galleries of finger-painted pictures and turning into a room full of youngsters, we got down to work (quite literally 'down' – on the floor, observing and assisting five-seven year olds). We all took a gamble by crossing a professional border into this new space, unsure if we would find anything among these young new readers that might benefit our adult ESL learners, some of whom are 60–70 years older and from an oral society on the other side of the globe. We realized, of course, that the learners we were observing in the K-2 settings had a definite advantage over our adult ESL learners: most of them were from English-speaking homes. With the exception of a few young learners from immigrant families, all the children we observed already had a strong grasp of oral English. This distinction was the subject of much discussion in our inquiry, as we worked to puzzle together how the literacy instruction we were drawn to replicating might require more oral language than our students had, and how quickly these young learners acquired reading skills, perhaps due to their strong foundation of oral English. Nevertheless, the children were still learning vocabulary daily and were being socialized to academic language in this formal school setting, much like our adult learners.

Over the course of two months, my colleagues and I engaged in a multifaceted inquiry into early literacy instruction. Acutely aware of the different contexts and learners, we worked to connect what we were seeing with kindergarten-second grade (K-2) learners with adult ESL students who are also new to literacy. We observed K-2 instruction and worked individually with young learners in a focal elementary school. We also completed assigned readings and tasks, and engaged in extensive discussions and reflective journaling and sharing with each other. As the facilitator, I encouraged the participants to make connections among the practices they were drawn to and to think together about how those practices might be wisely applied to their adult low-literacy ESL learners. By researching a new but related teaching and learning context, the participants uncovered key literacy practices in early elementary grades, identified what they thought might be useful to their own work, and transformed and applied these discoveries to their adult classrooms. This project brought teachers together as researchers and escorted them across a professional border. In doing so, they engaged in a complex, intellectually challenging series of meetings and tasks that encouraged collaboration, connection, and reflection.

Insights

Kindergarten literacy treasures found for adult ESL

What did we discover among those little desks and chairs? Findings show that the adult ESL teachers began organizing literacy instruction differently, such as implementing morning messages and daily sign-in questions like those they had seen in the K-2 classrooms. Such morning routines offer a way to focus attention on the day's topic and lesson, build community, and set plans for the day. Establishing sound routines was a key outcome of their experience. The adult ESL teacher researchers began assigning classroom jobs to their adult learners and implementing predictable blocks of literacy-focused instruction, much like what they encountered in the K-2 rooms. An extended definition of literacy also emerged, one that includes maths and integrates numeracy instruction into literacy-focused time. For example, a morning message regarding the day's topic of health and wellness led to a sign-in activity where adult low-literate ESL learners were asked: *Do you take medicine every day?* From the tallies of students answering 'yes' and 'no', maths work ensued with tasks of subtracting, adding, and creating number sentences with the symbols for greater than and less than.

In the K-2 classrooms, the adult educators learnt more about using literature in instruction and began reading aloud to their adult students and teaching about engaging with literature through text-to-text and text-to-self connections. The teacher researchers appreciated the classroom libraries in the K-2 classrooms and the time for independent reading the children enjoyed. While such practices are more challenging to implement in some adult education contexts, participants found ways to establish small collections of independent reading material in their classrooms and integrated time for 'read-to-self' during their adult ESL classes.

Another main finding was a heightened priority of self-directed learning and ways we might offer more choices and independent, individualized instruction to adult learners. In the K-2 classrooms, children had an abundance of choices during a portion of their literacy block. Strong routines around this 'choice time' had been established and children worked efficiently and productively on level-appropriate tasks while the teacher provided individualized instruction to learners as she moved about the room. This ability to nurture learners' independence as learners while at the same time attending to the multiple levels of literacy in the room impressed the participants and earned much attention in our discussions. Soon a variety of 'choice time' opportunities

78 *Patsy Vinogradov*

for low-literacy adult ESL students appeared in the teachers' classrooms who responded to various constraints with innovation.

Throughout the study circle, the teacher researchers were asked to think deeply about the K-2 practices they were drawn to and to make connections among them. We worked together and created Figure 6.1 and added statements that captured our discoveries about our classrooms in light of our encounters with K-2 literacy instruction:

By placing adult ESL learners as problem solvers in the centre, a shift in dispositions is evident. Low-literacy adult ESL teaching traditionally involves a great deal of hand-holding and teacher-fronted instruction. Viewing adult students as independent problem solvers shows a shift in thinking about our classrooms, as places where encouraging independence learning is prioritized in instructional choices. One teacher researcher's comment describes the traditional low-literate adult ESL classroom (note that names of participants are pseudonyms):

> It's not generally an expectation with low-literacy. I mean when most people think of good low-literacy instruction looks like, it's very teacher-structured. Very scaffolded, and all the students are doing the same thing, the teachers demonstrating each step. (Audrey, Meeting 5)

If our overall purpose is to assist our learners to become full participants in their communities outside of the classroom, then our classes need to be a place where independence and problem solving are nurtured. We can do this by attending to the following areas:

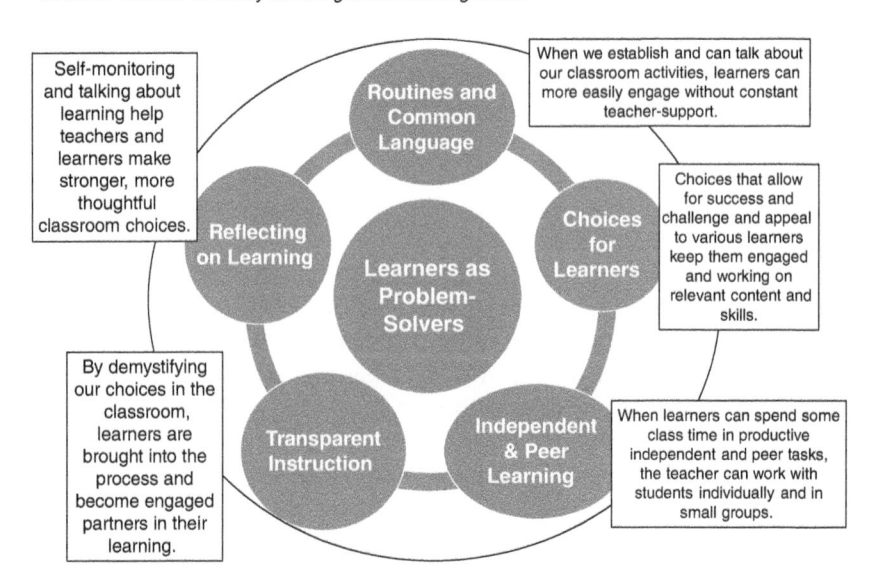

Figure 6.1 Learners as problem solvers and related components

However, by researching literacy in the early elementary context, we came to understand that a change in the expectation Audrey describes is both accessible and imperative. Low-literacy adult ESL teachers may assume, due to their learners' low English abilities and low-literacy abilities, that there is little that they can do in class that is not teacher-directed. Conversely, we saw in the K-2 classrooms that even very young, new readers were able to work efficiently on their own, leading to a host of benefits for both teaching and learning. Note this additional comment from Audrey:

> I was really struck by how self-directed the kids were during the independent work time. They were all engaged in their learning, completely focused on the task at hand, and needed virtually no instructions to get started on their work. Along with that, I was extremely impressed at how multi-level the classes were (1st and 2nd graders in the same room!), but how every child was working at their own pace and being challenged. The children seemed to have a great deal of personal responsibility with their learning, and were interested enough to stay motivated and work consistently. (Audrey, Online post)

Viewing learners as problem solvers to be nurtured, not simply low-level learners to be helped, represents a remarkable shift in disposition. This shift took place as a direct result of interacting with another educational setting, coming together with colleagues to investigate a related yet different context for early literacy development. Having researched across contexts, the adult educators could envision nurturing adult learners in a new way, as problem solvers, and how such a stance in fact mirrors our objectives for learners outside of the classroom.

Implications

Curiosity as a professional development goal

At the conclusion of our project, the teacher researchers were asked directly if this collaborative inquiry had sparked their curiosity, and if they felt challenged and stretched by the experience. These final written reflections were submitted anonymously to provide a space for complete honesty. Two excerpts are particularly revealing about the nature of intellectual activity in our work together:

> The study circle was a great way to ask questions, share issues, problems, concerns but more importantly it gave me a support system for trying out new activities in my class and gave me a way to reflect on why, how, and what I am doing to provide the most respectful learning/teaching situation.

> Made me take pause ... something I'm often too hurried to do. Reminded me what was important and why. Great opportunity to take teaching risks. (Anonymous, Final written reflection of study circle)
>
> Absolutely! Having been in ABE for 7 years, I sometimes feel like there aren't new and interesting presentations for teachers at my level. This opened my eyes to a whole new world of classroom ideas to explore. (Anonymous, Final written reflection of study circle)

In the first excerpt, the participant mentions taking risks and taking time to reflect on their work with others. The opportunity to investigate with others is an intellectual undertaking that can lead to change in practice. As the second excerpt mentions, seasoned teachers who are mid-career can benefit from such inquiries that open them up to new areas of knowledge. Too often, I believe, we assume teachers do not want to work any harder than they already do and that PD should be quick and painless and not ask too much of the participants. However, I submit that if PD is well planned, embraces a pedagogy of thoughtfulness, and treats participants as scholars and investigators, then it is more engaging, more satisfying, and in the end more beneficial for teachers and their learners.

In addition to the intellectual activity of our work, this project provided a way of building *adaptive expertise* in low-literacy adult ESL teachers. By taking part in this challenging work, participants were asked to be both innovative and efficient, the qualities of an adaptive expert (Darling-Hammond and Bransford 2007). They were innovative in that they were trying practices typically reserved for young learners (and that one teacher researcher, Mike, said were 'kind of wacky'), and they were efficient in that they were intentionally crafting the practice for our low-literacy adult context and to a specific programme and classroom and reflecting on its usefulness. The teacher researchers added to their teaching repertoires and deepened their understanding of their own classrooms. In fact, we noticed a fundamental shift in our thinking about our low-literacy classrooms; by the end of our time together we were seeing our classrooms as places where learners can be (and should be) nurtured as independent problem solvers.

Unlike professional development activities that are transmission-style, simply providing new information on policies, procedures, or techniques, collaborative inquiry, like a professional learning community, moves participants to think more deeply about their practice. They are provided the space and time to engage meaningfully with colleagues around a specific content focus. This type of PD honours and relies on the previous experiences and expertise of participants as they work through an intellectually challenging, worthwhile investigation together.

Conclusion

Teachers researching across contexts

> Learning cannot be designed: it can only be designed for – that is, facilitated or frustrated.
>
> (Wenger 1998)

Teacher change does not occur overnight, and scholars and educational leaders have devoted much time and energy to finding new ways to improve teachers' practice. As was described above, current trends in teacher PD involve job-embedded, longer-term efforts with teachers working in collaboration around specific topics (see Desimone 2009). Our findings from our cross-context research study affirm such efforts. They also add justification to designing intellectually challenging PD opportunities for teachers in formats such as collaborative inquiry, where teachers collectively investigate something of interest that is connected to their classroom practice. In this chapter's example study, a small group of teacher researchers investigated a new context for early literacy. Through observations, discussions, readings, and application tasks, we explored what might be useful for adult ESL learners. Below, some suggestions drawn from this experience are shared to assist other professional developers in designing such PD for teachers:

Shared experience

> There's something about being able to go into classrooms. We did readings, but the bulk of what we were discussing was based on observations of actual classrooms. I think that made such a difference ... you really had to be able to see it. (Audrey, Interview)

Audrey's comment highlights the power of visiting other classrooms to grow as an educator, and I submit that there is extraordinary benefit to not only observing others teach, but to observing others teach *together*. Every time we visited the K-2 classrooms, we did so in pairs, so that there would be at least one other person with whom to debrief who saw the same classroom. When teacher researchers have a shared experience, they are able to debrief, unpack, and assign meaning to what was observed.

Multi-level

Just as adult ESL learners represent a range of strengths and experiences, so do their teachers. One teacher researcher's (Mike's) classroom changed dramatically during our study circle, with a large number of new routines and practices, and for parts of his daily lessons, a new organizing structure emerged. For Audrey, however, change was more subtle. The morning message became more regular and more intentional, and she began adding a 'math morning' once a week. A 'choice box' time became part of one of her days of instruction, but the overall structure of her classroom remained the same. She described the study circle as 'enhancing' her practice (Interview). In PD such as this, the multi-levels of teachers and their experiences, programme restraints, and preferences are honoured. Each teacher can gain from the work, and that 'gain' can manifest in many ways, from strikingly new restructuring to slight tweaks to enhance a current repertoire.

Licence to experiment

Mid-way through our project, Mike decided to try reading a story aloud to his learners, a practice inspired from our K-2 classroom visits. Mike's path to this decision is a prime example of teacher learning; he went from never having considered a particular practice (reading literature aloud to students) to seeing it in action in another context, thinking about it with colleagues, transforming it for his particular context, trying it out, reporting back and processing with his colleagues, and ultimately advocating for this practice and articulating its perceived benefits. As he mentioned in his final interview, one of the main benefits of this study circle was the 'license to experiment' in his classroom (Mike, Interview). To re-energize a classroom takes intent and inspiration, and this cross-context research project provided that spark.

Ripple effect

> This really didn't feel like work to me. I have a renewed sense of creativity and my learners have been excited about the changes. I've had multiple conversations with colleagues both on and off my own teaching site about graphic organizers, implementing a library, setting up routines, and working toward independent learners. (Anonymous, Final written reflection)

An unexpected but pleasant finding from this PD is hearing how participants are sharing their experiences with their colleagues, and how they have grown to be professional developers via this project. While certainly the main impact rests with the participants themselves, they are not keeping quiet. There is a ripple effect to this research project. The teacher researchers were engaged in an intense experience together that challenged them as practitioners and scholars, and the kinds of shifts in thinking they experienced are being shared with others. Mike mentioned that he has spoken with his colleagues about the experience at staff meetings (Interview), and the anonymous comment above shows that she is continuing our conversations beyond our little group. Three of the four participants have presented with me at state, national, and international conferences about this project and its impact in our classrooms. One participant and I took an exciting next step recently when we created a new study circle experience for a new group of teachers, exploring a new border crossing (dyslexia education) and its connections to adult low-literacy ESL. We modelled this PD after our original study circle. While naysayers may claim that study circles are not efficient PD because they only impact a small number of people at a time, I propose that there is a ripple effect and that these participants continue to share their thinking and enhanced practices with others, creating even more change.

Implications for professional developers

For the professional developer thinking of designing a collaborative teacher research project across contexts, I share the following three suggestions.

1. Keep it small

Audrey, a teacher researcher in our project, says it best:

> In a small group you don't hear from a large number of people, but what you heard you really could flesh out, go more in depth, and follow up, and ask questions. In a bigger group that just doesn't happen nearly as much. I felt like this was the perfect size. (Audrey, Interview)

While we may be tempted to admit a large number of eager practitioners into a collaborative inquiry, I recommend (in agreement with Audrey above) keeping it small, perhaps four to six people.

2. Provide multiple ways for participants to connect

In this project, participants had two ways to interact – online and in person. Some teachers clearly felt more comfortable sharing off the cuff in person and had much to say in our six face-to-face meetings. Others preferred to process their thoughts and posted more extensively on the private website in the hours following our in-person meetings. People think and share differently, so I recommend providing different media for sharing. The website proved convenient as it held both written conversations and provided a single place for sharing photographs and files.

3. Be transparent

Just as transparency in instruction is good for new readers, so too is it for teachers. In our first meeting, we took time to read and talk about what a collaborative inquiry is and what is expected. I provided my research questions and shared my hopes and plans for our study circle. At each meeting, I began by handing out objectives for that session so that everyone knew the purpose of each piece of our time together. I recommend this level of transparency in any PD endeavour or collaborative teacher research.

In this research project, we literally reached across borders to learn more about early literacy instruction. At our first meeting, five adult ESL educators met in a community centre meeting room before walking around the block on a warm fall day to a local elementary school. Here we found ourselves in a completely different space; we had left our comfort zones. In time, together, we made sense of what we were seeing there and gained insight for our own teaching. By asking ourselves who knew more about our most pressing struggle, early literacy, and allowing our research to unfold in a new but related context, we grew both as practitioners and as scholars.

Engagement priorities

This chapter explored themes related to literacy development, crossing into new but related teaching environments, and connecting with colleagues to make meaningful change in the classroom. The example case in this chapter involved teachers of adult ESL with little or no first language literacy. When teachers research a related teaching context to enrich their own practice, sustained collaboration with colleagues can help make sense of what they discover. After reading this chapter, consider the following discussion points:

1. What were the two educational contexts described in this chapter? How do you think they are similar, and how they are different? Create a Venn diagram to illustrate your thinking. Reflect on these contexts' parallels and distinctions with a colleague. What are complicating factors that arise for adult learners acquiring literacy for the first time, particularly in a language they are still learning to speak?
2. Literacy development, in this chapter, is seen as a process that has parallels for adults and children. While adults as learners have unique characteristics that are to be honoured in the classroom, learning to read an alphabetic print language is seen as a process that, regardless of age, involves the same general steps and components. Do you agree? Why or why not?
3. The example project in this chapter asserts 'curiosity' as a professional development goal. Describe a time that you were genuinely curious about a topic related to your teaching and engaged with others to learn more. What happened? Would you consider this a 'collaborative inquiry'? Why or why not? What role did curiosity play in the resulting efforts?
4. Think about a current struggle or puzzle you are encountering in your teaching context. Consider, as the teacher researchers in this project did, 'Who knows more about this?' How could you reach across a professional border to learn more about that current puzzle? Who could you connect with, how so, and across what contexts?

Notes

1. ABE, or adult basic education, is the public education available to students 16 and older not enrolled at a high school in the United States. ABE programmes provide English language, basic skills, and college and career readiness courses.
2. K–12 refers to the kindergarten–12th grade general educational system in the United States. Children generally begin kindergarten at age 5 and may enter institutes of higher education after completing 12th grade.
3. While Webster-Wright's distinction between professional development and professional learning is important, with the exception of this paragraph when using Webster-Wright's terms, the term *professional development* is employed with a larger lens, referring to any and all activities a practitioner may take part in to become a better educator.

References

Auerbach, E. R. (1992). *Making Meaning, Making Change: Participatory Curriculum Development or Adult ESL Literacy*. McHenry, IL: Delta Systems.

Borko, H. (2004). Professional development and teacher learning: Mapping the terrain. *Educational Researcher*, 33(8): 3–15.

Cochran-Smith, M. and Lytle, S. L. (2009). Inquiry as Stance: Practitioner Research in the Next Generation. New York, NY: Teachers College Press.

Crandall, J. A. (1993). Professionalism and professionalization of adult ESL literacy. *TESOL Quarterly*, 27(3): 497–515.

Darling-Hammond, L. and Bransford, J. (2007). *Preparing Teachers for a Changing World: What Teachers Should Learn and Be Able to Do*. San Francisco: Jossey-Bass.

Darling-Hammond, L. and Youngs, P. (2002). Defining 'highly qualified teachers': What does 'scientifically-based research' actually tell us? *Educational Researcher*, 31(9): 13–25.

Desimone, L. M. (2009). Improving impact studies of teachers' professional development: Toward better conceptualizations and measures. *Educational Researcher*, 38(3): 181–199.

Johnson, K. A., Marchwick, K., and Liden, A. (2010). Who are Minnesota's adult ESL practitioners? *MinneWITESOL Journal*, 27: 18–41.

Kasl, E. and Yorks, L. (2010). 'Whose inquiry is this anyway?' Money, power, reports, and collaborative inquiry. *Adult Education Quarterly*, 60(4), 315.

Lave, J. and Wenger, E. (1991). *Situated Learning: Legitimate Peripheral Participation*. Cambridge: Cambridge University Press.

Little, J. W. (1987). Teachers as colleagues. In V. Richardson and D. Berliner (eds), *Educators' Handbook: A Research Perspective*. San Francisco, CA: Longman, pp. 491–518.

Marchwick, K. (2010). *Minnesota's ABE Workforce: Professional Experience, Challenges, and Needs Survey Results from ATLAS ABE Professional Development Survey*. St. Paul, MN: Hamline University. Available at: http://www.atlasabe.org/pd-system/research-surveys/abe-practitioner-survey-2009 [Accessed 14/7/13].

Roskos, K. and Bain, R. (1998). Professional development as intellectual activity: Features of the learning environment and evidence of teachers' intellectual engagement. *The Teacher Educator*, 34(2): 89–115.

Shulman, L. S. and Shulman, J. H. (2004). How and what teachers learn: A shifting perspective. *Journal of Curriculum Studies*, 36(2): 257–271.

Smith, C. (2010). The great dilemma of improving teacher quality in adult learning and literacy. *Adult Basic Education and Literacy Journal*, 4(2): 67–74.

Smith, C. and Gillespie, M. (2007). Research on professional development and teacher change: Implications for adult basic education. *Review of Adult Learning and Literacy*, 7: 205–244.

Smith, C. and Hofer, J. (2002). Pathways to change: A summary of findings from NCSALL's staff development study. *Focus on Basics*, 5(1): 3–8.

Smith, C. and Hofer, J. (2003). *The Characteristics and Concerns of Adult Basic Education Teachers*. National Center for the Study of Adult Learning and Literacy, Harvard Graduate School of Education.

Smith, C., Hofer, J., Gillespie, M., Solomon, M., and Rowe, K. (2003). *How Teachers Change: A Study of Professional Development in Adult Education*. NCSALL Report #25. Boston, MA: National Center for the Study of Adult Learning and Literacy (NCSALL).

Tarone, E. (2012, March 25). *Applied Linguists without Borders*. Presented at the American Association of Applied Linguistics, Boston, MA.

Vinogradov, P. and Liden, A. (2009). Principled training for LESLLA instructors. In I. van de Craats and J. Kurvers (eds), *Proceedings from 4th Annual LESLLA Symposium*. Antwerp, Belgium, pp. 133–144.

Webster-Wright, A. (2009). Reframing professional development throughunderstanding authentic professional learning. Review of EducationalResearch, 79(2): 702-739.

Wenger, E. (1998). *Communities of Practice: Learning, Meaning, and Identity*. Cambridge, UK: Cambridge University Press.

Wilson, B. and Corbett, D. (2001). Adult basic education and professional development: Strangers for too long. *Focus on Basics*, 4: 25–26.

Wrigley, H. (2008). From survival to thriving: Toward a more articulated system for adult ESL literacy. In I. van de Craats and J. Kurvers (eds), *Proceedings from 4th Annual LESLLA Symposium*. Antwerp, Belgium, pp. 171–185.

7
Participative Investigation: Narratives in Critical Research in the EFL Classroom

Gerrard Mugford

Introduction

In this chapter, I reflect as a research facilitator on the development of beginning non-native EFL teacher researchers in Mexico. My role in this process was to support the teachers in defining and evaluating modes of research which were locally relevant. I also wanted them to draw upon their first and second language experiences, perceptions, histories, and resources – what Bourdieu (1972) terms *habitus* – in order to critically question ideas, practices, and methodologies indiscriminately designed for global consumption. The goal of this chapter is to understand the challenges and obstacles facing the teacher researchers as they engaged in the above processes.

In terms of EFL teaching and learning, Mexico is positioned within the Expanding Circle of Kachru's (1992) model of concentric circles which represent the spread, acquisition, and use of English around the world. Whilst the Inner Circle reflects practices in long-established English-speaking countries such as Australia, the United Kingdom, and the United States and the Outer Circle embodies the use of English as a second language in countries such as India, Nigeria, and Pakistan, the Expanding Circle embraces those countries where English is taught and learnt as a foreign language. Pennycook labels Expanding Circle countries as 'norm-dependent' and appears to suggest that they take their teaching practices and methodology from 'norm-providing' Inner Circle countries (2007: 21). Whilst Kachru's concentric circles have been criticized because they are descriptive rather than explanatory (for an overview, see Canagarajah 1999; Pennycook 2007), I argue that the distinction helps to explain why countries like Mexico feel the need to follow native-speaker norms since they are not seen as having their own bona fide English language variety.

The problem of status differences is also taken up by Holliday through the distinction he makes between BANA and TESEP:

> Because of the hegemony of the received BANA [commercial British, Australasia and North American private language schools/cultural centres] English language teaching methodology, and because there are few examples of high status methodologies grown from the TESEP sector [tertiary, secondary, primary state education], the latter sector automatically becomes second class in that it is forced to make difficult adaptations of methodologies which do not really suit. (Holliday 1994: 12–13)

Consequently, BANA professionals are seen as superior since they 'come from the English-speaking West and are characterized as having an overactive professional zeal concerned with the notion that English and English teaching is originally theirs' (Holliday 2005: 3). To redress this bias, it is important to give non-native teacher researchers a sense of ownership in that English is also their language and that English language teaching belongs just as much to them as to members of the Inner Circle.

EFL approaches and methods are often considered to have a global application and it is thus believed that they can be implemented indiscriminately in any teaching situation or learning context. Challenges and problems can be confronted, overcome, and solved through blanket solutions regardless of the local environment. Pennycook emphasizes the need to address this issue through greater attention to the local:

> Rather than talk about human nature, universal cognition, or language structure, the focus has shifted towards the local, the grounded, the particular. ... there is a growing interest in the practices of everyday life. This is a move ... to capture what actually happens in particular places and at particular times. It is a shift away from broad abstractions about language, discourse and society towards local activity as part of everyday life. (Pennycook 2010: 1)

In the Mexican context, local approaches towards teaching and learning have been advocated (see, for instance, Clemente et al. 2006; Davies and Fraenkel 2003; Lethaby 2006). For instance, Clemente et al. argue that 'we need to find a way to connect the local with other "local" EFL contexts without having the gatekeepers of the global, who tend to come from dominant countries, regulating our interactions' (2006: 15). Meanwhile, Lethaby maintains that Mexican teachers need to 'look at their reality and situation and find methods that are suitable and appropriate for their learners' (2006: 57). Substantial and sustained progress has been made in research into local language teaching and learning practices by local researchers as seen in compilation publications such as Clemente (2006), Lengeling (2009, 2012) and Roux et al. (2012). However, little work has been done into the processes involved in becoming and being a non-native teacher researcher and how to support and facilitate teacher research.

One approach to examining and encouraging research at a local level is through the concepts of *voice* (Bakhtin 1984) and *habitus*. The concept of *habitus* reflects the non-native teacher researchers' first language (L1) and target language (TL) experiences, histories, and values. Grenfell uses the term 'biographical background' (2011: 82), which neatly summarizes what the non-native teacher researchers bring to the research context: their own histories and experiences of being foreign language learners and users; their own histories and experiences of being language teachers and their emerging histories and experiences of being researchers. Therefore, non-native researchers are in a unique position to relate how they embraced, accepted, questioned, resisted, or rejected the learning of English in their lives as a way of encouraging their students to do the same.

Context

As a research facilitator, I worked with 37 student teachers (16 males and 21 females) on an obligatory research course, *Proyectos de Investigación* (Investigation Projects), during their final year of a BA programme in Teaching English as a Foreign Language (TEFL) at a public university in Guadalajara, Mexico. My main goal during the course was to enable the teacher researchers to establish modes of research that validated their voice and the voices of their participants. As part of the BA programme, the students had already studied the theory of research methodology and had carried out small-scale projects, particularly employing ethnographic and action research techniques. I did not deliver a conventional research methods course; to the contrary, I wanted the student teachers to develop a healthy critical attitude towards standard ways of doing research in language learning contexts.

As part of the BA programme the student researchers taught actual students who came to English language classes at the university early in the morning as part of the BA in TEFL's *Programa Abierto de Lenguas* (PAL) – Open Language Programme – and, at the same time, they also taught at private language institutions. These student teachers, then, were already fairly experienced practitioners. So during the course I asked them how they would investigate how their own language students embraced, accepted, questioned, resisted, or rejected the learning of English in their lives. They were also given the freedom to choose their own participants to study.

My role was as a facilitator in encouraging the student researchers to put into practice (and to question) the theory that they had learnt. I wanted to focus their attention on developing localized modes of research rather than relying on conventional (and often ready-made) instruments such as questionnaires. I discussed with the teacher researchers the potential relevance of Sfard's participation metaphor as a way of participating in research. Sfard describes learning in terms of the acquisition metaphor whereby one builds up a range of possessions which cover labels such as 'knowledge, concept, conception, idea, notion, misconception' (1998: 5). In contrast, she sees the participation metaphor as learning in terms of 'situatedness, contextuality, cultural embeddedness and social mediation' (Sfard 1998: 6). The participation metaphor suggests that 'the learner should be viewed as a person interested in participation in certain kinds of activities rather than in accumulating private possessions' (Sfard 1998: 6). Such an approach sits well with encouraging teacher research as teacher researchers are encouraged to 'take part in' rather than learn about research. In a similar fashion, the teacher researchers' participants should also be encouraged 'to take part' rather than be the subjects of research.

As the research facilitator, I asked the teacher researchers, in the first stage, to consider how to go about undertaking the research and engaging their EFL students in the research in line with this participation metaphor. Given their own experiences as learners, teachers, and researchers, the teacher researchers were asked to consider how EFL students could be encouraged to talk about how they embraced, accepted, questioned, resisted, or rejected the learning of English in their lives. The aim was for the teacher researchers to use both their L1 and FL *habitus* to define effective research procedures.

In the second stage, I asked the teacher researchers to consider the best ways to collect data. They produced a range of approaches to gathering data. After initially discussing standard approaches such as interviews and questionnaires, we focused on more participatory strategies and considered such options as: interacting through discussion and narratives, chatting on Facebook, and designing and playing board games; reflecting on their own learning through the use of diary entries, journals, and collages; or doing group project work, sending emails and writing letters of advice. Through these involvement activities, the teacher researchers attempted to sensitize students to, and raise awareness of, different experiences, challenges, and problems which represented a variety of interactional patterns such as individual, pair and group work. In the final analysis, they identified language learner histories as the most effective instrument for putting the participation metaphor in practice as it allowed learners to tell their own story.

As teacher facilitator, I asked the teacher researchers to reflect on how they aimed to achieve their objectives. They had considered the end 'product' but not given sufficient thought to the process of collecting data. For instance, would their students need encouragement to tell their stories and perhaps need a model to follow? The researchers agreed that their students feel relaxed and less pressured when there is another person doing the same activity. As a result, teacher researchers felt that if they told their own language learner history first, they could encourage the EFL students to tell their own language stories. Therefore, the aim of the second stage was to encourage teacher researchers to identify locally sensitive and appropriate research tools.

After selecting the research instrument, in the third stage, the teacher researchers chose two EFL students with whom they would carry out the investigation. They were given the freedom to choose any student either from those students whom they taught on the university English language PAL classes or from those they taught at private language institutions. To understand the positive and negative aspects of learning English, one of the students should have to be successfully completing their English language programme whilst the other should have abandoned their study of the language. The teacher researchers aimed to give a *voice* to the EFL students so that, through language learner histories, they were able to say what they wanted to in a non-judgemental and understanding environment.

In the fourth stage, teacher researchers told their own language learner history to both EFL students and then encouraged the students to do the same asking them to focus both on agreeable and unpleasant experiences, successes and frustrations, and their attitude to teaching methods.

Finally, in the fifth stage, the teacher researchers were asked to present the results and, more importantly for the purposes of this chapter, to reflect on the processes of becoming and being a teacher researcher. The reflection focused on the effectiveness of the research approach in terms of achieving the desired results and the appropriateness of using the participation metaphor in their local context.

Insights

There are two particular aspects of this teacher research activity I want to reflect on in this section: what happened at the design stage and the use of narratives as a research strategy.

Research design stage

The teacher researchers' responses regarding how to encourage their students to reflect on learning English can be classified into three categories. First of all, there were participants who designed questionnaires that asked direct and perhaps invasive questions such as those from Beatriz (all names here are pseudonyms): *Why are you studying English? What is your main goal with it? Do you think that learning English is a good way to help you reach your goals?* These questionnaires reflect an acquisition metaphor approach where learning English is assessed in terms of costs and benefits. A second category reflected questions that asked language students to talk about experiences, feelings, and attitudes such as those offered by Andrea: *Can you talk about your best experience using English? Do you consider English as a helpful language? How so? What is your personal opinion about people who know more than one language?* These questions seem to refer to the respondents' *habitus* and reflect the participation metaphor as they talked about past experiences and current attitudes and values. A third approach which extends the second one above is much more autobiographical and calls for a high degree of involvement; the respondents were to personalize their experiences rather than just give them. For instance, Martin asked *What English teachers are the first ones to come to your mind, and why?* And *If a person asked you for advice about studying English, what would you say?* Meanwhile, Alberto wanted his respondents to narrate their experiences as he wanted

> to find out the story and motives that pushed both subject to study English, both for the student of English and the ex-student of English. The questionnaire, or rather, the questions that will be asked to the subjects (since this is not going to be a full-fledged questionnaire) are mostly the same, with the obvious exception that one of the questionnaires will also aim to find out why the subject quit studying English.

These approaches emerged as a result of discussions with the teacher researchers where I encouraged them to differentiate between the acquisition and the participation metaphors in terms of involving language users rather than just extracting information. I pushed them to base research approaches on the local context rather than framing investigation in conventional terms. Despite my efforts, I could see that one group of teacher researchers persisted in approaching the investigation as accumulating knowledge (i.e. finding out what the respondent knows and trying to categorize it). This highlights the challenges involved in displacing conventional modes of thinking about what it means to be a researcher. A second group tried to gain insights into and understandings of the respondents' world. They wanted to see learning and language use from the point of view of the learner rather than from the researcher's standpoint.

Narrative accounts

The teacher researchers said that they found language learning narratives useful as a research strategy in a number of ways. For example, they helped to develop their research relationships. Vicente said: 'I think it is an effective way to do research because the interviewee can feel a relation with the interviewer and give more data for the research'. Bernardo also emphasized the importance of relationships: 'Teaching is not only about sharing knowledge with students, it is interaction, that's an important part about teaching, and interaction takes place by narrating a story or an experience'. Therefore, Vicente and Bernardo underscored the importance of the participation metaphor in terms of teachers having a greater understanding of their students.

Bernardo also noted the degree of freedom that language learner histories gave respondents in expressing their views and reflected on the relative restrictiveness of forms of research that use structured questions: 'I think narrating the experience is a good way to do research because the person feels free of saying what he/she wants. I think questions make research more guided'. The freedom to speak openly was noted by Daniel who found that one of his research participants completely opened up about her feelings towards English: 'It is also interesting for me is the fact that she despises English, or at least that's the impression I got when she said "I'm pretty sure that there are many uses for it but in my case is not really that important. I'm sorry to hurt your ego teacher."' It is less likely that such attitudes would be expressed in a formal interview or questionnaire and that the respondent would apologize for giving an unexpected response.

Pablo noted that the language learner histories made the respondents feel they were making a valuable contribution to the study: 'In order to carry out a research project, it is important to make participants feel they are helping with something that might help to comprehend the problem that is unknown for the researcher. It is relevant because the participants are essential to gather information that will be helpful'. Another benefit that was noted was that the narrating of language learner histories also created scope for the unexpected, which is less likely with more conventional and structured research approaches. For instance, Teresa noted: 'It is very useful because a lot of unexpected things can come up such as, topics, feelings, perspectives'.

In their overall reflections on using narrative approaches to research the teacher researchers were generally positive. For instance, Nancy, who did not feel comfortable with this research approach, said, however, that 'it was a new experience for me and it helped me realize the role of English in my context. ... Somehow, I feel that I had the wrong perception towards research in general, and this experience changed the way I perceived it'. Meanwhile, Teresa's reflections suggested she had developed a more critical perspective on the teaching of English in her context: 'I can see that English teaching in Mexico is not being carried as it should, principles are not being applied as they should and the result is students with no motivation and unwilling to learn.' Meanwhile, Bernardo said that he had learnt a lot on a personal level: 'I think this research was so helpful because I had forgotten the problems that I encountered when learning a language, and by recalling them, I realized that maybe some of my students have these problems'.

It is important to highlight that not all participants liked the approach. For instance Nancy, as previously mentioned, said: 'I didn't feel very comfortable when using it and I didn't obtain all the information that I wanted. I think that structured interviews would have worked better for me'. Bertha also demonstrated a preference for the more conventional research approaches:

> These narrating experiences can definitely throw some information out, but I think they are not structural because you are not following a specific questionnaire, the questions are asked as they come out. I think I would apply a survey or questionnaire to get the information I want, and the information will be narrower down.

Through the research process, I encouraged the teacher researchers to critically view conventional data collecting methods and only to adopt those that allowed them to achieve their objectives rather than going for those that were conventional and convenient (in both data collection and analysis). Nonetheless, some teacher researchers resisted this idea, although I would hope that they still benefited from being exposed to alternative ways of doing research. Overall, I feel that as a research facilitator I was successful to some degree in encouraging teacher researchers to develop locally appropriate modes of doing research with their language learners.

Implications

Whilst this research project was carried out by a specific group of Mexican teacher researchers attempting to develop locally sensitive modes of understanding their own teaching-learning environment, the findings have implications for a wider audience.

First of all, encouraging teacher researchers to adopt, implement, and evaluate the usefulness of their chosen mode of research, in this instance language learner histories, give the researchers a *voice* as opposed to just following and implementing tried and tested research approaches. Such a process encourages teacher researchers to look at their own L1 and developing TL *habitus*, and relate research to the experiences, values, and attitudes of the EFL participants themselves.

Second, the use of narratives helped the teacher researchers reconnect with their students and develop closer interpersonal relationships. The interpersonal dimension is all too often lacking in EFL research where the focus is on producing tangible results that can be immediately translated into 'better' teaching methods and instant improvements in learner performance. Narratives take a long-term view of teaching and learning and see these as a process that has successes, failures, and frustrations.

Third, my experience highlights the value of collecting feedback from novice teacher researchers about their perceptions of the learning process they are engaged in. The feedback provided by my student teachers highlighted both the value they perceived in the work we were doing as well as the difficulties they experienced. Feedback also ensured I was aware of resistance to the approach to research I was encouraging. Collective feedback in this manner, especially formatively, can allow facilitators of teacher research to make sensitive adjustments to their work. Of course, this does not mean that all resistance can be overcome; but being aware of it certainly allows the facilitator of teacher research to consider what action might be taken to alleviate it.

One last point I should acknowledge here is that I am aware that what I was encouraging these novice teacher researchers to do was challenging – much more challenging, I would say, than asking them to design and administer a questionnaire (though this task too requires a certain level of technical skill). However, the approach to teacher research I was promoting involved much more than technique; the teacher researchers were being asked to reconceptualize their existing understandings of what research is, what researchers do, and what the role of research participants is. It is important, I think, for facilitators of teacher research to appreciate fully the level of challenge they are creating for those they work with, so that they can provide appropriate support.

Conclusion

I have found the participation metaphor to be a valuable perspective from which to introduce teacher research. It allows for inquiry that is methodical, and which is sensitive to participants and engages them meaningfully in the research process. Participatory forms of research can also enhance teachers' understandings of learners and these understandings can feed into what teachers do in the classroom. The example of narratives of language learning histories I have used here also illustrates an approach to teacher research that creates meaningful relationships between the researcher and the participants; again, this provides a welcome contrast to conventional views of research where such relationships are considered undesirable or are simply not feasible because of the limited time researchers have to interact with participants.

Engagement priorities

To promote further work on the issues addressed in the chapter, research facilitators and teacher researchers need to explore how participants can be more closely involved in the research process rather than just provide information that is used in the product. Below, I have taken the following four key concepts from the chapter for further discussion, exploration, and debate: participation metaphor; language learner histories; narratives; and language as local practice:

1. Participation metaphor: the participation metaphor suggests that 'the learner should be viewed as a person interested in participation in certain

kinds of activities rather than in accumulating private possessions' (Sfard 1998: 6). Is this realistic with regard to teacher research? How feasible is this approach when teachers and language learners' time is limited?
2. Participation metaphor: The participation metaphor aims to give developing teacher researchers a *voice*. As argued by Borg (2013), research needs to be disseminated in some way? How can teacher researchers project their voice and participate in the EFL community and beyond?
3. Participation metaphor: in the chapter, I argued that teacher researchers and participants are mutually dependent in creating knowledge rather than passively acquiring knowledge. What practical ways and methods can be developed to achieve this aim?
4. Language learner histories: what different ways are there for encouraging teachers and language learners to 'produce' their own histories as part of a research approach?
5. Language as local practice: Where is the balance between encouraging developing teacher researchers to build on, and refer to, their own *habitus* and learning from global aspects of research?
6. Language as local practice: in the chapter, the emphasis is placed on the non-native teacher researcher. Is there a real and substantial difference between non-native teacher researchers and native teacher researchers? If so, what are they?

References

Bakhtin, M. M. (1984). *Problems of Dostoevsky's Poetics*, edited and translated by Caryl Emerson. Minneapolis: University of Minnesota Press.

Borg, S. (2013). *Teacher Research in Language Teaching: A Critical Analysis*. Cambridge: Cambridge University Press.

Bourdieu, P. (1972). *Outline of a Theory of Practice*. Cambridge: Cambridge University Press.

Canagarajah, S. (1999). *Resisting Linguistic Imperialism in English Teaching*. Oxford: Oxford University Press.

Clemente, A. (ed.) (2006). Critical pedagogies (Special Issue). *MEXTESOL Journal*, 30(2): 1–133.

Clemente, A., Crawford, T., Garcia, L., Higgins, M., Kissinger, D., Lengeling, M., Lopez Gopar, M., Narvaez, O., Sayer, P., and Sughrua, W. (2006). A call for a critical perspective on English teaching in Mexico. *MEXTESOL Journal*, 19(2): 11–16.

Davies, P. and Fraenkel, A. (2003). *The Language in English Teaching*. London: Richmond.

Grenfell, M. (2011). Language variation. In M. Grenfell (ed.), *Bourdieu, Language and Linguistics*. London: Continuum, pp. 67–96.

Holliday, A. (1994). *Appropriate Methodology and Social Context*. Cambridge: Cambridge University.

Holliday, A. (2005). *The Struggle to Teach English as an International Language*. Oxford: Oxford University Press.

Kachru, B. J. (1992). Teaching world Englishes. In B. J. Kachru (ed.), *The Other Tongue: English across Cultures*. Urbana: University of Illinois Press (Second edition), pp. 355–365.

Lengeling, M. (ed.) (2009). *Selección de Artículos del Segundo Congreso de Investigación Cualitativa/Selection of Articles from the Second International Qualitative Research Conference*. Universidad de Guanajuato, Mexico.

Lengeling, M. (ed.) (2012). *Investigación Cualitativa e Interpretación Selección de Artículos del Tercer Congreso de Investigación Cualitativa/Qualitative Research and Interpretation Selection of Articles from the Third International Qualitative Research Conference*. Universidad de Guanajuato, Mexico.

Lethaby, C. (2006). Appropriating English in Mexico. *MEXTESOL Journal*, 30(2): 51–58.

Pennycook, A. (2007). *Global Englishes and Transcultural Flows*. Abingdon, Oxon: Routledge.

Pennycook, A. (2010). *Language as Local Practice*. London: Routledge.

Roux, R., Mora, A., and Trejo, N. P. (eds) (2012). *Research in English Language Teaching: Mexican Perspectives*. Bloomington, IN: Palibrio/COLTAM/UAT.

Sfard, A. (1998). On two metaphors for learning and the dangers of choosing just one. *Educational Researcher*, 27(2): 4–13.

8
Facilitating Teacher Research: Course Design, Implementation, and Evaluation

Simon Borg

Introduction

Teacher research is a viable form of professional development with significant transformative potential. However, while several texts are available that provide advice on the conduct of teacher research, discussions of how to *teach* teacher research remain very scarce. I begin this chapter by highlighting this gap in the literature before outlining the context of a teacher research initiative I recently facilitated. I will then analyse this initiative to highlight key issues in the design, implementation, and evaluation of teacher research courses. It is important to consider such issues because giving teachers opportunities to do teacher research will in itself not guarantee that productive inquiries will be carried out. Teachers very often need to *learn* to become teacher researchers and it is therefore important to think about the ways in which such learning can be supported.

Starting from a consideration of the literature on research methods more generally, it is clear that pedagogical issues have been periodically discussed in a range of disciplines; for example, Saville (2008) discusses the teaching of research methods in psychology, DesJardins (2005) does so in computer science, while Booth and Harrington (2003) examine research methods courses in business programmes. More general analyses of the teaching of research methods have been provided by Onwuegbuzie and Leech (2005) and Birbili (2003), while specific discussions of teaching particular areas of research are also available (Page 1997 and Glesne and Webb 1993 both focus on the teaching of qualitative research). Overall, though, the volume of literature which examines the teaching of research methods remains very small compared to the very substantial range of resources focusing on research methods themselves. Specific attention to the teaching of teacher research seems even more limited, with McKernan's (1996) chapter on teaching action research being an exception here.

In the field of language teaching, the contrast between the volume of literature on doing research and on teaching is similarly pronounced. Thus while several texts exist which provide practical advice on doing research (e.g. Dörnyei 2007; Nunan and Bailey 2009) and teacher research (e.g. Burns 2010), limited attention has been paid to how research methods for language teachers are taught. The few relevant sources that do exist are also written with undergraduate and postgraduate contexts in mind (Diab 2006; Kiely et al. 2004; Lorch 2005) and analyses of how to support teacher research outside such academic contexts are thus lacking. One exception here is my own recent work (Borg 2013) in which I discussed two teacher research initiatives and identified the features of them that contributed to their success. More recently, Burns (2014) has also analysed a teacher research scheme in Australia and identified a range of factors that contributed to its success; for example, teachers were volunteers, resources were available, and opportunities for dissemination were available.

Despite limitations in the literature on teaching research methods, though, an overall analysis of this material does suggest a range of parameters which provide a useful framework in discussing the design of teacher research courses. These parameters are:

1. *Objectives* – what impacts on teachers' knowledge, skills, beliefs, and practices does the course seek to achieve? Are impacts on students also being targeted?
2. *Content* – what issues in research methods generally and teacher research specifically does the course cover?
3. *Organization* – what are the components of the course and how are these sequenced?
4. *Pedagogy* – what instructional strategies are utilized by the course facilitator and what learning activities are participants engaged in?
5. *Assessment and evaluation* – if the course is assessed, what forms of assessment are used? How is the course evaluated?

The decisions that are made in relation to the many of the above course parameters will themselves be underpinned (explicitly or implicitly) by assumptions about teacher learning and research which facilitators should make explicit at the design stage of teacher research courses.

Context

The English Language Teaching Reforms (ELTR) initiative, as Coleman (2010) notes, has been supporting ELT in higher education in Pakistan since 2004. Within this reform scheme, I facilitated a teacher research course for teachers of English in universities and colleges in Pakistan initially between May 2012 and March 2013 (Phases 1–3), with an additional period of report writing and dissemination (Phase 4) continuing until May 2014. In the first year there were three face-to-face workshops (all lasting five days and conducted in Islamabad) with online support in between. Phase 1 equipped participants with a basic understanding of research, particularly of teacher research. During this phase participants also developed a research proposal and conducted a pilot study. In Phase 2, participants developed a deeper understanding of data collection methods, and collected the data for their studies. In Phase 3 the focus was on data analysis and report writing. Additionally, in the final workshop some time was dedicated to a discussion of how participants might act as research mentors for others in their contexts. Phase 4 was dedicated to the further development of the teachers' reports and the production of an edited volume of these (Borg 2014). This list of contents from this volume illustrates the themes examined by the teachers:

- undergraduate students' attitudes to pair work;
- using group work in large classes;
- introducing interactive learning in higher education;
- student and teacher views about using the L1 in English classrooms;
- university students' attitudes towards code-switching;
- using simulation in teaching oral skills to hotel management students;
- language anxiety in university learners of English;
- markers' criteria in assessing English essays;
- improving writing skills through written corrective feedback;
- improving coherence in university students' writing;
- dropout of students from English language courses;
- student and teacher perspectives on the use of technology.

Although all the teachers had experience of studying research methods (many had MA degrees and some were close to completing doctorates), teacher research was a novel concept for them – they initially saw research as a complex, theoretical activity which high-level academics did to or on others. Thus we invested a substantial amount of time during Phase 1 to 'unlearn' some of these deeply-rooted views about what research is; we emphasized the fact that teachers could be researchers in and of their own contexts and that there was considerable value in them being so.

In terms of outcomes, 16 of the 18 teachers who started the course completed it and, of those 16, 12 produced written reports which were included in the final publication. Also, teachers' perceptions of the course, as measured through evaluations after each phase and exit interviews at the end of the project, were very positive. For example, on a scale of 10 (1=low, 10=high), the mean level of overall participant satisfaction with the course was 9.4, while in individual exit interviews conducted with the teachers, they mentioned the following benefits:

- greater awareness of what research is;
- improved practical skills in doing research;
- enhanced professional independence ('You have made me an independent individual, I believe that I can now carry on plenty more research');
- enhanced understanding of their own teaching;
- increased motivation to learn about and do research;
- increased self-esteem as a result of being recognized by colleagues as experts ('I find myself in a position where I can advise others ... and I felt good about it');
- changes in their teaching ('It made me look at my own teaching methodology and there has been a change in the way I teach');
- changes in their attitudes or mentality as teachers ('I think this course has brought a lot of inward change').

My focus in the next section is to understand, using the framework introduced earlier, what factors contributed to what was generally seen to be a successful initiative (though later I will also highlight areas where impact was perhaps less obvious).

Insights

Although teacher research has been advocated for many years as a valuable form of professional development (e.g. Nunan 1989), it has generally been difficult to translate relevant theoretical ideas into sustained professional activity leading to meaningful outcomes. In recent years, though, our understandings of how teacher research can be productively supported have developed significantly and we are increasingly better informed (especially through the literature on teacher professional learning more generally, e.g. Muijs et al. 2014) about how to promote teacher research effectively. I will now use the framework introduced above to examine the features of the course under discussion here which contributed to its success.

Objectives

The course aimed to promote change in five areas: beliefs, knowledge, skills, attitudes and practices. Attention to each is, I think, central in maximizing the impact of teacher research initiatives. As noted above, beliefs were the starting point in the course, and it was important to give participants the chance to articulate their existing views about research and opportunities to review these.

Thus, initially, the predominant view of research the teachers held (shaped undoubtedly by their prior experiences and the research culture in Pakistan more generally) was that it was a complex, exclusive, academic activity; by the end of the course this had been modified so that the participants saw research as a feasible, practical activity which teachers (and not just an academic elite) could engage in. Teacher research courses cannot be effective unless teachers' beliefs about research are appropriately aligned with the notions of research that teacher research is based on.

Knowledge was a second area of intended impact – teachers needed to develop an understanding of basic concepts in educational research (e.g. key terms and their meaning). Formal knowledge development of this kind was important because good-quality research cannot be conducted without the foundational knowledge required. However, the theoretical element of the course did not occur at the expense of the other areas of impact I am discussing here. Thus, the development of practical research skills were also given due importance. This was important because I wanted the teachers not just to know about research but to do it – in this respect research, like teaching, is ultimately a practical activity. The course, therefore, as discussed below, had a strong practical component, both during the workshops and, even more prominently, in between workshops when teachers were doing their fieldwork.

Two final areas of impact were attitudes and practices. By attitude here I mean teachers' general dispositions towards research as a form of professional development. Their beliefs, knowledge and skills may grow, but without corresponding changes in their attitudes it is unlikely that teachers will become enthusiastic about doing teacher research. The course, therefore, aimed to create positive attitudes to research throughout and to give teachers a strong sense of achievement. Finally, the course also aimed to impact on teachers' classroom practices – it was hoped that the research they did in their own classrooms would feed into their work and lead to developments in teaching and learning in their English courses. Beyond the feedback provided by the teachers themselves, this is one area of the course where direct evidence of impact is less evident. The importance of this range of objectives was an important feature of this course; a narrow and exclusive focus on theoretical knowledge was avoided and learning about research was linked throughout to teachers' own classroom practices.

One additional objective for the course was the publication of the teachers' reports. I have always argued that research needs to be made public in some way and from the outset it was my hope that a volume of teachers' work might be produced (although this was not part of the original brief for the course). This objective motivated the teachers, for although they understood the value of teacher research for their teaching, achieving a publication was also in their context an important professional achievement.

Content

The content of this course (particularly in Phases 1 and 2) was fairly conventional in that standard issues in doing research were covered; thus we progressed from a discussion of the components of the research process to specific analyses of the planning, fieldwork and dissemination phases of a research project. Each of these phases was discussed in particular detail – for example, under 'Planning' we examined issues such as choosing a topic and defining research questions, while under 'Fieldwork' different ways of collecting and analysing data were considered. What was less conventional about the course, though, was the space allocated to an initial examination of teachers' beliefs – as explained above, this was central to the course given teachers' previous experiences of research. Phase 3, too, was much more loosely structured content-wise, with an increasingly flexible and responsive approach being taken to decisions about which issues to focus on. Another area of content that received significant attention was oral presentations – the teachers each gave two presentations (once in Workshop 2 and again in Workshop 3) and received peer feedback on them. Overall, though, I would not say that the content of this course was radically innovative – its impact stemmed more from its organization and pedagogy, from its constructive orientation and the positive relationships that were established within the group.

Organization

The organization of the course was shaped by the practical constraint that I would need to travel to Pakistan for the workshops but would not otherwise be available to provide face-to-face support to the teachers. This consideration apart, though, the structure of the course was informed by a number of principles:

- an extended course is preferable to an intensive one, to allow more time for the teachers to engage with ideas, to interact, to experiment in their classrooms and to benefit from feedback on the work they are doing. The in-country workshops were thus organized in three phases with a few months in between each.
- intensive periods for the teachers to focus wholly on the course are beneficial, allowing them to concentrate on learning to be teacher researchers without competing demands on their time. For this reason, the teachers were given official release from work for the three one-week intensive workshops.
- a practical component is essential; thus in between the workshops the teachers were developing and doing their teacher research projects in their classrooms. Without a practical element, teachers will learn *about* teacher research rather than learning to *do* it.

- a clear progressive course structure provides teachers with a helpful sense of direction. The course was structured in a logical manner to proceed from foundational issues, to the development of research proposals, and then to the design, implementation and reporting of the teacher research projects. There is nothing innovative in this; what the teachers found helpful, though, is that this progression was explicit, as were the various phases of the course and the tasks that needed to be accomplished within each.
- support structures are vital in maximizing completion rates and enhancing the quality of teacher research. Particularly in between the workshops, it was essential that teachers received ongoing support to help them cope with the challenges that novice teacher researchers face. In our case, support was provided through an online platform (Wiggio), via email and Skype. This allowed both peer support among the teachers and individual support from me to them. I have no doubt that without support in between the workshops the outcomes of the course would have been substantially less positive.

Pedagogy

As noted above, I believe that the organizational and pedagogical features of the course were more influential than the actual course content in facilitating the outcomes that were achieved. Here are some aspects of teaching and learning on the course that contributed in a positive way:

- teachers' expectations were addressed. The teachers were an experienced group who were expecting a 'serious' course delivered by an 'expert'. They had strong views about what good 'lecturers' did. It was important that, especially initially, they were reassured on all these fronts, so early sessions on the course involved a certain amount of frontal teaching, PowerPoint presentations and theory. Once my credibility had been established, the course pedagogy became less input-driven and more inductive.
- collaborative learning was emphasized. During workshops, the teachers worked together on a range of tasks and discussions; during oral presentations, the teachers supported one another with constructive feedback; online, the teachers shared materials and ideas. A strong sense of community was thus established.
- a constructive climate was established. Although it was important that I was seen as authoritative, it was possible to achieve this while being approachable, sensitive to the teachers' needs, open to feedback, and positive in the way I commented on teachers' work. Teachers were also constructive in the manner in which they interacted with each other.

- the teachers were increasingly involved in course decisions. During the workshops they provided written feedback every day and I adjusted our subsequent work accordingly. Particularly after Phase 1, they made suggestions for the areas of teacher research they wanted to focus on and their suggestions were incorporated into the course. And decisions about the focus of their teacher research projects and their conduct were made by every individual teacher.
- the teachers were required to produce regular written work and they received prompt and detailed written feedback on this. Writing regularly meant that the teachers gained ongoing practice in writing in English about their research. It also meant that by the end of the project they had produced drafts of many of the individual sections needed for their final reports. Writing also provided concrete evidence on which I was able to comment; it gave me a clear sense of the progress each teacher was making and allowed me to personalize the support the teachers received.
- the importance of quality was emphasized throughout the course. Although there is intrinsic value in the process of teacher research in its own right, if the aim is to generate insights which teachers can use as the basis of subsequent decisions about their work, it is important that the projects they do meet basic quality criteria – e.g. ethical, technically competent, unbiased, evidence-based. I would not want to over-emphasize the technical dimension of teacher researcher but neglecting it will inevitably mean that, while teachers may experience a reflective orientation to their teaching, they will not generate trustworthy findings.
- an attempt was made to make the experience as enjoyable as possible for the teachers. Although research is a serious topic, this does not mean there is no room for humour and fun on a research methods course. For example, research terminology was learnt and revised through the kinds of vocabulary games teachers can use in their own classrooms with learners of English.

Assessment and evaluation

This teacher research course was not assessed – there were no tests or assignments and I did not grade the teachers' final reports. Certificates were awarded to all teachers who attended all phases of the course. It could be argued that assessment increases motivation; it is also necessary where a formal qualification is being awarded or when teacher performance on a course is to be used as the basis of subsequent decisions (e.g. about scholarships). However, given the choice, I would avoid formal assessment on teacher research courses; it can be stressful and may overshadow developmental goals (i.e. teachers may focus more on passing and less on doing teacher research in a way that maximizes their development – though if appropriate assessment criteria are defined, this risk can be minimized). In terms of evaluation, as noted already, the teachers provided written feedback every day during the workshops; fuller evaluations were completed at the end of each phase and I also produced a final course evaluation report based on all the data available. The course was sponsored by the Higher Education Commission in Pakistan and the British Council; both bodies collected their own evaluation data from the teachers.

Implications

I will now consider the broader implications of the experiences discussed above for the design of teacher research courses. One initial question to ask is whether learning to be a teacher researcher actually has to take place within the formal structure provided by a course. In the context described above, and in many similar to it, I would say without hesitation that a suitably designed course offers many more benefits to a wider range of teachers than teachers working individually or even collaboratively but without external support can achieve. I am not saying that it is not possible for teachers to develop independently as teacher researchers; however, a structured course such as that described above will be desirable in contexts (of which many exist globally) where (a) conventional notions of research dominate; (b) teacher research (and reflective practice more generally) is a novel idea; (c) professional development is associated with externally-driven activity rather than teacher-led; (d) teachers' research skills are not well-developed; and (e) the conditions for teacher research within institutions are unfavourable. In such contexts, it is unlikely that teachers will be able to develop independently as teacher researchers. A course, however, will provide a supportive framework within which the development of teacher researchers can be fostered, as my experience here and elsewhere has shown. Examples do exist, of course, of one or more teachers working alone or together to conduct systematic inquiry in their classrooms (e.g. Denny 2005); however, such contexts are typically amenable to high levels of teacher autonomy and involve teachers who are accustomed to reflective and collaborative forms of professional development. Even in such contexts, though, there is increasing evidence that a structured approach, where external support is available and a cohort of teachers work together on a course, is an effective model for promoting teacher research (e.g. Burns 2011).

A second issue of general relevance highlighted by my experience relates to the degree of formality that teacher research courses need to have. In its content, the course I have described here was not very different from that you might find on an MA TESOL programme at many universities around the world (though I am not certain that many of these pay as much attention to teachers' beliefs about research as they should). The course also led to a fairly standard research report (as opposed to alternatives such as narratives, blogs, scrap books, and photo-based accounts). What scope, therefore, is there for teacher research courses to cover alternative topics and to lead to alternative forms of dissemination? My answer is that the exploration of such alternatives is very desirable, with some caveats. One is that teachers' expectations and previous learning experiences cannot be ignored. In contexts where these are fairly traditional, alternatives need to be introduced gradually. In such contexts, too, a standard output such as a research paper may be more valued by teachers and more officially recognized than alternatives. Also, in contexts where teacher research is a novel concept and teachers have had to make significant cognitive and attitudinal adjustments to complete a teacher research project, expecting them, additionally, to devise alternative written formats for dissemination is perhaps too much to expect. Having said that, though, we did organize an event in Lahore where the teachers were able to share their studies orally, not through formal plenary presentations but through ten-minute small group discussions repeated three times (to different groups). This was a refreshing and engaging way for the researchers and the audience alike to take part in a dissemination event. A third proviso relates to the time and support available. In the course described here I was fortunate to have an initial ten months for the course and a final phase of over a year in which reports were drafted, revised after feedback, edited and published. Even though a conventional template for research papers was followed, the teachers needed substantial support in preparing these. Much additional time would have been needed to support them in considering and developing alternatives. This does not imply that alternatives to conventional forms of reporting research should not be considered; rather, my point here is that the decision to be 'alternative' cannot be taken simply on paradigmatic grounds and careful consideration of the feasibility of the idea (e.g. the readiness of the teachers) is essential. Also, no matter how 'alternative' a teacher research course is, it is hard to see how a concern for foundational concerns such as ethics, rigour, evidence, and impact can be avoided.

Earlier in this chapter I noted that teacher evaluations of this teacher research course were positive and that teachers also reported that the research they had done had led to changes in their teaching. I also noted that this was one course outcome for which strong evidence was not available. Another issue of broader relevance to consider, then, is how the impact of teacher research on what teachers do can be assessed more systematically (i.e. beyond summative self-reports). It was not feasible for me to visit teachers' classrooms and, even if I had been able to, a one-off visit would not have allowed me to make any connections between the teachers' research and their teaching. It would seem useful, then, to build a focus on this kind of impact into the ongoing evaluations of the course from the outset. For example, when teachers are developing their initial proposals, they can be asked to think about the impact they think the project will have on their work; then they can be asked to revisit this issue at periodic points during the course. Teachers can also be asked to include a specific section on impact in the reports (oral and/or written) that they produce. I am not suggesting that teacher research must always result in immediate concrete changes to what teachers do; for example, the outcome of an action research project might be an awareness that current practices are better than those experimented with during the research and in that case the outcome is a change in teachers' understandings of what they do rather than any behavioural change. This is, of course, important. However, we would hope that in many cases what teachers learn through teacher research can be utilized by them to make positive changes of some kind, no matter how modest, to how they teach.

Pedagogically, I have noted that the way the teacher research course was taught was a major contributor to its success. However, the way I characterized it earlier – a collaborative, interactive, constructive, practical, scaffolded experience – is nothing more than a summary of the kind of good practice that I would seek to apply (but not necessarily achieve with the same degree of success) on any course I teach. The point I want to make here is that I doubt there is a specific pedagogy for teacher research courses; rather, what we know about learning generally can inform the way we support the development of teacher researchers. For example, if we accept the constructivist principle that learning is the interaction between what people know and new experience, then it becomes important to give teachers space to examine their prior experiences and beliefs about research early in a teacher research course; and if we embrace socio-cultural notions which stress the social and situated nature of learning, then learning to be a teacher researcher will be enhanced through practical opportunities for teachers to be researchers in their classrooms and for them to reflect on this learning with peers. Additionally, the literature on teacher education provides specific insight into how *teachers* learn and this, too, should underpin the facilitation of teacher research; for example, one contemporary argument is that professional learning should be driven by the need to support students in specific ways (Timperley et al. 2008). This implies that teacher research will be a more meaningful task for teachers, and of greater value to students, when it is driven by a challenge, problem, or puzzle that teachers have identified in their own classrooms. Overall, the point here is that it is beneficial for facilitators of teacher research to articulate the pedagogical principles that underpin their work. Once they have, the principles are available for scrutiny and review if needed; it also becomes possible to share these principles with teachers, thus enhancing their awareness of why they are being engaged in particular kinds of learning experiences.

Another point worth examining is the role of students in teacher research. Proponents of exploratory practice (Allwright and Hanks 2009) argue that students should be co-researchers rather than subjects who are studied by their teachers. In the course under discussion here, students (and other participants) generally functioned as conventional research subjects – they provided data but otherwise played no active role in the research the teachers were doing. And, to be fair to the teachers, our course did not pay particular attention to this issue. It is, though, one that merits explicit attention when teacher research courses are being developed.

The final issue I will consider here relates to the conditions surrounding the course under discussion which facilitated or hindered its effectiveness. Starting from the former, several facilitative conditions were in place:

- motivated teachers;
- official support;
- funding;
- external advisor;
- ongoing support (including online);
- some release from teaching;
- sufficiently long course duration;
- clear course structure;
- well-defined target outcome;
- projects relevant to the teachers;
- flexible (as opposed to fixed) course content.

At the same time the following conditions were not conducive to teachers' development as teacher researchers:

- limited access to resources such as literature;
- no face-to-face support outside workshops;
- challenging working conditions (e.g. no Internet, civil unrest, regular power cuts);
- conflicting motivations for doing research.

This last point is particularly interesting; although the focus of the course was teacher research, some participants were motivated by academic concerns related to getting published or completing a project that would support a higher qualification they were studying for. Teacher research does not exclude such motivations (see Arnold 2012; Edwards and Willis 2005 for collections of teacher research conducted as part of academic study), yet, as I have discussed elsewhere (Borg 2013), when academic goals become a teacher researcher's main concern, there is a distinct risk that attention to the development of teachers' own understandings and practices may be obscured. I have also encountered (on a different course) cases where some teachers said they wanted to do academic research, not teacher research, because they saw their research as preparation for a career outside teaching rather than a way of growing as reflective practitioners. Such cases have implications for the selection of participants on teacher research courses and the need for the purposes of courses to be made explicit from the outset.

Conclusion

Increasing global activity indicates that teacher research is being recognized as a valuable form of professional development for teachers of English. It is also noticeable that many current teacher research initiatives take the form of a course, providing teachers with the structure and support to facilitate the task of carrying out good quality investigations in their own classrooms. These initiatives provide opportunities for the development (through research) of deeper understandings of how teacher research courses can be made more effective. I hope that the insights provided in this chapter contribute to this goal.

Engagement priorities

Based on the analysis provided in this chapter, key questions in the design, conduct, and evaluation of teacher research courses that merit further attention are:

1. Before teacher research is chosen as a professional development strategy, it is important to assess the extent to which it is an appropriate option for the target teachers. In what kinds of contexts might teacher research *not* be appropriate?
2. Teacher research creates opportunities for teachers to experiment with alternative ways of making their work public. What options exist for doing so and are practical examples of these available that can provide models for teacher research facilitators to use on their courses?
3. How can teacher research be made more participatory, in the sense of involving students and colleagues more directly in different phases of the research and not just as a source of data? How willing and able are students and colleagues to assume these extended roles?
4. What criteria should be used to judge the quality of teacher research (see, for example, Anderson and Herr 1999)?
5. What approaches to monitoring and evaluation can generate systematic data about the immediate and longer-term impacts that teacher research courses have on teachers, students, and organizations?

References

Allwright, D. and Hanks, J. (2009). *The Developing Language Learner: An Introduction to Exploratory Practice*. Basingstoke: Palgrave Macmillan.

Anderson, G. L. and Herr, K. (1999). The new paradigm wars: Is there room for rigorous practitioner knowledge in schools and universities? *Educational Researcher, 28*(5): 12–21.

Arnold, C. (2012). *Improving Your Reflective Practice Through Stories of Practitioner Research*. London: Routledge.

Birbili, M. (2003). Teaching educational research methods. Available at: http://escalate.ac.uk/resources/teachingresearchmethods/index.html [Accessed 28/07/14].

Booth, C. and Harrington, J. (2003). Research methods courses in undergraduate business programmes: An investigation. *The International Journal of Management Education, 3*(3): 19–31.

Borg, S. (2013). *Teacher Research in Language Teaching: A Critical Analysis*. Cambridge: Cambridge University Press.

Borg, S. (ed.) (2014). *Teacher Research in Pakistan: Enhancing the Teaching and Learning of English*. Lahore: British Council.

Burns, A. (2010). *Doing Action Research in English Language Teaching. A Guide for Practitioners*. New York: Routledge.

Burns, A. (2011). Embedding teacher research into a national language programme: Lessons from a pilot project. *Research Notes, 44*: 3–6.

Burns, A. (2014). Professional learning in Australian ELICOS: An action research orientation. *English Australia Journal, 29*(2): 3–20.

Coleman, H. (2010). *Teaching and Learning in Pakistan: The Role of Language in Education*. Islamabad: British Council.

Denny, H. (2005). Can busy classroom teachers really do action research? An action research study in an EAL tertiary setting. *New Zealand Studies in Applied Linguistics, 11*(2): 59–73.

DesJardins, M. (2005). Case study: Teaching research skills to computer science graduate students. Available at: http://maple.cs.umbc.edu/papers/eista05-dj.pdf [Accessed 28/07/14].

Diab, R. L. (2006). Teaching practice and student learning in the introductory research methods class. *TESL-EJ, 10*(2). Available at http://www.tesl-ej.org/ej38/a6.pdf [Accessed 28/07/14].

Dörnyei, Z. (2007). *Research Methods in Applied Linguistics*. Oxford: Oxford University Press.

Edwards, C. and Willis, J. (eds) (2005). *Teachers Exploring Tasks in English Language Teaching*. Basingstoke: Palgrave Macmillan.

Glesne, C. and Webb, R. (1993). Teaching qualitative research: Who does what? *International Journal of Qualitative Studies in Education, 6*(3): 253–266.

Kiely, R., Clibbon, G., Rea-Dickins, P., Walter, C., and Woodfield, H. (2004). Teachers into researchers: A study of learning to research on a Masters in TESOL programme. Available at: http://www.llas.ac.uk/projects/1454 [Accessed 28/07/14].

Lorch, M. (2005). Turning students into researchers: Introduction to research methods in applied linguistics. Available at: http://www.llas.ac.uk/resources/gpg/2273 [Accessed 28/07/14].

McKernan, J. (1996). *Curriculum Action Research: A Handbook of Methods and Resources for The Reflective Practitioner* (2nd ed.). London: Kogan Page.

Muijs, D., Kyriakides, L., van der Werf, G., Creemers, B., Timperley, H., and Earl, L. (2014). State of the art – teacher effectiveness and professional learning. *School Effectiveness and School Improvement, 25*(2): 231–256.

Nunan, D. (1989). The teacher as researcher. In C. J. Brumfit and R. Mitchell (eds), *Research in the Language Classroom*. London: Modern English Publications/The British Council, pp. 16–32.

Nunan, D. and Bailey, K. M. (2009). *Exploring Second Language Classroom Research*. Boston: Heinle.

Onwuegbuzie, A. J. and Leech, N. L. (2005). Taking the 'q' out of research: Teaching research methodology courses without the divide between quantitative and qualitative paradigms. *Quality and Quantity, 39*(3): 267–296.

Page, R. N. (1997). A thought about curriculum in qualitative research methods. *International Journal of Qualitative Studies in Education, 10*(2): 171–173.

Saville, B. (2008). *A Guide to Teaching Research Methods in Psychology*. Oxford: Blackwell.

Timperley, H., Wilson, A., Barrar, H., and Fung, I. (2008). *Teacher Professional Learning and Development: Best Evidence Synthesis Iteration (BES)*. Wellington, New Zealand: Ministry of Education.

9
Supporting Teacher Research through a Practical In-Service Course

Anisa Saleh Al-Maskari

Introduction

Recent literature has stressed the value of teacher research as a means of supporting teacher professional development. In this chapter I will report, from my perspective as a teacher trainer, on an INSET course offered to teachers of English in Oman and entitled *Research for Professional Development* (henceforth RPD). Participant feedback on the course has been generally positive and I would like to reflect on the features of the structure and the processes of RPD which have contributed to the positive evaluation of it by teachers. Such insights can, I believe, be of value to facilitators elsewhere who want to promote teacher research. I will first discuss some literature relevant to the analysis that will follow.

Teacher research involves inquiry by teachers into what happens in their classrooms and which takes place through systematic reflection using a range of data collection tools (Farrell 2007; Wallace 1998). Teacher research, as Crookes (1992: 137) notes, is seen to be important for teachers' 'educational renewal and professional growth' and, more specifically, is considered to be a strategy that can lead to improvements in teachers' classroom practices (Burns 2010). Teacher research can also enhance teacher confidence while, as Borg (2013) notes, it can have a positive effect on student learning and schools more generally. There is general agreement in the literature that teacher research has the potential to contribute in significant ways to teaching and learning.

In practice, though, teachers often find it challenging to do teacher research and Borg (2013) has listed a number of conditions that can facilitate efforts to help teachers overcome such challenges. These are:

- support for teacher researchers offered by teacher trainers, schools, supervisors, or other teachers;
- time;

- input which helps promote development in teachers' beliefs, knowledge, and skills;
- access to literature;
- opportunities for teachers to share their work.

In contexts such as Oman where, until recently, the idea of teachers as researchers was very new, one key obstacle to promoting teacher research lies in the misconceptions teachers have about what research is. For example, as Borg (2009) has shown, teachers often equate research with large-scale statistical studies and, as a result, teachers do not feel research is an activity that is feasible or relevant to them. Some research has also been conducted in Oman about the RPD course (Al-Abri 2011; Al-Raesi 2013). While these studies indicate that teachers benefited through expanded knowledge of teacher research, increased confidence in their abilities as researchers, enhanced reflectivity and positive changes in their teaching, it was also found that a lack of time, resources and a heavy workload were major obstacles to the engagement in research of Omani teachers of English.

Context

Since 1998, when a major reform of Basic and post-Basic education started, the Ministry of Education in Oman has offered teachers of English a range of in-service courses (Etherton and Al-Jardani 2009). Currently, such courses are run by over 22 Omani trainers in 11 regions across the country. They range from two-day workshops to 80-hour courses and cater for both newly appointed and more experienced teachers. Teacher research has become an increasingly important theme in the Ministry's work since the educational reform started and RPD was originally developed for trainers and supervisors as part of their professional development programme. It introduced them to small-scale classroom research and required them to conduct research into their own practices. It also prepared them to support teacher research with practitioners across the country:

> Having studied on the course, the trainers were involved in developing a revised version of the course to be taught by them in their regions to English teachers. Studying on the course not only helped them to explore their own practice, but also ensured they had the knowledge and confidence to teach the course themselves and support and supervise the research of teachers. (Etherton and Al-Jardani 2009: 196)

I was one of the trainers who did the original RPD course and who subsequently conducted it with teachers of English in my region. In the following paragraphs, I will describe key features of RPD in terms of selection of participants, objectives, content, structure, teaching methods, and evaluation.

Selection

Teachers who want to take RPD fill in an application form which asks about their background, language level, previous research experience, and beliefs about research. This information allows trainers to select applicants who are felt to be suitably equipped to benefit from the course, both in terms of their level of English and their motivation to be teacher researchers. Having clear selection criteria for teachers makes it more likely that those who start the course will complete it. To make sure that participants get adequate attention and support, places on the course are limited to 12, and in most cases, the course is delivered by two trainers.

Objectives

According to the official course description, RPD has the following objectives:

1. to develop an understanding of the need and value of teacher research;
2. to develop the participants' understanding of the theory and practice of conducting teacher research into practice;
3. to enable participants to conduct meaningful and appropriate research into their own practice as a form of professional development;
4. to support participants through the process of conducting their own research project;
5. to develop language skills through reading academic texts, writing reports, taking part in seminar discussions and presentations;
6. to develop presentation and workshop skills;
7. for participants to go on to become a research 'resource' in their schools to support other teachers in their research ideas.

While most of these focus on enabling teachers to complete a teacher research project, the objectives also refer to developing teachers' English, equipping them to disseminate their research and also to making them teacher research 'champions' who can support colleagues in their schools.

Content

RPD covers standard topics in research methods, as the following list illustrates:

- exploring understandings about research and introducing action research;
- types of research;

- action research and developing research questions;
- research methods, triangulation, and researching children;
- research ethics and developing a focus for the inquiry;
- developing a research proposal;
- case study research and sampling;
- observation;
- writing questionnaires and conducting interviews;
- an introduction to qualitative data analysis;
- analysing qualitative interview data;
- analysing interaction transcripts;
- sharing research through presentations and reports;
- analysing and presenting quantitative data;
- designing workshops and evaluating the course.

One feature of RPD, though, is that these topics are tackled in detail and teachers have ample time to engage with them both theoretically and in practice. Breaking the content of teacher research down for the teachers is one way in which RPD makes this content more accessible for them.

Structure

In terms of structure, RPD is organized through 16 full-day sessions divided into an initial six-day intensive study period followed by ten weeks of day-release sessions (one day a week when teachers are released from school). Day-release courses are favoured by trainers and teachers. Trainers value the opportunities that time between sessions gives them to reflect on their work, to discuss the course with other trainers, to adjust the course in response to teacher feedback, and to provide more thorough feedback on teachers' course work. For teachers, weekly sessions enable them to experiment with research in their classrooms and to feed practical experiences into the workshops the following week. Overall, RPD seeks to address the components of teacher research identified by Freeman (1998) – inquiry, question/puzzle, data collection, data analysis, understandings, and making public.

Teaching and learning

During RPD teachers engage in the following forms of learning activity:

- seminars – input from trainer and plenary discussions;
- group tasks – participants working together on tasks;
- workshops – practical tasks often resulting in poster displays;
- presentations – prepared and delivered by participants;

- tutorials – one-to-one discussion between trainer and participant to provide research support;
- library study – individual study.

Through this range of teaching and learning strategies, RPD seeks to provide a balance of trainer-led and teacher-led activity, as well as a range of whole class, smaller group, and individual teacher work.

Evaluation

Participants are evaluated through two oral presentations, in which they give progress reports on their research, and a final 3,000-word report. The course itself is evaluated through a range of data:

- summative and formative evaluation questionnaire at the end of the intensive block;
- an evaluation questionnaire at the end of the course (see Appendix 1);
- reflection sheets after each session;
- evaluation of documentary evidence – the final reports;
- follow-up evaluation of workshops and presentations given by teachers after they have completed RPD.

Insights

RPD has been conducted for several years and I will now discuss evaluations of the course by teachers and trainers and identify what we can learn from these about supporting teacher research.

As noted above, evaluation data for the course are collected from a variety of sources, and my analyses of these over different years indicate that teachers feel they benefit from RPD in the following ways:

- enhanced knowledge of teacher research;
- added confidence in their ability to conduct meaningful, systematic, and ethical research in their own contexts;
- increased motivation to do research and to encourage others to do it;
- deeper understanding of the value of reflection;
- improved awareness of their own teaching;
- greater confidence in their ability to promote learning in their classrooms.

The evaluation data also highlighted the key challenges teachers faced and there were no surprises here: they felt they needed more time to do the research and greater access to relevant literature. Increased individual support was also a recurrent suggestion made by teachers when evaluating the course.

Trainer evaluations of the course have also identified ways of strengthening it. Recurrent suggestions were:

- extending RPD over a school year rather than limiting it to one semester;
- incorporating peer feedback into the course – i.e. structured opportunities for teachers to receive feedback from one another rather than just from the trainer;
- reducing the amount of reading given for teachers to do out of class and doing more in-session reading instead;
- increasing trainer visits to teachers' classrooms during the day-release phase;
- organizing a research symposium at the end of the course where teachers can share their work.

Despite these suggestions, RPD has been evaluated very positively by teachers and trainers and this leads to a consideration of the factors which have allowed the course to support teachers in ways that have been conducive to their work as teacher researchers. Based on my experience of conducting the course, I believe that attention to six particular issues has been influential in the success of the course. These are:

1. modifying misconceptions about research;
2. developing knowledge about teacher research;
3. doing (rather than just learning about) teacher research;
4. providing appropriate support for teachers;
5. monitoring teachers' progress;
6. promoting reflective practice.

I will now discuss each of these in turn.

Modifying misconceptions about research

RPD seeks to modify teachers' initial negative attitudes towards research in different ways. One key strategy is the discussion of their beliefs about research throughout the course. The relationship between teachers' beliefs and practices has been widely discussed (e.g. Basturkmen 2012; Phipps and Borg 2012) and it is clear that teachers' beliefs about research will influence how they approach the task of being teacher researchers. It is therefore important to give teachers opportunities to express, discuss, reflect on and modify (if needed) their views about what research is and about its relevance to teachers' work. For example, in the very first session of the course teachers write down what they think research is, compare their ideas in groups, and produce a summary on the board which reflects some kind of consensus. This activity also alerts me to aspects of their beliefs which need to be addressed and which I should focus on in later sessions on the course. At the end of the course, the teachers once again articulate their beliefs about research, compare them to those they expressed at the start, and reflect on any changes.

Developing knowledge about teacher research

While appropriate beliefs are important if teachers are to be teacher researchers, they also require knowledge of what research and teacher research involve. RPD thus provides teachers with substantial time to deepen their understandings of basic concepts in research generally and teacher research specifically (keeping in mind that teacher research is, after all, a form of research). For example, as the list of course topics above illustrates, teachers learn about key issues in the design and conduct of research and more specifically about different ways of collecting data in their classrooms. Teachers need a sound understanding of such foundational issues if they are to function effectively as teacher researchers.

Doing (rather than just learning about) teacher research

Teachers on RPD all complete a teacher research project in their own classrooms and this is seen to be the core learning activity on the course. The practical orientation of the course is emphasized from the outset and teachers are encouraged early on to think about issues relevant to their classrooms that they want to investigate; by the end of the intensive block the target is for them to have developed some specific research questions to study. During the day-release block the practical orientation of the course is even more evident as in between each session the teachers experiment with research tools in their classrooms. The theory that is covered on the course is meant to support the practical activity of doing teacher research. The final research report that teachers produce, while supported by theory, is expected to be a practical account of teachers' investigations of their work.

Providing appropriate support for teachers

It is difficult for teachers with full workloads to conduct and disseminate teacher research unless appropriate support is available to them. RPD recognizes teachers' need for support. As discussed already, the course is designed so that theory supports teachers in conducting research in their classrooms. Another form of support comes from the access to literature which teachers are given (RPD is normally run in a centre which has a library). Trainers also provide support through feedback on coursework and through two individual tutorials for each teacher. Teachers also receive further support through sessions late in the course which provide advice on ways of sharing their work, orally and in writing. One final example of support is peer support (though I acknowledge that this is not extensive and could be developed further). In sessions 10–12 the teachers give oral reports on their progress to the whole group and peers are then encouraged to ask questions and make suggestions to support one another.

Monitoring teachers' progress

This is linked to the previous point but I discuss it separately here to emphasize the important role that the trainer has to play in monitoring teachers' progress during RPD. Trainers do this in a range of ways, informally (i.e. through observing teachers' contributions during sessions) and more formally (e.g. through tutorials and written progress reports). By monitoring teachers' progress in an ongoing manner I am able to identify the kinds of support that specific teachers or perhaps the whole group need. I am also able to identify at an early stage cases where teachers are making limited progress and are at risk of not completing their project.

Promoting reflective practice

Course participants are advised to keep daily reflection notes and to complete session summaries where they make a record of key learning points (see Appendix 2). At the end of each session the teachers are asked to write a short summary of the key learning points and these provide the basis for further reflection and discussion. Another reflective tool is the research journal, which teachers are encouraged to keep throughout the day-release phase of the project. All sessions involve activities which require teachers to examine, evaluate, and discuss different aspects of teacher research and during the day-release phase of RPD teachers have regular opportunities to reflect together on their experiences in the classroom during the week between course sessions. Creating a reflective mentality in teachers is central to their development as teacher researchers.

Collectively, the six facets of RPD I have discussed here interact to create a context in which teachers can develop, over time and with appropriate support, as teacher researchers.

Implications

Although RPD is a course for teachers of English in Oman, it has implications for different global contexts where teacher research is valued as a tool for teacher development. What this course does is give teachers effective support by breaking down the teacher research process into manageable portions, introduced and practised one at a time and which feed into teachers' own projects. The tutorials and library time also play an important role and give the teachers access to resources that they do not normally have. The reflective and analytical course activities in and after each session enable participants to absorb new ideas and to integrate them into their own research repertoire. Overall, RPD takes its participants on a trip of self-discovery where they realize how relevant and effective teacher research can be.

As a result of the discussion in this chapter, some practical recommendations can be made for teachers, trainers, supervisors, and course designers who wish to create a culture of teacher research among ELT professionals. First of all, it is important that teacher research be seen as an extended form of reflective practice rather than an academic activity. Reflection is a central process in teacher development and thus provides a suitable perspective through which to introduce teacher research. There are of course different forms of reflection and teacher research is a more structured and formal approach. But teachers should never lose sight of the fact that on in-service courses such as RPD the enhancement of professional practice, and not academic development for its own sake, is the goal. A second recommendation is that teacher research courses will be more effective when they are driven by practical problems or puzzles that teachers wish to address. Unless teachers identify an issue in their own work that they are genuinely motivated to explore, it will be difficult for them to maintain the motivation that is needed to complete a course such as RPD. A further recommendation I would make based on my experience is that those who facilitate teacher research courses should have experience of teacher research themselves. As I explained earlier, before I supported other teachers through RPD, I did the same kind of course myself and that experience allowed me to function more effectively as a teacher research facilitator: I was better able to understand the challenges the teachers would face and was able to refer to my own experience at various points during the course. This in turn enhanced my credibility in the eyes of the teachers I worked with. I would also encourage facilitators of teacher research to think carefully about how much reading teachers are expected to do and how teachers will gain access to these resources. Of course, research should make connections with existing work of relevance, but there will always be limitations to how much reading in-service teachers on a part-time course can be expected to do, for reasons of both time and access. RPD is fortunate in that it normally takes place in training centres which have libraries; however, this will not always be the case and trainers may very often need to assist teachers in getting access to a modest selection of material to read.

It is also clear from my experience that teachers value very much the personalized support they have received from me. A balance is of course needed here between what is ideal and what is possible, because there will be limitations to how much individual support trainers can provide. I have found that a combination of in-person and online support works well, including giving the teachers the chance to contact me by email with quick queries whenever they need to.

Another recommendation I will make relates to the structure of teacher research courses. RPD utilizes a combination of intensive and day-release work which complement one another. The initial six days of full-time work allow the teachers to focus on the course in an intensive way that six weekly day-release sessions would not allow. The intensive start allows teachers to build momentum quickly and also facilitates the development of relationships between trainer and teachers and among the teachers themselves. The day-release phase, in turn, allows teachers to do teacher research in their classes, to experiment with different ways of collecting data and to meet each week to share experiences. I would conclude from my experience that a combination of intensive work and distributed sessions provides a useful model for supporting teacher research, though this is an issue which would be a good focus for continuing research.

Finally, while it is desirable to encourage teachers to produce written reports and to share their work orally and in writing in their ELT communities, for most teachers such tasks will present a substantial challenge. It is important, then, that teacher research courses provide teachers with opportunities to learn about such activities and with support in doing them.

Conclusion

Although teacher research has been a popular idea for many years, it is only more recently that it is becoming part of formal in-service programmes provided by organizations such as Ministries of Education. In Oman, RPD has been established for some time now and the Ministry sees it as an important way of enabling teachers of English to contribute to the development of a research culture. My experience as a trainer on this course over several years, and my analyses of relevant course evaluation data, suggest that it does function effectively in promoting teacher research and my focus in this chapter has been on identifying some of the features of the course which have contributed to its success. I hope that by highlighting these I can assist ELT professionals elsewhere who want to promote teacher research.

Engagement priorities

Although it is generally accepted that in-service courses can be effective in supporting teachers in doing research into their own practices, such courses have not been widely studied. Examples of aspects of teacher research that require more systematic investigation are:

- What alternatives to standard research reports are available to teachers when it comes to sharing their work? What do teachers feel about these alternatives? How can teachers be introduced to them?

- What contribution to teacher development does reading books and articles make during the process of teacher research?
- What happens to teachers after teacher research courses? To what extent do they sustain their engagement in teacher research and what factors influence whether they do?
- What kinds of professional development do facilitators of teacher research require? How might that professional development be provided (e.g. through self-study, collaboration among trainers, or training courses?).

References

Al-Abri, S. (2011). *Teachers' Perceptions of Action Research as a Tool for Professional Development: The Role of the 'Research for Professional Development' (RPD) Course for In-Service Omani Teachers*. Unpublished Masters Dissertation, Graduate School of Education, University of Manchester.

Al-Raesi, R. (2013). *Omani Teachers' Perceptions of the Research for Professional Development (RPD) Course*. Unpublished Masters Dissertation, School of Education, University of Exeter.

Basturkmen, H. (2012). Teacher beliefs and teacher training. *The Teacher Trainer*, 21(1): 8–9.

Borg, S. (2009). English language teachers' conceptions of research. *Applied Linguistics*, 30(3): 358–388.

Borg, S. (2013). *Teacher Research in Language Teaching: A Critical Analysis*. Cambridge: Cambridge University Press.

Burns, A. (2010). *Doing Action Research in English Language Teaching*. Routledge: New York.

Crookes, G. (1992). Action research for second language teachers: Going beyond teacher research. *Applied Linguistics*, 14(2): 130–144.

Etherton, S. and Al-Jardani, M. (2009). Recent developments in in-service language teacher education in Oman. In J. Atkins, M. Lamb, and M. Wedell (eds), *International Collaboration for Educational Change: The BA Project*. Muscat: Ministry of Education, pp. 191–200.

Farrell, T. S. C. (2007). *Reflective Language Teaching: From Research to Practice*. London: Continuum.

Freeman, D. (1998). *Doing teacher research: From inquiry to understanding*. Boston: Heinle & Heinle.

Phipps, S. and Borg, S. (2012). Exploring the relationship between teachers' beliefs and their classroom practice. *The Teacher Trainer*, 21(1): 8–9.

Wallace, J. M. (1998). *Action Research for Language Teachers*. Cambridge: Cambridge University Press.

Appendix 1: End of course evaluation questions

Please fill out this evaluation so we can improve the course for future participants

1. Do you think this course has provided you with a good introduction to the idea of teacher research?
2. What were the most interesting and useful aspects of the course for you? Give reason.

3. What things would you like to change in the course?
4. How confident do you feel in your ability to conduct meaningful research?
5. How motivated do you feel to do further research?
6. What were the most important things you learnt from this course about undertaking research?
7. What did you learn in your own research?
8. How useful did you find the readings? What were the most useful readings?
9. How do you feel your language has improved as a result of the course?
10. How do you feel about your final research report?
11. Have you got any plans to disseminate the findings of your report? If Yes, how do you plan to do this?
12. Do you feel satisfied with the support you received while doing your research?
13. Would you advise another teacher to take the course?
14. Any other comments

Appendix 2: An example of a session summary

Session Summary

   Session Nine (Focus on writing questionnaires and conducting interviews)
Aims:

- To explore the use of questionnaires and interviews in teacher research
- To review and develop reading and note-taking skills
- To identify and record appropriate information from research literature
- To review referencing norms
- To continue to develop your own research proposals

Summary of learning:

10
Action Research as a Professional Development Strategy

Servet Çelik and Kenan Dikilitaş

Introduction

In today's increasingly interconnected and interdependent world, foreign language education has become a matter of great importance. English – with its prominent status as an international *lingua franca* – has become the most widely taught foreign language, and over 100 countries currently provide English instruction as part of the public education process (Crystal 2003). Turkey is no exception in this respect. In the years following the Second World War, English language instruction has been continually emphasized by the Turkish Ministry of National Education, and a series of educational reforms has established English as a compulsory subject from the early years of public schooling (Republic of Turkey, Ministry of National Education, Board of Education 2013).

Yet, despite ongoing attention to the importance of developing competence in English, a desirable level of learner success has yet to be realized. Numerous problems, ranging from motivation of students to class size to inadequate teaching materials, have been faulted for poor learning outcomes; and in particular, Besimoğlu et al. (2010) note that ineffective teaching practices play a significant role. As a result, the need to improve the standard of foreign-language teaching in Turkey has been widely acknowledged.

However, Çelik et al. (2013) point out that, in spite of efforts to address this issue through modernization of the country's teacher preparation programmes, the importance of ongoing professional development (PD) for practising teachers has received little emphasis. In Turkey, as in many other educational contexts, there are few opportunities for instructors of English as a foreign language (EFL) – particularly those at the university level – to engage in meaningful professional development beyond their initial teacher training (Altan 2006; Bayrakçı 2009; Çelik 2011). The existing opportunities for professional growth, such as in-service workshops, are often seen by language teachers as deficient in content and irrelevant to their practice. Furthermore, little incentive is offered to individuals for involvement in PD beyond what is required of them as a condition of employment (Çelik et al. 2013).

As a result of these shortcomings, maintaining high standards in EFL education in such contexts requires exploring new avenues to motivate English language teaching (ELT) professionals to expand their pedagogical and practical skills. One aspect of PD that has been widely recognized as beneficial on an international level (Richards and Rodgers 2011) but has been relatively underutilized in the Turkish context concerns language teachers' engagement in action research. This chapter details a project that was designed to involve Turkish EFL teachers in action research and to draw attention to its advantages in terms of their professional development.

Context

As a means to address the need for effective professional development for EFL professionals in the Turkish context, the second author of this chapter (referred to in the following sections as the *trainer*) was recruited as a PD supervisor at a private university in Izmir, Turkey. In this capacity, his responsibilities included creating a programme for in-service university EFL teachers who were asked to engage in a PD programme in addition to their teaching duties over the course of an academic year.

Implementing action research as a professional development strategy

In reviewing and considering numerous formative strategies, the trainer recognized that effective acquisition of new knowledge entails interaction with the surrounding environment (Kincheloe 2000; Thayer-Bacon 1999). With this in mind, he consulted with the first author, an experienced researcher and teacher trainer. Through their discussion of the issues, they concluded that an experiential approach to professional development might be most effective in expanding EFL instructors' understanding of their teaching practice. Accordingly, the trainer decided to implement a guided action research project that would engage the participants in observing problems in the classroom and formulating solutions to address them (Norton 2009).

For the training experience to succeed, the authors agreed that it was essential to ensure the teachers' awareness of action research and its potential role in their professional development, as well as to encourage them to think about the learning theory and logic behind the approaches they took in their practice. Because not all of the teachers could be expected to have the research skills necessary to conduct an empirical study, the authors concurred that the programme participants would need extensive guidance and support throughout

Table 10.1 Outline of the project phases

Project Phase	Activities
1	An introductory meeting to review the objectives of the programme and encourage the participating teachers to express their expectations and preferences with respect to their professional development.
2	An attitude training session designed to address the teachers' questions and concerns related to their ability to carry out a full-scale research project in addition to their regular teaching tasks.
3	A number of sessions describing and exemplifying the stages involved in action research.
4	Training on the application of the stages of action research.
5	Selection and development of a research topic.
6	Group presentation of research proposals.
7	Data collection and analysis.
8	Preparation of a research report.
9	Oral presentation at a mini-conference.

the process. Furthermore, to provide additional motivation for the project, they decided that the trainer would bring the completed studies together in a mini-conference and publish them in a book of proceedings. Accordingly, the phases presented in Table 10.1 were incorporated into the project, which took place over the course of an academic year:

The first author, as an experienced teacher educator, continued to serve as a mentor and informal consultant throughout the course of project. This mentorship centred on an exchange of ideas about the problems that arose in helping the teachers, along with specific questions regarding the content of the teacher research topics. On completion of the research phase, the authors collaborated in editing the studies and compiling them into a book.

The project participants

A total of 25 English language teachers, all of whom were working as university-level EFL instructors, participated in the PD programme. Both males and females were included; the majority of the teachers were Turkish, but a number of them were foreign nationals – both native and non-native speakers of English.[1] All of the teachers had earned their Bachelor's degrees, and several had graduate degrees in their fields. Their ages ranged from 22 to 32 years, and they had between one and five years of teaching experience. While all of the participants were currently teaching English as a foreign language, their original fields of study included majors such as graphic design and English language and literature, in addition to English language teaching.

Insights

In the following section, each phase of the project is described in detail. In addition to the implementation of each phase, the issues that became apparent during the process are discussed, together with any insights that emerged from them.

The introductory meeting

The initial session consisted of an introductory meeting in which the trainer encouraged all of the teachers to express their views on professional development and discuss what they expected from the programme. Two contradictory views arose at this point; while one group of participants indicated that they preferred a PD strategy that would allow them to play an active role, a small number of the teachers indicated reluctance to engage themselves in such a hands-on process. Instead, they hoped for one-shot, lecture-type sessions in which they would not be expected to take an active part. Aside from these conflicting ideas, a few of the teachers had no preference and were satisfied to be directed by the trainer in terms of any plan he might propose. Keeping these issues in mind, the trainer went on to outline the project plan before moving to the training phase.

Because the instructors had an average teaching load of 24–28 hours per week, combined with responsibilities such as marking papers, proctoring exams, and carrying out administrative tasks, the necessity of finding time to attend the PD sessions and carry out a research project met with some resistance. One of the participants expressed the general view of the group:

> We were all in a panic when we heard that we are supposed to do action research, because of restricted time. How to spare enough time and how to be both researcher and teacher were our biggest concerns.

To address this aspect of the teachers' apprehensions about the project, they were encouraged and guided throughout the process to integrate their research into their lessons as much as possible and make it a part of the normal course period.

Attitude training sessions

Given the initial resistance of the teachers, the trainer consulted the first author with his concerns. Drawing on his experience as a teacher educator, the first author stressed that comprehension of how action research might be used in teacher development and its potential impact on their knowledge and classroom practices was needed to minimize the likelihood that the participants would become demotivated before the project had even begun. Accordingly, the trainer planned and carried out a lecture-oriented and question-answer session that was designed to alleviate the teachers' uncertainty by explaining the concept of action research, outlining its basic principles, and highlighting its advantages and disadvantages. The discussion helped to stimulate changes in the teachers' attitudes toward the project; one of the participants, in particular, expressed a growing awareness that 'research can be valuable if we can see a correlation to our work environment.' As a result of these sessions, the trainer observed that the teachers appeared to be increasingly motivated by the literature they covered on action research and began to focus on its application in their own contexts, evidencing a new appreciation for the process of observation and reflection.

Research methods training

After completing the attitude training session, the trainer moved on to the next phase, which involved developing the research skills the teachers would need to carry out their individual studies. A series of group training sessions – four in all – were conducted to provide information on the action research cycle and on developing competence in research methodologies. These sessions covered the various types of data collection tools used in action research; and the quantitative and qualitative methods of data analysis were also explored. As the teachers had little to no experience in carrying out research of any kind, many of them were anxious about this aspect of the project, which led to problems with self-confidence. The methodological and pedagogical guidance provided by the trainer assisted in overcoming the participants' concerns. In this respect, the first author provided ongoing support for the trainer in terms of methodological issues related to carrying out research in educational settings.

In conjunction with the training sessions that were carried out with the whole group, one-on-one meetings with the teachers constituted the core of the project. These sessions, which were held regularly throughout the year, were used to address the teachers' individual needs in carrying out their research and to provide ongoing support for their efforts. This individualized support is discussed in greater detail in the following sections.

Selection and development of a research topic

At this stage, each teacher was first asked to consider and list the issues he or she had encountered during classroom teaching in order to determine a specific research problem – an undertaking which presented a greater challenge than anticipated for many of the teachers, who were not generally accustomed to critical thinking about their practice. One area that turned out to cause considerable difficulty involved getting the teachers to focus on a particular problem, rather than on broad issues related to teaching in general; furthermore, they struggled when it came to asking answerable questions related to issues they were experiencing in their own lessons.

To support the teachers in this process, the trainer asked them to elaborate on their individual teaching contexts and to identify specific problems they had encountered. As one of the teachers remarked, 'I started to reflect on the problems in my classroom, which I had never done before', as a result of the trainer's guidance. Thus, they were able to gain deeper insights into the issues they planned to explore, which in turn helped them to narrow their focus and select appropriate topics for their research.

Review of the related literature

In order to develop greater insight into their research problems, the teachers were required to find and summarize the most significant literature related to their proposed topics. This phase was relatively easy, because most of the teachers were proficient enough to locate, read, and interpret articles relevant to their subject; and at the later stages, when they were preparing their research reports, they were able to summarize the literature effectively. By spending time reading the work of other researchers, they broadened their awareness of the scope of their research and were able to identify gaps in the existing literature. According to one of the teachers, in particular, carrying out the literature reviews allowed them to better comprehend the related educational theory and its application in their practice. As he explained, 'we all had a chance to refresh and/or learn something new to take back to our teaching arenas'. His colleague also remarked on this benefit, noting that 'it's very helpful, because it gives you an understanding of what other people have done and how this has been applied in a practical way'.

Framing of the research questions

The identification of research topics was followed by another full-group session centred on developing the research questions. Sample research questions from previous action research studies were presented, and the teachers were asked to develop their own questions based on the topics they had previously identified. The questions were later discussed individually in trainer-trainee meetings.

Selection of data collection tools

After developing their research questions, the teachers were asked to decide on appropriate data collection tools and analysis methods, drawing from the research methods training sessions that had been held prior to beginning the studies. Due to their lack of research experience, this phase turned out to be one of the most difficult aspects of the project. The initial training on research skills had not been as effective as anticipated, and as a result, the teachers needed intensive one-on-one support in designing their studies.

For instance, in terms of data collection tools, most of the teachers proposed only Likert-type questionnaires; however, as the first author and the trainer debated, the use of interviews to corroborate the numerical data was appropriate in many cases. Accordingly, the trainer guided the teachers in understanding the purpose of interviews to develop deeper insights and worked with them to identify suitable interview questions. Initially, the teachers tended to produce questions that were leading, or that required only yes/no answers, which could create bias or limit the students' answers. Another issue that arose at this stage was whether they should ask students these interview questions in their native language or in the target language. To address these problems, the trainer worked with the teachers to consider both the content of the questions and the proficiency level of the respondent students.

An interesting development in these one-on-one meetings was the exchange of ideas concerning research design that, in a few instances, turned into collaborative efforts between the teachers and the trainer. In these cases, the trainer was directly drawn into the projects as a researcher; thus, in addition to modelling, he also contributed directly to some of the studies as a co-author.

Group presentation of the research proposals

After determining their research questions and developing the research instrument(s) to be used, the teachers were asked to prepare a research proposal to be handed in to the trainer. In order to guide them in writing their proposals, the trainer provided ongoing support for each of the individuals or research groups. This was accomplished, in part, through asking the teachers to think about critical questions related to the core problem, context, participants, appropriate data collection tools, and their expectations from the research. The trainer also provided the participants with a sample research proposal to better illustrate how different parts of research are interconnected. This written form of guidance helped them to understand the structure of the research design and keep moving in the right direction. See Table 10.2 for an example of a completed research proposal; in this case, the teacher had planned to carry out a study concerning hyperactive behaviour in university students.

In addition, each individual or study group presented their proposals in a group session. This was especially helpful in stimulating discussion and peer feedback on different aspects of the studies; equally importantly, the teacher researchers inspired one another in ways that were not initially planned. One of the teachers, in particular, noted that the presentations of the research proposals gave him an opportunity to identify the scope of the study he was planning to undertake:

> From the beginning of school year, in [the] professional development meetings, I started hearing my colleagues talk about the problems that students were having in terms of the outcomes. Their achievement levels were below expectations and this seemed to be coming across the different levels with the different teachers.

Table 10.2 Sample research proposal

	Action research proposal
	University Teacher Training Program
Researcher(s):	
Research area:	Hyperactivity in the classroom: what methods and activities are effective in keeping a class focused and attentive (without patronising young adults)?
Titles of articles to be read:	
Research question(s):	1. What is hyperactivity and how is it related to university students? 2. What problems do they face in language learning? 3. What is their idea of a 'good lesson'? 4. Which methods are suitable for classroom management? 5. Which activities keep them focused, attentive and engaged in the learning process?
How it will contribute to classroom practice and your professional development.	I think we will always be confronted with the modern phenomenon of hyperactivity in class. Hopefully, the research project will help to understand students' needs as well as to find one useable method or activity to implement in class. Personally, it will help me to remain in charge and therefore to be able to continue with teaching.
	Methodology
Target participants: How many? Turkish or international?	• Students: focus on Class 302, around 24, Turkish
Data collection instruments: *(Add if you have a different choice)*	• Questionnaires • Interviews • Observation

At first I'd like to find out more about the concept of hyperactivity in theory. After that, I am going to find out in class (using a questionnaire) what sort of problems students are confronted with that are related to hyperactivity. After that, I plan to practice at least 2 methods and activities each that are said to be helpful and useable in hyperactive classroom surroundings over a certain period of time (each 4 weeks). The class will be questioned afterwards again on how they perceived these activities (second questionnaire).

A final questionnaire will be given at the end of the testing period, as well as personal interviews and teachers' observations.

According to the above mentioned outcomes, at least one method or activity should be selected as useful.

In his case, the presentations had given him greater insight into the experiences that many of his colleagues were facing; recognizing a common problem may have been a motivating factor for many of the teachers as they proceeded with their investigations.

Collecting and analysing the data

As with the research design, the data collection and analysis phases of the studies presented a challenge for the teachers, due mainly to their lack of research experience. Therefore, throughout this process, the trainer met with them frequently and checked their progress systematically. Unlike the more generalized information provided during the research training sessions, the trainer focused on the specific skills that were relevant to each study, including the appropriate techniques for analysing the data and interpreting and verifying the results.

In particular, the trainer guided the teachers in working with the qualitative and quantitative data they collected, showing them how to identify themes and categories in the qualitative data and to carry out simple calculations of means, percentages, and frequencies with the statistical data they had obtained. The first author provided considerable input at this stage, especially in terms of handling qualitative interview data – a more challenging concept than the numerical data for many of the teachers. This learning-by-doing approach helped the teachers to experience the stages of analysis, while encouraging them to think critically about the data and connect their findings to the research questions.

To keep the teachers motivated to move forward with their projects and to provide ongoing support where needed, the trainer asked them to report on their research progress during the second and third quarters of the academic year. In the second quarter, these reports consisted of the planning and actions taken to that point, their plans to move forward during the term, the challenges they anticipated, and any plans they had for dealing with challenges as they occurred. Likewise, in the third quarter, the teachers provided details on their current progress. They also noted any methodological changes they might have made to their original research design, detailing any obstacles they had faced and explaining how they had dealt with them. At this point, the trainer asked them to report on any preliminary results they had reached. The written reports were submitted to the trainer, who collaborated with the first author in providing detailed written feedback. Afterwards, the trainer met with the individual teachers and research groups and discussed the feedback with them in order to assist them in developing their own solutions. On the whole, the teachers were open to suggestions and advice, as they were first-time researchers. The trainer took a non-judgemental stance in this respect, mentioning aspects of their research that they might not have considered and asking them what they thought in order to stimulate critical thinking on the issues.

Organization and writing of the research report

While some of the teachers had prior experience in writing research reports, the majority of them had limited competence in this area. The trainer met with the participants on an individual basis to address their weaknesses. Relating their research questions to the data was especially problematic; therefore, the trainer utilized graphic models at this stage in order to illustrate the connections more clearly. The teachers were also guided in terms of appropriate reporting of the results, linking them to the existing research, and forming logical conclusions about their research findings. A process writing approach was followed, with the trainer providing feedback and suggestions for improvement until a final manuscript was produced.

Presentation of the research at a mini-conference

At the conclusion of the programme, the teachers presented their papers at a mini-conference that was designed to allow them to showcase their work and to discuss their findings with their colleagues. A number of the teachers found the presentations useful, citing the opportunity to learn more about their colleagues' practice; to converse on common issues; and to give and receive feedback. On the other hand, some of the teachers reported that the presentations had little meaning for them, as they felt that the studies carried out by others had no direct relevance to their own practice. Because they were unable to draw a correlation between their own work and that of their colleagues, they viewed this aspect of the project as ineffective and disappointing.

At the completion of the project, the authors compiled the presentations in a teacher research book, as the opportunity to see their work in published form was viewed as an additional motivating factor for the participants.

Implications

As discussed in the previous sections, a number of challenges arose during the course of the programme, such as heavy teaching loads, little time for carrying out research, lack of research experience, and a degree of unwillingness to participate in PD. A taxonomy of the major issues that were encountered and the efforts made to address them is provided in Table 10.3.

In spite of these difficulties, the majority of the participants reported that the project had a positive impact on their practice and changed how they approached a variety of classroom issues. Several of the teachers expressed that they planned to expand on their original studies or to carry out additional research in the future. For instance according to one of the teachers:

Implementation of action research in my classroom has solved some of my teaching problems, but that doesn't mean that I have solved all my problems. What I need to do now is to continue my investigation. It seems it will be a career-long process.

From the trainer's perspective, one aspect of the study that did not provide the expected results involved the research skills training sessions. Because each study required a different approach, many of the topics covered in the initial sessions turned out to have little relevance for the participants, and a great deal of time was spent in individual meetings reviewing and explaining the approaches that were best suited to each project. As a result, the trainer concluded that providing individualized instruction and omitting the group training sessions would be more effective in future teacher development programmes. While conducting one-on-one or small-group sessions of this nature is more time-consuming than holding full-group meetings, this constraint may be mitigated in many situations by careful organization. In this case, the trainer opted to schedule regular weekly meetings with the teachers, rather than having them contact him on an as-needed basis, allowing for more effective time

Table 10.3 Issues encountered in carrying out action research as a PD strategy

Issue	Intervention
Lack of time for carrying out research	The teachers were encouraged to integrate their research in their lessons and make it a part of the normal course period.
Lack of self-confidence in carrying out research	One-on-one meetings, individualised support, presenting their studies to the rest of the teachers and then to a wider community, and collaborating and discussing the issues were major factors in minimising the teachers' lack of self-confidence.
Lack of understanding of basic research methods	Group training sessions and individual meetings were carried out to provide general information on conducting research; individualized support was also given for the more specific needs of each teacher/research group.
Difficulty in creating a critical stance toward classroom issues/a tendency to want to be told what to do	Asking open-ended questions that prompted the teachers to support their methodological decisions helped them to develop a more critical, questioning view of their practice.
Difficulty in sustaining the teachers' focus on their research	Progress reports to be submitted in the 2nd and 3rd quarters prompted the teachers to focus their attention on each stage of the project.

management. Furthermore, while these individual sessions were focused on the individual teachers or study groups, all participants were encouraged to attend these whenever possible to give them the opportunity to benefit from the feedback. In addition to the weekly meetings, the trainer made himself available via email for ongoing support.

Conclusion

While this project was carried out in the context of a Turkish university, many of the issues that the teachers faced in this instance are relevant to diverse English language teaching contexts. Providing language teachers with ongoing support in carrying out action research can have significant benefits in terms of improving their practical skills, deepening their knowledge of both the theoretical and practical aspects of language teaching and learning, and motivating them to continue their PD efforts on their own in the future.

It is the authors' hope that the project described here will provide other professional development trainers in a variety of EFL teaching contexts with a useful framework for designing a similar programme. In addition, this material may offer insights to guide teacher trainers in anticipating and addressing the challenges that may arise in the process of carrying out action research as a means of professional development.

Engagement priorities

In this chapter, we have described an approach to facilitating teacher research at a higher education institution as a means of teacher development. This project involved 25 teachers who conducted their research simultaneously, coming together to discuss the project and offer feedback on one another's progress throughout the implementation. This close interaction provided them with the opportunity to gain deeper insight into their practice within their specific context, enabling them to create their own solutions as they reflected and elaborated on a range of teaching and learning issues. For teacher trainers working to implement a similar programme, the following points should be considered:

1. As was the case in the project described in this chapter, teacher researchers require a variety of qualifications and skills for conducting a classroom-based study. What are the basic methodological or research competences that you believe a teacher researcher should have before and during the process of carrying out an investigation in their practice?
2. Knowing the context is at the heart of doing teacher research. In what ways do you think you can raise teacher researchers' awareness in the context of their individual teaching environments?

3. Teacher researchers often try to present quantitative evidence to show the positive impact of what they do in the classroom. However, such measurements are often impossible, even with numerical data. The trainer in this project encouraged the teachers to consider the impact of students' opinions, evidence of learning in their writing or speaking, and other personal observations, in addition to quantifiable evidence. How might you guide teachers in exploring other means for designing their research and demonstrating its impact on their practice?
4. In the case of our project, there was a tendency among the participants to see teacher research as academic research. To address this misconception, the trainer encouraged them to view the output of their projects primarily in terms of its impact on their own practice. While teacher research may, in fact, be carried out in accordance with academic standards, the findings of such investigations are not always regarded by the wider educational community as having scientific merit. On the other hand, the insights obtained from teacher research may be valuable to classroom practitioners who are facing similar issues. How could teacher researchers in the field of English language teaching be supported in presenting their findings to the wider ELT community?

Notes

1. The authors recognize the conceptual and linguistic difficulties presented by the terms 'native' and 'non-native' speakers of English (e.g., Rampton 1990). However, as there is no generally accepted alternative, these terms are used in this chapter to refer to individuals who speak English as a first (native) or foreign (non-native) language.

References

Altan, M. Z. (2006). Preparation of foreign-language teachers in Turkey: A challenge for the 21st century. *Dil Dergisi*, 134: 49–54.

Bayrakçı, M. (2009). In-service teacher training in Japan and Turkey: A comparative analysis of institutions and practices. *Australian Journal of Teacher Education*, 34(1): 10–22.

Besimoğlu, S., Serdar, H., and Yavuz, Ş. (2010). Exploring students' attributions for their successes and failures in English language learning. *Hasan Ali Yücel Eğitim Fakültesi Dergisi*, 14(2): 75–89.

Crystal, D. (2003). *English as a Global Language* (Second Edition). London: Cambridge University Press.

Çelik, S. (2011). Characteristics and competencies for teacher educators: Addressing the need for improved professional standards in Turkey. *Australian Journal of Teacher Education*, 36(4): 73–87.

Çelik, S., Bayraktar-Çepni, S., and İlyas, H. (2013). The need for ongoing professional development: Perspectives of university-level EFL instructors in Turkey. *Procedia Social and Behavioral Sciences*, 70: 1860–1871.

Çelik, S., Mačianskienė, N., and Aytın, K. (2013). Turkish and Lithuanian EFL Instructors' professional development experiences: Worth the effort, or waste of time? *Erzincan University Faculty of Education Journal*, 15(2): 160–184.

Kincheloe, J. L. (2000). Rethinking critical theory and qualitative research. In N. K. Denzin and Y. S. Lincoln (eds), *The Handbook of Qualitative Research*. Thousand Oaks, CA: Sage, pp. 279–314.

Norton, L. S. (2009). *Action Research in Teaching and Learning. A Practical Guide to Conducting Pedagogical Research in Universities*. Abingdon: Routledge.

Rampton, M. B. H. (1990). Displacing the 'native speaker': expertise, affiliation, and inheritance. *ELT Journal,* 44(2): 97–101.

Richards, J. C. and Farrell, T. S. C. (2011). *Practice Teaching: A Reflective Approach*. New York, NY: Cambridge University Press.

T.C. Millî Eğitim Bakanlığı Talim ve Terbiye Kurulu Başkanlığı [Republic of Turkey, Ministry of National Education, Board of Education]. (2013). İlköğretim kurumları (ilkokullar ve ortaokullar) İngilizce dersi (2, 3, 4, 5, 6, 7 ve 8. sınıflar) öğretim programı [Elementary (primary and lower secondary) English language teaching programme (Grades 2–8)]. Ankara: T.C. Millî Eğitim Bakanlığı.

Thayer-Bacon, B. J. (1999). Closing the split between practical and theoretical reasoning: Knowers and the known. *Educational Philosophy and Theory,* 31(3): 341–358.

11
Practices and Principles of Pre-Service Action Research

Maureen Rajuan

Introduction

All the flowers of tomorrow are in the seeds of today

In our context, student teachers are called 'teaching flowers' in Hebrew, alluding to the process through which teacher candidates are nurtured toward their eventual blooming. This process is a challenging one for teacher educators, who must prepare future teachers to cope with a multitude of changing roles and job descriptions (Ben-Peretz 2001). As a teacher trainer, I find myself trying to do more in less time with each successive year. This is especially difficult in the third, and final, year of our teacher training programme as I envision my students standing on the threshold of their new teaching jobs. The responsibility of preparing student teachers to be full-time novice teachers weighs heavily on my shoulders. I seek to integrate the knowledge and skills that they have learnt in the previous years with a new heightened sense of autonomy in the classroom, the ability to make their own decisions based on thoughtful and sensitive considerations together with an awareness of social issues that go beyond the classroom. For many years now, I have looked to action research as a way to integrate theory with practice, reflection on self (Schön 1983) with a focus on pupils, and EFL subject matter with broader educational values. In an attempt to bring coherence to pedagogical coursework and clinical experiences, the purpose of this chapter is to suggest an integrated framework for student-teacher learning which has action research at the core in the final year of study.

A working definition of teacher research, as suggested by Cochran-Smith and Lytle (1993: 23), is 'systematic, intentional inquiry by teachers about their own school and classroom work'. We adopt action research in our training programme to promote grounded inquiry of this kind; we also want student teachers to reflect on their classroom experience; and, longer-term, we hope action research will impact positively on student teachers when they graduate and start teaching full time.

Edge (2001) attributes the growth of action research in foreign language teaching to Nunan (1991), who placed the focus of methodology on data from real classrooms rather than on theory. Burns (2010) has written a guidebook for the implementation of action research specifically for teacher researchers in the English language classroom. Finch (2000) believes action research to be especially empowering to teachers in the EFL classroom because language learning situations are more unpredictable than in other learning contexts. Action research enables EFL teachers to define problems they are having, design procedures for investigating them and implement solutions in their classrooms while assessing the results (Kemmis and McTaggart 1988).

Action research for practitioners is becoming increasingly widespread and accessible. Some school districts and educational programmes now have websites where teachers can post their research papers. One example is the 'Classroom Action Research' site provided by Madison Metropolitan School District (https://staffdevweb.madison.k12.wi.us/car). Among the research papers provided there are some on second language learning. Another example is the website of the City University of New York that posts PowerPoint presentations of college students' drafts and completed action research papers (httnp://actionresearchprojects.wikispaces.com/home).

The benefits and use of action research in pre-service contexts have been discussed widely in the literature (e.g. Levin and Rock 2003; Noffke and Stevenson 1995; Price 2001; Smith and Sela 2005; Zeichner 2001). Despite the proliferation of writing on action research, the task of designing a framework that uniquely fits the needs of a specific teacher training programme and student-teacher population is a challenge. In this chapter, I will report on a model of action research in use in the English Department of Achva Academic College of Education in Israel. The ideas discussed here have been developed over a number of years and have been found useful in our specific context, and I hope that they may also be relevant to action research courses on pre-service teacher training programmes elsewhere.

Context

Our teacher preparation programme integrates academic and pedagogical courses with a mentored student teaching practicum throughout the three years of study leading to the internship in the fourth year in which teachers assume full responsibility and take on Ministry-recognized jobs. The rationale behind this curriculum is the integration of theory with practice (Rajuan 2012). However, it is the teacher trainer's responsibility to make explicit the connections between course materials and teaching experiences.

The action research project comes in the third, and final, year of teacher preparation. As such, it is called the Final Project and is intended to show the culmination of what student teachers have learnt to know and do at the end of their studies. Student teachers do their teaching practice once a week in Professional Development Schools (PDS). They work under the supervision of their cooperating teachers and their teacher trainer in 'someone else's classroom' (Feiman-Nemser 2012). As such, they have limited authority in the classrooms in which they are expected to succeed. Often, they have limited freedom to try out new and innovative ideas, having to navigate between the sometimes different requirements and demands of their school and college mentors and the needs of the pupils in their classrooms (Rajuan et al. 2007). Despite these limitations, student teachers and cooperating teachers have collaborated well over the years to support the action research project for the welfare of the pupils in the classroom.

Results of a questionnaire sent to student teachers after the submission of their final action research projects over a period of three years show that the overwhelming majority reported positively on the experience of engaging in action research, despite the fact that they were given no credit points for the project, nor was the grade entered into their final GPA. In addition, they reported that they felt capable of independently undertaking some form of action research in the future after having been guided through the process the first time. To provide a broader context for the deeper discussion of our action research programme, I will now summarize some of the recurring themes that emerged from the responses of the student teachers to the question, *'Do you think action research will help you in your future teaching? If so, explain in which ways you think it will be helpful'*:

- *An increase in confidence and empowerment.* Many student teachers expressed the desire to repeat elements of action research in their future teaching for various purposes, such as to deal with problems or to better understand their pupils ('It will help me focus on finding solutions to problems that may come up'). Rather than commenting on specific issues that were the subject of the research, the majority of student teachers reported in their evaluations that the method of action research, in general, provided a way of coping with unforeseen problems. This appeared to be important in increasing their confidence to manage in the classroom in the future.
- The action research experience promoted a more *pupil-centred approach to teaching* – for example, one student teacher saw it as 'a way to get feedback from my pupils'. Student teachers learnt not only how to obtain ongoing feedback from pupils concerning their feelings and attitudes, but also discovered that there is no need to be afraid of negative feedback from learners. Such negative feedback thus came to be seen as a call for change rather than a sign of failure and it helped student teachers see things from the pupils' point of view ('I can see what the problems of the pupils are').

Action research, through reflection on data collected from their pupils and peers, supported student teachers in shifting from initial teacher-centred approaches to a more learner-centred pedagogy.

- Action research encouraged *the use of multiple approaches* and student teachers reported 'trying different ways to solve problems by trial and error; by checking what works and what doesn't'. Action research gave student teachers the courage to try innovative things in the classroom in the understanding that not everything has to succeed:

> The subject has interested me so much that I wanted to know everything and try everything. But I understood that it was impossible to apply and try everything in the research, especially when I have less than a school year to do the research. Moreover, even if I were the regular teacher in the classroom and had the whole year, it would be impossible and not recommended to start applying everything without trying approaches step-by-step and deciding whether they benefit the pupils.

Action research encourages experimentation with multiple teaching approaches and methods. This is in contrast to the focus on one strategy as a hypothesis to be accepted or rejected that is typical of more traditional kinds of experimental forms of research.

- *Persistence and confidence in the face of delayed results.* In the words of one student teacher, 'desired results that we aspire to require a gradual process of ups and downs'. Knowles and Holt-Reynolds (1991) note that student teachers often give up quickly on new methods learnt at university because they do not reflect those the student teachers experienced as learners themselves. Student teachers are more likely to give up when positive results supporting these new methods are not immediately forthcoming. Action research emphasizes the process of experimentation rather than the search for immediate results; it promotes a more authentic way of viewing how children learn, for such learning is characterized by unanticipated and irregular patterns and action research, as a process, allows student teachers to learn to cope with such patterns.
- *Action research narrows the gap between theory and practice.* We encourage student teachers to seek solutions in the literature and search for articles that are practically relevant to them, instead of asking them to read a bibliography provided by the teacher trainer. Student teachers' evaluations showed that they appreciated the way that using the literature allowed them to connect theory with practice, and many expressed a desire to continue doing so in their future teaching. They saw the academic literature as an important resource for classroom practice. Engaging with the literature also exposed

student teachers to conflicting theories and approaches, enhancing further the idea that education is a complex undertaking with no single correct answer:

> My focus on the subject changed many times since I started doing my research. In the beginning, I thought that the term Differentiated Instruction is an approach that helps teachers to engage all the pupils in the classroom. However, as I started reading the literature, I discovered that the term includes many different approaches, methodologies and tools.

- Action research gave student teachers scope to *define the focus* of their own investigations. Student teachers are individuals who are engaged in developing their own teacher identities (Beijaard 1995) and personal teaching styles. On an emotional level, student teachers have a need to identify and 'own' their learning processes as reflected in their need for choosing their own focus of study. In the initial stage of choosing a focus, teacher educators must be flexible and allow student teachers to pursue their own agendas and passions (Price 2001). Initial research topics that may appear unduly vague and abstract (such as motivation), or, alternatively, narrow and limited (such as the use of a specific game for vocabulary acquisition) should not be rejected. They can serve as starting points for the development of the process in which student teachers must participate in order to reflect on their personal choices, agendas, and values. These topics take shape and become practical research issues through the action research process as student teachers implement them in their classrooms.
- *Self-reflection*. Action research promotes personal and professional reflection. It helps student teachers focus on a specific issue or problem that is relevant to them in their practicum, helping them to overcome the seemingly endless number of problems they face in their initial 'survival stage' (Fuller 1969). One student teacher reported that although she was not convinced that her action research project had been beneficial to her pupils, she was certain that it had supported her development as teacher:

> I had many difficulties and new things to learn as I went along. I was definitely inexperienced and I learned things along with the pupils ... it made me flexible and open to new ideas (that is why, for example, I have changed some of my requirements as things progressed).

- Finally, student teachers' evaluations noted how action research promotes *a sense of community with other teachers* through collaboration in the research process and in dissemination in local and global contexts (Mullen 2000). In our programme, action research is carried out within a learning community of fellow student teachers, supported by the practices of cooperating teachers in the schools and facilitated by theoretical knowledge gained in course work. Action research papers are posted on the college website as exemplary models for student teachers in subsequent years, thereby, providing current student teachers with an intrinsic reward and empowering them to see their efforts as being of value to others. We have organized a student conference in collaboration with the national English Teachers Association in Israel (ETAI) in which students presented their research projects. Mullen (2000) presents a model for the co-mentoring of teachers as equals in the design, implementation, and reporting of action research. As in her work, relational inquiry between myself, as a teacher trainer, and selected student teachers, as 'colleagues who are equal but different' (Mullen 2000: 4), have resulted in conference presentations and publications at local and international levels.

Insights

Clearly, then, student teachers have generally appreciated the benefits of being asked to engage in action research. I will now analyse key stages in the first phase of our action-research programme, as the structured guidance provided there does, I believe, contribute to the overall effectiveness of the work the student teachers do.

Choosing a focus for research

In our scheme, the first stage of action research consists of the following assignment:

Assignment 1: Pedagogical journal
Keep a weekly record of the progression of your action research that includes:

- Observations of other teachers or student teachers that are related to your research topic.
- Reflections on your teaching experiences that are related to your research topic. This should help you formulate your evolving ideas, actions, or changes in practice.

Reread what you have written in your journal and highlight recurring significant issues.

Summarize the recurring significant issues that you found that are related to your research topic.

This assignment requires student teachers to write observations of classroom teaching in their pedagogical journals, beginning with an open and general focus in the first month, similar to what they have done in the two previous years of their participation in the student teaching programme. In the second month of student teaching, student teachers are instructed to reread their journals and choose a focus for their continued observations. Given the range of challenges they may face as classroom novices, some student teachers find it difficult to identify a focus and may approach the exercise perfunctorily; others, though, see this as an opportunity to focus on what concerns them most, rather than simply to complete an assignment stipulated by their teacher trainer.

The second stage, in the second month of the academic year, also coincides with the time that most of the student teachers begin their teaching practice in the classroom. They are now encouraged to write reflections on one issue of their choice. While I am aware of the disadvantages of a strategy that is aimed at limiting the focus of observation and reflection, I believe that this does lead to a richer and more in-depth reflection on one subject. This first assignment seeks to outline the steps of developing a research focus that is grounded in the reality of the classroom and the needs of the student teacher.

Writing the introduction

In order to provide the student teachers with opportunities to learn about action research according to their preferred learning styles, I use a wide array of teaching and learning strategies over the academic year. These include frontal lectures, class discussions in which student teachers raise problems they are experiencing, discussions of articles about action research and of published action research studies, class presentations by student teachers of their ongoing action research projects, group work, individual meetings, and comments on written drafts.

Having been mentored online from abroad throughout my doctoral studies, it was only natural for me to request that my student teachers submit their drafts by email. I comment in writing on these drafts and a large portion of the work is carried out online. I want to allow student teachers to progress at an individual pace, but they also need a framework for their activity and I provide this through the following set of questions:

Assignment 2: Questions related to the focus of research:
1. What is the problem, issue, or question that you want to learn more about?
2. Why is this important to you as a teacher?
3. Why is this important to your pupils?
4. What underlying assumptions, beliefs, and values are embedded in your focus?
5. What are some of the possible ways of answering this question from your readings, observations, and teaching experiences?

6. What are the approaches you prefer and why? What theoretical ideas support your approaches? What practical observations support your approaches?
7. How will you plan your lessons according to this way/approach?
8. How will you record/document what happens as a result of your approach?
9. Has your approach or focus changed since you began the project? If so, explain.

The purpose of these questions is to further the student teachers' writing about the subject of their research, both by narrowing the focus and by opening up the subject to more general issues. The questions are aimed at connecting theory and practice, linking external information found in the literature and in the classroom with internal meanings, values, and beliefs.

Rather than working through the above list of questions in a linear manner, student teachers are encouraged to note down thoughts, observations, reflections, or feelings as they occur in relation to any of the issues listed. They are told that the final organization will be done at a later stage and that they should concentrate on recording ideas that emerge spontaneously. This serves to reduce the anxiety of writing and the writers' block of not knowing how to begin at the stage when the research focus may still be rather vague.

Still in relation to the introduction to their project, after choosing a topic and starting to write notes related to the above questions the student teachers are asked to engage with the literature, and the following guidance is provided:

Assignment 3: Theoretical Background

Find, at least, **10 sources** that help develop your topic.
Elaborate on the sources in the introduction:

1. Present theories, ideas, or concepts that support your thesis.
2. Present theories, ideas, or concepts that gave you ideas for solutions.
3. Present theories, ideas, or concepts that present underlying beliefs and values.
4. Reference these sources in the body of your introduction according to APA.
5. Write a bibliography according to APA.

Student teachers are instructed to insert relevant ideas from the literature into what they have already written in a purposeful way in order to support and strengthen their initial thoughts, observations, and experiences. The purpose of the literature search is also to expose student teachers to opposing or contradictory ideas or to ones that challenge what they believe, know and see others doing. Adding ideas from the literature to what they have already written, rather than summarizing the literature as a separate section of the paper, has prevented plagiarism and the all-too-familiar copy/paste phenomenon found in many student papers.

Assessing the results

The design and use of rubrics for planning and assessment of teaching and learning is part of the Pedagogy curriculum for third-year students based on the national English Curriculum (Israeli Ministry of Education 2002). For this reason, early in the action research project I involve student teachers in the process of designing their own rubrics for the action research project. The choice of criteria and standards for the research project by the student teachers themselves serves to clarify the requirements of the project. The rubrics also serve as a practical reference guide for the implementation and writing of the research. In addition, the rubrics encourage transparency in terms of what the expectations of the final grade are. Teams of student teachers engaging in group work in Pedagogy lessons design the different parts of the rubric for the action research study (introduction, method, results, and discussion). Each rubric is presented to the entire class and changes are suggested and made until consensus is reached. In the final stage, the class rubric is compared to rubrics that have been used in previous years and further adjustments made if necessary. The additional advantage of the process is the feeling of ownership gained by the student teachers who are able to choose their own standards for assessment, as opposed to being subjected to an imposed grading system. An example of a rubric devised by the student teachers is given in Table 11.1.

Implications

The design and implementation of our action research programme, as discussed above, has implications for the ways in which action research can be embedded in pre-service language teacher education programmes.

First, although it is often said that student teachers do not have enough time or experience to do research during teaching practice, our model shows that this is possible and that it can be a valuable way of helping student teachers establish links between theory and practice.

Second, in terms of addressing student teachers' anxiety concerning the seemingly formidable task of doing and writing research, our experience suggests that a step-by-step approach of structured assignments is useful in supporting the initial stages of focusing on a topic, finding background literature and formulating a plan for implementation. Once they have completed the introduction to their action research projects, student teachers link ongoing lesson planning to their topic, and see the collection of data and reflection on it as natural parts of the process of teaching.

Table 11.1 Example of rubric for assessment of final action research project

INTRODUCTION (20 points) 8–15 pages

Criteria	Description	Excellent 5	On the way 2-3-4	Try again 0-1
1. Statement of problem	What do you want to change or improve in the classroom?	Clear and focused presentation of the problem	Partial presentation of the problem	Very broad or very narrow presentation of the topic Presentation of problem is not clear or far too broad
2. Rationale for study of topic	Why is the topic important to you and to others?	Clear and convincing argument for importance	Vague argument for importance of study	Lack of ideas that show importance of study
3. Integration of theoretical background	Sources are relevant to ideas presented	10 or more relevant sources are presented	Less than 10 sources are presented or not all sources are relevant	Less than 10 sources are presented and some are not relevant
4. Action plan	Possible approaches/ strategies that can be used to solve the problem	Many possible approaches/ strategies that are relevant to solving the problem	Few possible approaches/ strategies or approaches/ strategies that are not relevant to the solving of the problem	Very few approaches/ strategies mentioned. Those that are mentioned are not relevant to the solving of the problem
TOTAL				

Third, it is also important that student teachers are given space to make mistakes. Through action research, the fear of failure common among student teachers is replaced by the perception that making mistakes is part of the learning process and that mistakes are a basis for alternative ways of acting in the classroom.

One final implication that stems from our work is that student teachers need to feel that they have some ownership of the action research process. This cannot be achieved if the process is defined for the student teachers by their trainers and the role of the student teacher is to simply execute instructions they have been given. There is a clear need for structured guidance, as I have illustrated above, but within this structure we provide students with many opportunities to contribute to the process, such as in designing the evaluation criteria.

Two areas where our action research programme could be strengthened are collaboration within the school community and empowerment beyond the classroom. We need to send a stronger message to student teachers that teaching is not done behind closed doors and that success is directly related to the amount of collaboration sought from colleagues and expert teachers in the field (Mitchell et al. 2009). Lack of involvement on the part of the cooperating teachers in the schools is one of the major factors that we will strive to improve in the future through greater collaboration with and supervision of the cooperating teachers (Rajuan et al. 2011). We also believe that involving the school principals in the projects of the student teachers will do much to further this goal.

Also, although we are very satisfied with the programme and its immediate impacts on student teachers, we have no way of knowing what the longer-term effects of action research are. Indeed, some researchers claim that teachers only retain training course content that confirms their pre-existing beliefs about teaching (Pajares 1992). Tracking the student teachers once they graduate would help us attain longitudinal results about the value of action research in helping our graduates cope with their new roles as full-time teachers. It would be advantageous to learn whether action research supports and sustains new teachers in implementing innovations in their classrooms, in withstanding the pressures to conform to school norms and in decreasing the amount of regression to familiar ways of teaching.

Conclusion

The process of action research ends with new questions and new challenges for future learning (Zeichner 1995) in relation to specific pupils, classrooms, and methods, rather than with solutions that can be implemented in a fixed manner. The focus on action research in the final year of our teacher training programme serves as a core around which student teachers can integrate theories of education from their readings and other courses with their classroom practices. Key ideas that have been learnt theoretically, such as feedback, pupil-centred classrooms, and reflection, are all activated in practice through action research.

In addition to the many benefits derived by student teachers, teacher trainers who facilitate action research are likewise engaged in ongoing professional development by implementing inquiry-based and reflective practices. Teacher trainers must engage in ongoing professional development as role models and mentors as they prepare the 'seeds of today' for the future 'flowers of tomorrow'.

Engagement priorities

To promote further work on the issues addressed in this chapter, the following questions are raised for discussion based on the recommended texts:

1. Many of the ideas and recommendations in the chapter are based on the assumption that the Pedagogical Advisor serves as a role model of an educational researcher and author who, through experience, has developed expertise as a teacher of writing. How can this process be initiated and supported for those in need of more information and support as teachers of writing and as authors in their own right?
2. Student teachers deal with a myriad of issues and concerns of immediate management of the classroom in their initial teaching experiences. Is there a need for student teachers to become more engaged with social and ethical issues that go beyond the classroom or is it sufficient that they be exposed to a research approach that deals with practical classroom issues?
3. Collaborative research partnerships can enhance the value and outcomes of action research. In the context of pre-service teachers doing action research during their practicum, how can cooperating teachers be motivated to take a more collaborative role in the process when faced with time limitations and their dual obligations to fulfil their roles as teachers of pupils and mentors of student teachers?
4. Our action research programme empowers student teachers to disseminate their research beyond the framework of the course requirements. What different mechanisms can be created to enable action researchers to share their work in such ways?

References

Ben-Peretz, M. (2001). The impossible role of teacher educators in a changing world. *Journal of Teacher Education*, 52(1): 48–56.

Beijaard, D. (1995). Teachers' prior experiences and actual perceptions of professional identity. *Teachers and Teaching: Theory and Practice*, 1(2): 281–294.

Burns, A. (2010). *Doing Action Research for English Language Teachers: A Guide for Practitioners*. New York: Routledge.

Cochran-Smith, M. and Lytle, S. (1993). *Inside Outside: Teacher Research and Knowledge*. New York: Teachers College, Columbia University.

Edge, J. (2001). Attitude and access: Building a new teaching/learning community in TESOL. In J. Edge (ed.) *Action Research*. Alexandria, VA: TESOL, pp. 1–12.

Feiman-Nemser, S. (2012). *Teachers as Learners*. Cambridge, MA: Harvard Education Press.

Finch, A. (2000). Action research: Empowering the teachers. Korea: Kyungpook National University. Available at: http://www.eslteachersboard.com/cgi-bin/articles/index.pl?noframes;read=950 [Accessed 24/07/14.].

Fuller, F. F. (1969). Concerns of teaching: A developmental characterization. *American Educational Research Journal*, 6: 207–226.

Israeli Ministry of Education (2002). *Standards for Pupils of English: A Curriculum for Israeli Schools.* Pedagogical Secretariat, English Inspectorate, State of Israel.

Kemmis, S. and McTaggart, R. (eds) (1988). *The Action Research Planner.* Third Edition. Geelong, Victoria: Deakin University Press.

Knowles, G. J. and Holt-Reynolds, D. (1991). Shaping pedagogies through personal histories in preservice teacher education. *Teachers College Record,* 93: 87–111.

Levin, B. B. and Rock, T. C. (2003). The effects of collaborative action research on preservice and experienced teacher partners in professional development schools. *Journal of Teacher Education,* 54(2): 135–149.

Mitchell, S. N., Reilly, R. C., and Logue, M. E. (2009). Benefits of collaborative action research for the beginning teacher. *Teaching and Teacher Education,* 25: 344–349.

Mullen, C. A. (2000). Constructing co-mentoring partnerships: Walkways we must travel. *Theory into Practice,* 39(1): 4–12.

Noffke, S. E. and Stevenson, R. B. (eds) (1995). *Educational Action Research: Becoming Practically Critical.* New York: Teachers College, Columbia University.

Nunan, D. (1991). *Language Teaching Methodology.* London: Prentice Hall.

Pajares, M. F. (1992). Teachers' beliefs and educational research: Cleaning up a messy construct. *Review of Educational Research,* 62: 307–332.

Price, J. N. (2001). Action research, pedagogy and change: The transformative potential of action research in pre-service teacher education. *Journal of Curriculum Studies,* 33(1): 43–74.

Rajuan, M. (2012). Mentoring student teachers in professional development schools in Israel. In S. Fletcher and C. A. Mullen (eds), *The SAGE Handbook of Mentoring and Coaching for Education.* Los Angeles: Sage, pp. 322–336.

Rajuan, M., Beijaard, D., and Verloop, N. (2007). The role of the cooperating teacher: Bridging the gap between the expectations of cooperating teachers and student teachers. *Mentoring & Tutoring,* 15(2): 223–242.

Rajuan, M., Tuchin, I., and Zuckermann, T. (2011). Mentoring the mentors: First-order descriptions of experience-in-context. *The New Educator,* 7(2): 172–190.

Schön, D. (1983). *The Reflective Practitioner: How Professionals Think in Action.* New York: Basic Books.

Smith, K. and Sela, O. (2005). Action research as a bridge between pre-service teacher education and in-service professional development for students and teacher educators. *European Journal of Teacher Education,* 28(3): 293–310.

Zeichner, K. (1995). Designing educative practicum experiences for prospective teachers. In R. Hoz and M. Silberstein (eds), *Partnerships of Schools and Institutions of Higher Education in Teacher Development.* Be'er Sheva, Israel: Ben Gurion University of the Negev Press, pp. 123–144.

Zeichner, K. (2001). Action research and the preparation of reflective practitioners during the professional practicum. *Conference proceedings: Opening Gates in Teacher Education.* Tel Aviv: The Mofet Institute.

12
Teacher Research in the English Language Teacher Development Project

Rachel Bowden

Introduction

This chapter discusses factors which can facilitate teacher research, drawing on case studies from Malaysian English teachers as part of the English Language Teacher Development Project (ELTDP). The ELTDP operated in East Malaysia from 2011 until 2013 (later extended from 2014 until 2016) and involved British Council mentors supporting Malaysian teachers' development as reflective practitioners through a range of activities, including teacher research. The case studies in this chapter present reflections from mentors on processes, outcomes, challenges, and enabling factors related to teacher research. The chapter concludes with a discussion of the factors that facilitated the research and which others might draw on.

I worked on the ELTDP as a Project Manager from the start of the project in January 2011 until September 2013. I was involved with the initial design of the project, and in supporting a team of up to 21 mentors in over 100 schools to implement, monitor, and evaluate project work. The case studies in this chapter were written by mentors in collaboration with teachers.

The design of the ELTDP was based on research. This included research into effective teacher development, research into the education system in Malaysia, and a baseline survey conducted in schools by mentors in the first phase of the project (Bowden 2012; ELTDP 2011). The research informed the project's approach of developing teachers as reflective practitioners within a professional development 'system', rather than a training based programme. In practice, the project consisted of a wide range of development activities, undertaken in response to local contexts and with the active involvement of teachers (and often other stakeholders) in their selection, implementation, and evaluation (Kaplan 2013). Teacher research was seen as a key activity which all mentors were encouraged to facilitate, although when and how it was undertaken remained flexible (ELTDP 2011).

This chapter begins with a review of literature which informed the design of the ELTDP. More information about the ELTDP and the role of teacher research within the project is then provided, followed by the three case studies. The chapter concludes with a discussion of factors which enabled teacher research drawn from the case studies that others interested in supporting teacher research might find useful.

Learning and teaching

Conceptions of learning and teaching have shifted considerably since the Victorian era, when elementary school pupils were seen as passive recipients of knowledge designed to prepare them for menial tasks within a hierarchical and fixed industrial society (Alexander 2009). Nowadays, at least within the international literature, learners are seen as citizens with the right to influence the societies they inhabit through participation in democratic decision-making. In addition, increased economic competition between countries means that education systems are tasked with developing different skills and knowledge in learners (Villegas-Reimers 2003). This demands a very different model of schooling, and has important implications for teacher development (UNESCO 1997).

However, as late as the 1970s the Victorian model of teaching and learning remained dominant in the research literature (Dunkin and Biddle 1974, in Borg 2006). The model assumes direct causal links between teacher input and learner output; sees learning as a product of teaching, and teaching as a series of behaviours to be performed by teachers in class (Borg 2006). From this viewpoint there is little need for teachers to engage with theory or their learners, either as part of teaching or to develop their teaching.

Socio-cultural theory and constructivism challenge such views about teaching and learning. Socio-cultural theorists demonstrated the importance of what learners think and are able to do as the basis for development (Lantolf 2000). Within socio-cultural theory, learning is seen as progress through a zone of proximal development (ZPD) from the current state (what I currently know and do) to what can be known or done with support and finally 'internalized', known or done independently. 'Support' is fundamental in mediating new learning as individuals interact with existing constructs in order to integrate them into their own thinking. Therefore, learners' current knowledge should be drawn out and built upon as the basis for new learning, which is facilitated through social interaction, interaction with theory, and practical experience (Lantolf 2000). For constructivists, concepts are open and dynamic, existing inside individuals based on the sum of their knowledge, assumptions, and experience. From this perspective learning is an active and transformative process where 'Knowledge is not only transmitted but also negotiated and re-created' (Alexander 2009: 19). In contrast, passive learning approaches such as memorization can fail to engage with existing concepts or reformulate ideas, limiting the 'depth' of learning which occurs (Sterling 2001).

It is important to recognize that the value of a pedagogical approach can only be assessed in relation to aims and contexts. Gregory Bateson's two orders of learning and change are helpful in differentiating types of learning and considering the educational aims they might be appropriate for (Bateson 1972). First order change, or learning *about* things, implies a finite view of knowledge which is 'bolted on' to existing frameworks (Sterling 2001). Also termed 'transmission', this approach is underpinned by behaviourist theory and the educational aim of preparing people to fill existing roles in society and uphold cultural norms (Fien 1993).

The Malaysian Ministry of Education (MoE) recently published an 'Educational Blueprint', which calls for 'fundamental changes' to the education system in order to 'better prepare young Malaysians for the challenges of the 21st century' (MoE 2012: 1). These educational reforms aim to equip learners with 'higher order thinking skills, ... creative and critical thinking' to meet the demands of a knowledge economy (Malakolunthu 2007: 153; Yaacob 2006: 227). Bateson's second-order change captures the kind of 'deep' learning needed for this transformation, arguably for students *and* teachers within the system. Second-order change requires not only learning about things, but also reflection on learning itself (Sterling 2001). This takes into account constructivist models of change, and the view that 'education not only informs people, it can change them' (UNESCO 2002: 8).

Teaching and teacher education

The shift in thinking about learning is reflected in the language of teaching and teacher education. For example, Ohata, with reference to changes in second language teacher education, differentiates between 'training' on one hand and 'development' on the other. He sees the term 'training' as indicative of a 'process-product' view while 'development' implies changes in thinking and attitudes as well as practice (Ohata 2007: 2–4). Ohata recognizes that there are certain elements of teachers' practice which are effectively learnt through training, but points out that training is not suitable for developing higher-level cognitive processes. In Malaysia there has been sustained pressure from policy makers for teachers to adopt constructivist approaches, seen as essential for developing citizens for a 'knowledge economy'; therefore 'training' as the sole means of professional learning is insufficient (MoE 2012).

The proposed 'new paradigm' of teacher development is founded on the recognition that there is no universal 'best' model or activity but rather a range of approaches which may be appropriate for different teachers at different times, underpinned by certain principles of learning and change. Indeed, Villegas-Reimers (2003) suggests that teacher development be seen as a broad 'system' rather than a single model or activity. This system encompasses

> goals, objectives and purposes; contexts; personal and professional characteristics of participants; models, techniques and procedures; costs and benefits; determination of who makes which decisions; a process to assess and evaluate success; infrastructure support. (Villegas-Reimers 2003: 16)

Several researchers (e.g. Villegas-Reimers 2003; Walter and Briggs 2012) have identified features (often through extensive reviews of literature describing teacher development activities) which they see as being fundamental to effective teacher development. I summarize these below:

1. It is considered a system, underpinned by objectives and principles. Within this system, diverse methods, tools and processes are differentiated for teachers' varying needs and contexts.
2. It is informed by 'research on children's development, learning, needs and capabilities' (Alexander 2009: 12–13).
3. It takes into account teachers' current knowledge, beliefs, values, experiences, and practices.
4. It engages teachers actively in the choice of areas to develop, the activities to undertake and in evaluating their effectiveness.
5. It engages teachers as reflective practitioners; developing through exploration of theory and practice connected to the contexts in which they operate.
6. It is collaborative and supportive; including mentoring or coaching with peers, others within the wider system and external supporters.
7. It is seen as a long-term process, including regular support sustained over time.
8. It is context-based, for example located within the school or classroom.
9. It is linked to school reform and/or changes in the wider education system with effective school leadership.

Teacher development in Malaysia

In Malaysia, while the discourse around teacher education reflects a move from a 'technicist model, to reflective practitioner constructivist'(Lee 2002: 60), the evidence suggests that policy reforms have not impacted practice. Courses are reported to be overly focused on technical competence or a 'cook-recipe' approach and fail to engage teachers' thinking (Lee 2002: 61). Where the term 'reflective practice' has been applied, the emphasis has been on the technical over the practical or critical, and activities have not sought to engage with the teachers' thinking (Lee 2002). In-service training follows the 'cascade' model where key teachers receive centralized training which, often several 'levels' later, is repeated for teachers in schools resulting in 'dilution and distortion' (Nalliah and Thiyagararajah 2002: 447). Malakolunthu notes that such 'traditional, episodic in-service training is not effective in helping teachers learn and change their practices' (2007: 161). There have been efforts to introduce school-based learning, led by head teachers. However, teachers have complained that this has remained too generalized to be relevant (Lee 2002). It seems that while constructivist theory is espoused in policy and by teacher educators, it has not been internalized or put into practice. Indeed, teachers' own perceptions of professional development reflect a rudimentary understanding of PD that includes 'attending conferences or courses', 'participating in workshops or seminars' or 'attending training'. Many teachers seem to view themselves as passive recipients in the process 'dependent on the MoE and other stakeholders to provide PD programmes/activities' (Kabilan and Veratharaju 2013: 17).

Context

In this section I provide more information about the ELTDP, where the research described in the case studies below was undertaken. The project was described by an external evaluator as follows:

> The ELTDP as a mentoring programme has been designed to foment and support changes in thinking and practice. Based on reflective practice, project stakeholders have been engaged in looking into current practices, and formulating and evaluating interventions. Thus, rather than working to a standard format or course, project work has centred on what teachers and other stakeholders know, do and value. This has resulted in diverse, exciting and meaningful activities and development. (Kaplan 2013: 6–7)

An overarching theoretical model for conceptualizing and communicating the project's approach was the 'reflective learning cycle' (see Figure 12.1). The cycle emphasizes the need for reflection in and on action, and portrays learning as a context bound and social process (Schön 1983).

Rather than training teachers, mentors were tasked with: 'supporting teachers and other stakeholders through processes of enquiry and action' where they:

> identify what the current situation is, and areas they want to learn more about or change ... work together with teachers to plan research, development or classroom intervention activities based on this (plan and do), and then evaluate the success of the activities (look/review). Mentors and

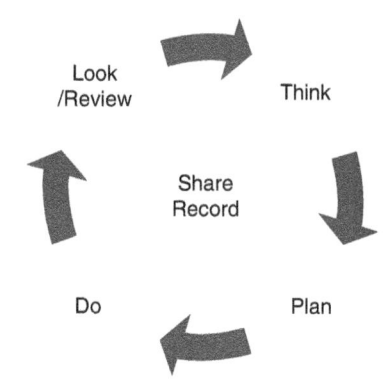

Figure 12.1 ELTDP's reflective cycle
Source: Mentor handbook (ELTDP 2011: 21)

> teachers prioritise objectives to focus on and decide how they wish to work in terms of interactions, tools and activities. (ELTDP 2011: 20)

Classroom research methods were suggested as a means for teachers to gather and evaluate evidence from their own classrooms to inform changes in practice (Hopkins 2008). However, when and how teachers undertook research was left intentionally flexible, which resulted in a variety of approaches. In the mid-project evaluation report, the external evaluator noted:

> There is clear evidence that mentees are engaging in research based on their own concerns and interests. However, the ways in which this research is facilitated by mentors differs; some using more structured approaches … and others going about the process more loosely. (Kaplan 2012: 24)

I believe that the ELTDP represented the characteristics of the 'new paradigm' of teacher development outlined above. Unlike many in-service training interventions, ELTDP mentors had the advantage of working alongside teachers in schools for up to three years and were able to offer regular and ongoing support. The project's emphasis on developing teachers as reflective practitioners meant they were actively engaged in the development process with their own values, assumptions, knowledge, beliefs, and practices as the starting point for development work. The ELTDP was part of wider educational reforms, as outlined in the Educational Blueprint, which lent broad support for development interventions (MoE 2012). Surrounding reforms, which include a new constructivist curriculum and a formative assessment system, were complementary to the project's emphasis on evidence gathering as the basis for differentiated practice (MoE 2011). Within the frame of developing teachers as reflective practitioners, mentors and teachers were encouraged to choose from an array of models and tools for development. This engaged them actively in the process of selection, implementation, and evaluation of activities and challenged the idea of a single 'best practice' for professional development. Project activities were developed within schools and sought to involve other teachers, school administration, and surrounding communities.

Insights

In this part of the chapter, three case studies of teacher research, written by mentors in consultation with the teachers involved, are presented. The case studies included here highlight the processes which facilitated teacher research and which are discussed further in the concluding section of this chapter.

Case Study 1

In the first case study, mentor Carolina shares her experience of supporting ten mentees to undertake action research, over a period of several months. She describes how she developed her own and her teachers' interest in research, the challenges they faced, and the positive outcomes they experienced. For Carolina, the intrinsic value of action research, i.e. for developing research and reflective skills, is as important as answering research questions. Carolina finds support for teachers (from school management, colleagues, and their mentor) to be a crucial enabling factor; along with the relationships and skills developed from a year on the project before the research was undertaken.

Action Research (AR) was a foreign idea to me and my mentees. I had doubts as whether it would be viable and of interest and relevance to the teachers and their contexts. I also felt that I lacked the legitimacy and confidence to use it as a mentor, as I had never been involved in AR as a teacher. I started by collecting ideas and resources from my colleagues who were already doing AR. Googling and reading Anne Burns' *Doing Action Research in English Language Teaching: A Guide for Practitioners* (2010) provided a great start. Later on, the experience of reading some critical voices deploring an over-emphasis on problem-solving and stressing the importance of teachers' critical involvement made me much more motivated to start AR.

All the teachers were vaguely familiar with AR. Most of them expressed strong reservations, as they had little or no experience in any form of research. Some had done AR in college, following what seemed to be a very prescriptive and restrictive model. I decided to introduce AR in a workshop with all ten teachers as a way to bring different perspectives together, generate more ideas, and create a stronger sense of purpose and responsibility. I felt that it was important to build confidence and interest, so that the teachers could appreciate the potential of AR as a development tool and be genuinely motivated to make use of it. The initial of choice research questions was supported by a process approach:

- individual self-reflection questionnaire to build awareness of own interests, concerns, etc. (e.g. 'What do I feel passionate about? What needs of my students are not being met?');
- then, group brainstorming of possible topics;
- then, individual stream of consciousness activity: writing as many possible interesting questions as quickly as possible;
- then, choice of one question that fits criteria:
    Exciting? I love my research question, it really suits me
    New? I will find and learn something new with it
    Specific? It's not too big and general
    Relevant? It's directly meaningful to my context
    Feasible? I can do it with the time and resources I have

The initial planning was based on some guiding questions:

- Why did I choose this topic? To ensure strong personal interest and sustained commitment.
- What do I want to find? To clarify ideas, redefine questions, and keep in mind AR is more about discovery than confirmation of assumptions.
- What resources and tools will I be using? To identify the appropriate resources and tools, plan or design them with the appropriate purpose and audience in mind, plan ways to analyse and act on gathered data.

From the beginning there was an emphasis on mentee ownership and responsibility through increased self-initiative and agreed weekly action points and the final workshop in mind. Mentees used a variety of tools to collect information: reading (usually online), discussions with mentor and peers, interviews, questionnaires, observing their classrooms, observing other teachers, etc. I saw my role as one of responsiveness and motivation, raising relevant questions to help mentees develop their analytical and planning skills and have confidence in their judgements and decisions. The level of support varied, depending on each mentee's level of autonomy and the different phases they were going through. It ranged from active guidance – planning and designing tools; treating and analysing information; summarizing results; structuring content; suggesting ideas and alternatives during stalemates in research; to receptive support – keeping focus, prioritizing, anticipating problems, clarifying thoughts and intentions, identifying strengths and interesting research clues and encouraging mentees to build on them, promoting group sharing, encouraging involvement in peers' projects, offering constructive feedback and inviting mentees to observe and celebrate smaller steps and achievements, motivating, spreading enthusiasm, projecting an attitude of trust and faith in individual abilities and outcomes.

The challenges and difficulties I faced in my role included: managing mentees' breaks in motivation and commitment; managing stalemates and exhaustion of ideas; responding to mentees' expectations of my role as a provider of ideas and solutions; dealing with mentees' inconsistencies in purpose and critical involvement; avoiding plagiarism and shaping projects to merely confirm previous assumptions; and building my own confidence and skills in a more receptive role. In their subsequent reflections, all mentees identified lack of time as the biggest challenge. Some reported lack of support from GB (head teacher), PKs (senior teachers), and being burdened with extra work. Other reported challenges included: finding suitable reading references for specific local topics; defining and narrowing their research question; lack of confidence in feeling they were doing 'the right thing'; lack of response from their pupils when trying something different; finding the right adjustments to the changes they had initiated in their practice. As to strategies to overcome these difficulties, they mentioned developing time-management skills, discussing and getting motivation from mentor and peers, positive thinking and open-mindedness.

The final presentations evidenced a high level of professionalism, complexity, relevance, and originality of issues and analyses. Mentees felt they became more: 'positive', 'creative', 'open-minded', 'independent', 'confident', 'patient', 'professional', 'happy to complete the research and present it'; and more able to: 'understand pupils', 'make pupils not afraid of English', 'change teaching style', 'save time', 'use and reuse materials', 'know where to find and look for methods, skills and new ideas' and 'write for research'. They also reported some positive impacts on their pupils, including 'improved student achievement', 'changes in behaviour and discipline' and being 'more comfortable with English'. In general, mentees developed a range of important skills, namely researching, planning, prioritizing, managing time, designing tools, anticipating problems, analysing information, summarizing, creating presentations and public speaking.

In terms of beliefs and attitudes, I feel that mentees developed an appreciation of the value of AR, self-reflection, exploratory teaching and collaboration. There has also been a boost in group confidence – since then all the workshops have been mentee-led. I think AR has given my work an edge, making it more purposeful and effective – helping me sharpen my listening skills, detach from suggesting, understand my mentees better and develop more personalized ways to help each of them.

Overall, these are some of the issues that made an important contribution to the process of doing AR:

- building on existing foundations and allowing the necessary time. We started AR a year after the beginning of ELTDP;
- conceiving AR beyond a generalizable intervention formula to find solutions to problems and rather as a tool to enable a deeper personal understanding of local issues in teaching and learning;
- balancing the importance of process (skills development and autonomy) and product aspects (quality of results, records, and final presentation) – though a bit more emphasis on process is entirely appropriate for first-time researchers, in my opinion;
- planning ways to make AR attractive and engaging to ensure intrinsic motivation and critical involvement;
- setting a clear purpose with clear time-frame and audience that motivated teachers to act upon a visualized final outcome;
- reassuring teachers that the research question often needs to be redefined, and that this is a valuable part of the research process;
- investing time with teachers to develop underpinning research skills such as: googling, choosing appropriate search terms, refining search results, selecting information and websites, recognizing local sources of information;
- encouraging any kind of presentation format other than Power Point – one mentee preferred to make a scrapbook;
- motivating, motivating, motivating!
- agreeing accountability for deadlines and results and responsibility for developing initiative and resourcefulness to find own ideas and solutions;
- being flexible about timeframes if justified: we started with a three-month horizon for the completion of the projects, but then extended it to four months as the mentees were getting more involved and their projects gaining more complexity.

Case Study 2

In the second case study mentor Cathy describes research undertaken by teacher Roszita on engaging parents with their children's learning. The research focus emerged from discussions with colleagues as part of the ELTDP, and the process was facilitated through regular meetings with the mentor. Activities included reading both international and Malaysian literature on parent-school relationships, a local survey of parents' behaviour and attitudes, and an intervention aimed at enabling greater involvement of parents. The research had broad impacts including the development of the teacher's skills and confidence; improved parent-school relationships and pupil engagement with English; and the involvement of other teachers and the head teacher. Cathy finds that support is an essential factor in enabling the process, and notes that the impact of research can be increased by ensuring channels for teachers to share their research.

Roszita teaches English in a semi-rural state primary school of approximately 600 pupils on the island of Labuan, East Malaysia. As a mentee on the ELTDP, she was often involved in discussion with her mentor and other mentees about the role of parents in their children's education. Roszita believed that parents were enthusiastic about their children's English education but could see that her school did little to involve them.

Roszita began by reading academic articles about the advantages and difficulties of involving parents in their children's education. She then sent out a questionnaire to Year 1 parents to see if they were interested in learning about how to support their child's studies at home. The majority of parents expressed interest. Roszita then decided to experiment with a homework-signing project. During 2012, she asked parents of the three classes she was teaching to sign homework every time she sent it home. She kept records of whose homework was signed. The aims were to give parents a chance to find out what their children were studying in their English lessons and to show to school management that if you give parents a chance to work with their children and the English teacher this has an impact on their children's achievement.

From her reading Roszita learnt that the education system in Malaysia focuses on teachers as the key players in the children's education with little concentration on having parents as co-partners in the children's learning process. She also learnt that Western studies show that children perform better at school when they have support from parents at home. From the data recorded from the homework-signing project, Roszita noticed that pupils who were getting homework signed regularly tended to achieve higher assessment scores than those who did not. From informal discussions with pupils, she found that they enjoyed sharing with their parents what they had learnt at school. From a follow-up survey of parents, she found that 100% of parents who replied liked the homework-signing project and wanted to continue with it. Roszita realized that parents *are* interested in their children's education and that if the school gives them a chance to be more involved they will take it.

There have been some positive outcomes from this project. Roszita's findings that parents want to be more involved in their children's education led her to hold two Saturday morning workshops for parents this year to show them how to enjoy reading at home with their children. This involved other English teachers and the librarian. The head teacher of the school also attended, and was impressed by the level of interest from parents. The main difficulty is to disseminate the results of the project and to involve the whole school in engaging parents. Many teachers are still hostile to the idea of parental involvement. Roszita has been trying to encourage other teachers to do the homework-signing project with their classes but so far they have not been disciplined about giving homework regularly and collecting data.

This is a long-term project, which is still ongoing, and needs the teacher to be disciplined and organized in collecting and analysing the data collected. Weekly meetings to discuss Roszita's progress were invaluable in helping her to maintain focus. Teacher research is not a solitary pursuit. Teachers need support when carrying out a project – to discuss findings, difficulties, and successes – and they need a formal channel for presenting and disseminating their findings. With the support of her mentor, Roszita has presented her research at school meetings, at district-level meetings for English teachers, and at a regional conference. It would be helpful to have research groups set up at school and district level to formalize support for teacher research, to provide a forum for sharing research, and to ensure that findings are used to influence school and district policies.

Case Study 3
In the third and final case study mentor Tim summarizes work done with teachers from three schools in rural Sarawak who used research to investigate involving parents in supporting children to learn English outside school. The process started by looking into parents' behaviours and attitudes, which challenged teachers' assumptions and informed the subsequent interventions. The teachers appear to have moved towards increasing parents' involvement, and the case suggests that their participation in framing the aims of research as well as in the process is valuable. The project was seen to benefit relationships between the school and surrounding communities and pupils' engagement with English. The mentor also notes that teachers transfer aspects of the research approach to developing skills in other areas of their practice. He reports that the teachers, who see the work as ongoing, found being the drivers of their projects essential. It is suggested that the support of school administration is vital in enabling such projects to happen.

Following discussions about the purposes and challenges of parental involvement, the teachers gathered information on families' attitudes through home visits, interviews, structured discussions and surveys. The teachers discovered, among other things, that parents were willing to help children but needed support. The teachers and mentor reflected on these findings, and then planned parental involvement and home learning pilot activities. Once established they further developed the programme based on their experience and the input of parents and children. The teachers are still exploring new activities for parents to use at home.

From this research and reflection process the teachers learnt that working in partnership with parents is possible; indeed some parents were always actively involved in their children's learning. They found that many parents, even if uneducated, were willing to do home learning activities, talk regularly to teachers, and make the time and space to help their children and discuss school with them. Teachers found that interacting with the parents improved relations and reduced problems and misunderstandings about school. Parents and children often had their own ideas about learning outside the classroom so that as parental involvement increased, new ideas and working methods emerged. Having parents visit the school to practise home learning activities helped the children see English as something valuable and important. Their confidence and motivation definitely increased. Reflecting on parental involvement helped teachers think about other issues e.g. making learning fun, exploiting storytelling. The constraints on parental involvement identified were primarily practical – transport, time, money, ideas for activities. For the teachers, key challenges were finding locally appropriate activities and creating suitable materials.

What we learnt from this project was that:

- teachers have to decide the research methods themselves;
- you have to build trust and closeness with the stakeholders you are researching and be open about your aims;
- you will need to explain yourself many times;
- social events help the research process;
- teacher research needs support from head teachers, as sustained time commitments are necessary to produce anything valuable;
- if the objects of the research/stakeholders know how the research might benefit them and can be actively involved, it is helpful.

Implications

These case studies indicate the potential of teacher research as a means for teachers to identify and address specific issues; to develop critical, creative, and analytical skills; to access and interpret wider research; to form collaborative and constructive professional relationships; to build professional confidence and motivation; and to interpret theories, policies, and training in practice. In this section factors which facilitated teacher research in the case studies, and may be of use to others in the field, are discussed. As the research was undertaken within the broader context of teachers' involvement with the ELTDP, many of the elements relate to the project's approach and the characteristics of the 'new paradigm' of teacher development described earlier.

The diversity shown in these case studies reinforces the view that there is no single 'cook-recipe' model for teacher research to be followed. While research has certain fundamental principles, research design depends upon the aims of the research, the beliefs of the researcher and other pragmatic concerns (Bartlett and Burton 2012). Therefore, those supporting teachers to undertake research need an understanding of research principles, knowledge of a range of research methodologies and methods, and the skills to learn as they go along. For instance, initially both Carolina and her teachers had negative views about research based on assumptions and previous experience. Carolina found it necessary to learn more about teacher research herself before identifying ways to engage her teachers. As a result of reading and discussions with colleagues, her conception of action research changed and she gained in confidence and motivation. Ultimately Carolina found that the process of facilitating her teachers' research helped her to develop as a mentor, and led to teachers taking more responsibility for other development activities within the project.

The research described in the case studies was based on established professional relationships among teachers and mentors and a shared understanding of the context of investigation. This was part of the design of the ELTDP, which included an initial phase of non-intervention where mentors and teachers explored together the context of practice (the 'look' stage of the reflective cycle – see Figure 12.1) through observations, focus groups, and discussions among other methods. This phase served to familiarize mentors with the context they were working in, encouraged teachers to re-assess their contexts, and provided time for mentors and teachers to get to know each other (ELTDP 2011). Carolina describes how the research 'built on the foundations' of the previous year of the project which included the development of research skills such as classroom observation and Internet research. In addition, she used the group of teachers she was mentoring (approximately ten, from five different schools) to motivate each other, share insights, and provide a level of accountability.

In addition, in all three case studies it is apparent that the regular and ongoing support mentors provided was an important factor. All mentors note that regular meetings helped to sustain teachers' motivation and focus. The case studies also demonstrate how the focus of teacher research can change along the way; therefore, regular opportunities for teachers to take stock of new knowledge and the overall process may enable the degree of responsiveness required. For both Tim and Cathy's teachers, initial research into parents' attitudes to education led to research into how they could be more involved. ELTDP teachers were allocated weekly time for project activities, in addition to their regular classes (which mentors might also attend). These activities included discussions with the mentor and other colleagues, reading and meetings with other stakeholders such as parents. Carolina and Tim note that allocated time for teacher research was an essential enabling factor.

Two further factors for facilitators to consider are the levels of structure and flexibility appropriate to ensure teachers benefit from the guidance the research framework offers, while ensuring enough differentiation to be practical and meaningful. Carolina found providing a time-frame for teachers helpful (although the end-point was later extended), in addition to agreeing expectations and responsibilities in a group setting. She also found it necessary to intervene at times to ensure that teachers were thinking critically and not simply reinforcing assumptions. She recommends being creative about how teachers share information – for example, one teacher created a scrapbook of her experience. For Tim and Cathy's teachers the research process was highly flexible, included several iterations and was seen by the teachers as an ongoing process. Carolina reports adapting the level of support offered for each teacher at different times in the research process, with an overall focus on increasing teachers' ownership of the research. All of the mentors ensured the initial research focus came from the teachers, and adapted to changes as teachers' understandings developed. Tim also highlighted the need to engage teachers actively in choosing the research methods.

All of the mentors agreed that some involvement from school management and other teachers is essential for the practical and psychological support they can offer. In addition, including other stakeholders may help to build shared understandings of common issues and mitigate resistance that teacher researchers may otherwise face. Head teachers' involvement can ensure teachers have the time for research activities, lend legitimacy, and ensure findings are acted upon or shared more widely. For Carolina, working with her teachers in a group increased motivation, boosted confidence, and ensured a level of commitment from teachers. Roszita's research focus emerged from discussion with other teachers in her school and she attempted to involve them in the intervention in order to broaden her initiative and mitigate hostility, although this was a challenge. For Cathy and Tim's teachers, learners' parents were central to the research process. Tim's teachers found that being open about research aims and involving the research 'objects' as active subjects in the research was beneficial.

Both Cathy and Carolina found that identifying forums for teachers to share their research was important. Carolina suggests this acted as a goal for teachers, providing useful structure and helping teachers stay focused and motivated. In addition, she found that teachers' confidence improved as a result of sharing and the teachers were able to get ideas and inspiration from each other. Cathy believes that establishing formal forums for sharing research would help to prioritize teacher research within schools and the wider system, and ensure that teachers' experiences and findings are used to build understanding of the complex context of schools and to inform policy making and implementation.

Conclusion

The ELTDP represented a professional development system within which teachers received regular mentoring support for a period of up to two and a half years. This often involved teachers working with school stakeholders within and between schools and engaging in a wide variety of activities where they were asked to consider their own teaching contexts as a basis for development. Activities included sharing ideas, issues, and activities with other teachers, observing their own and others' classes, planning lessons, and assessing pupils' learning, and reading and applying learning theory to their classes.

Teacher research, in various forms, was presented as a model mentors could use with teachers. Whether, when, and how mentors and teachers undertook the research was up to them. This flexibility meant that, where it did occur, research focused on issues or priorities and adopted methods for data collection and analysis selected by teachers.

Shifting beliefs about teaching and teacher development is crucial if practices are to change in line with educational discourse in Malaysia. Teachers sharing their processes of research with teachers and other educational stakeholders is a powerful means of demonstrating what reflective practice is, the complexity and diversity of teaching contexts, and the agency of teachers in developing their own practice. It is therefore important that there are both formal and informal forums for teachers to share their work and indeed, where possible, involve others in research processes. As a teacher development system the ELTDP provided the environment, including professional support and a high degree of flexibility, to enable meaningful research to occur. A key challenge for Malaysian schools is to ensure that teachers have this kind of support in the future.

Engagement priorities

While it is possible to identify certain features which may support teacher research, there is no 'cook-recipe' model to follow. In order to develop context appropriate approaches those supporting teacher research will need to act as reflective practitioners themselves. This may include learning, alongside those they work with, about teacher research and about the context of the research. Ultimately, facilitators (and teacher researchers) should aim for an understanding of the principles of research, a knowledge of a range of research methodologies and methods, and the skills to learn as they go along. In this section questions are used to stimulate further discussion and reflection.

1. Interpretations of teacher research
Assumptions about research can limit teachers' willingness to get involved. However, there is no single 'correct' way of defining research. What different but appropriate ways of defining teacher research do teachers in different contexts find useful?

2. Support
Practical and psychological support were identified as key factors in enabling teacher research. What other kinds of support have a significant impact on teachers' ability to be teacher researchers?

3. Involving others
In Malaysia, involving stakeholders such as parents, school administration, and other teachers in research was seen as beneficial. Further examples from

different contexts of how these and other stakeholders influence the process of teacher research would be valuable.

4. Forums for sharing
Sharing the findings and processes of research can be valuable in gaining support for teacher development. What different ways for sharing teacher research exist and what do we know about their relative effectiveness?

Acknowledgements

The author would like to thank the following mentors and teachers for the case studies they contributed to this chapter: Carolina Cruz and the ELTDP teachers of Kudat, Sabah; Cathy Layne and Roszita Asma Abd. Rahman (ELTDP, Labuan), Tim Hughes and the ELTDP teachers of Sri Aman, Sarawak. Cathy, Tim and Carolina worked on the ELTDP between 2011 and 2013.

References

Alexander, R. J. (2009). *Introducing the Cambridge Primary Review*. Available at: http://www.primaryreview.org.uk/publications/introductory_booklet.php [Accessed 11/2/2011].
Bartlett, B. and Burton, D. (2012). *Introduction to Education Studies*, (Third edition). London: London.
Bateson, G. (1972). *Steps to an Ecology of Mind*. San Francisco: Chandler.
Borg, S. (2006). *Teacher Cognition and Language Education: Research and Practice*. London: Continuum.
Bowden, R. (2012). The English Language teacher development Project (ELTDP): Enquiry-based project design and teacher development. In T. Pattison (ed.), *IATEFL 2012: Glasgow Conference Selections: 46th International Conference*. Kent: IATEFL, pp. 150–152.
ELTDP (2011). *The English Language Teacher Development Project: Project Introduction*. Available at: http://schoolsonline.britishcouncil.org/english-language-teachers-development/project-introduction [Accessed 10/7/13].
Fien, J. (1993). *Teaching for a Sustainable World*, Australia: Griffith University.
Hopkins, D. (2008). *A Teacher's Guide to Classroom Research* (Fourth edition). Maidenhead: Open University Press.
Kabilan, M. K. and Veratharaju, K. (2013). Professional development needs of primary school English language teachers in Malaysia, *Professional Development in Education*, 39(3): 330–351.
Kaplan, I. (2012) ELTDP *Mid Project Evaluation Report* http://schoolsonline.britishcouncil.org/participatory-project-evaluation/reports [Accessed 10/07/2013]
Kaplan, I. (2013). *ELTDP Final Project Evaluation Report*. Available at: http://schoolsonline.britishcouncil.org/participatory-project-evaluation/reports [Accessed 10/7/13].
Lantolf, J. P. (2000). Introducing sociocultural theory. In J. P. Lantolf (ed.), *Socio-cultural Theory and Second Language Learning*. Oxford: Oxford University Press, pp. 1–26.
Lee, M. (2002). *Educational change in Malaysia*. Penang: Universiti Sains Malaysia, School of Educational Studies, Monograph Series No: 3/2003.
Malakolunthu, S. (2007). *Teacher Learning in Malaysia: Problems and Possibilities of Reform*. Kuala Lumpur: University of Malaya Press.

Ministry of Education Malaysia, (2011). *KSSR Teachers' Guide Level 1*. Available at: http://www.moe.gov.my/bpk/v2/kssr/dokumen_kurikulum/tahap_i/modul_teras_asas/bahasa_inggeris [Accessed 3/7/13].

Ministry of Education Malaysia, (2012). *Malaysia Education Blueprint 2013–2025*. Available at: http://www4.unescobkk.org/nespap/sites/default/files/Preliminary-Blueprint-ExecSummary-Eng_0.pdf [Accessed 21/12/12].

Nalliah, M. and Thiyagarajah, R. (2002). Teacher education for TESOL in Malaysia: The pursuance of conformity in the context of cultural diversity. In Y. Cheng, K. Tsui, K. Chow, and M. Mok (eds), *Subject Teaching and Teacher Education in the New Century: Research and Innovation*. Hong Kong: The Hong Kong Institute for Education and Kluwer Academic, pp. 439–456.

Ohata, K. (2007). Teacher development or training? Recent developments in second/foreign language teacher education. *Language Research Bulletin, 22*(1): 1–16.

Schön, D. (1983). *The Reflective Practitioner: How Professionals Think in Action*. London: Basic books.

Sterling, S. (2001). *Sustainable Education: Re-visioning Learning and Change*. Totnes: Green Books for The Schumacher Society.

UNESCO (1997). Universal declaration on democracy. 161st session of the Inter-parliamentary Council Cairo Available at: http://www.unesco.org/cpp/uk/declarations/democracy.pdf [Accessed 12/12/2013].

UNESCO (2002). Education for Sustainability. From Rio to Johannesburg: lessons learnt from a decade of commitment. UNESCO. Available at: http://tinyurl.com/kb2b66z [Accessed 27/02/2014].

Villegas-Reimers, E. (2003). *Teacher Professional Development: An International Review of the Literature*. IIEP. Available at: http://unesdoc.unesco.org/images/0013/001330/133010e.pdf [Accessed 25/6/13].

Walter, C. and Briggs, J. (2012). [online] What professional development makes the most difference to teachers? A report sponsored by Oxford University Press. Available at: http://www.academia.edu/3294074/What_professional_development_makes_the_most_difference_to_teachers [Accessed 8/6/13].

Yaacob, A. (2006). *Malaysian Literacy Practices in English: 'Big Books', CD-ROMs and the Year 1 English Hour*. [Online] PhD. English Language Teaching and Applied Linguistics. University of Warwick. Available at: http://wrap.warwick.ac.uk/4076/1/WRAP_THESIS_Yaacob_2006.pdf [Accessed 2/1/13].

13
Encouraging Teacher Research through In-House Activities: The Approach of a Finnish University Language Centre

Tuula Lehtonen, Kari Pitkänen, and Johanna Vaattovaara

Introduction

This chapter discusses approaches a university language centre or any similar educational institution can opt for in order to promote and enable the combination of teaching with research and development. While focusing on ways that encourage teachers' engagement both with research (by reading and using it) and in research (by doing it) (Borg 2010), our particular interest is on the necessary social or institutional requirements, on the type of opportunities that may arise in a positive environment as well as on the role of personal incentives. We deal with these questions in the context of the Language Centre at the University of Helsinki, Finland, which has, during recent years, gained a reputation as an active, development-oriented and research-friendly language centre in both national and international language centre networks.

Teachers' engagement with and in research cannot be taken for granted. Borg (2010) has identified various barriers to teacher research: non-collaborative school culture; limitations in teachers' awareness, beliefs, skills, and knowledge; limited resources; demotivators such as teachers' lack of ownership in their research; economic matters; leadership attributes such as no support from the leaders; and political issues. Many of these barriers are familiar to us. For example, our staff have different understandings of what constitutes research (partially because of their varied backgrounds), not all are experienced in research, and the resources available for research are limited.

These barriers to teacher research may pose a risk of paralysing the workplace and blocking the incentives the employees may have. In our view, the most 'high-risk' barriers are, however, *non-collaborative culture* and *leadership attributes* (see Borg 2010), which need to be overcome first in order to focus on lowering some of the other barriers. Without a proactive approach to collaboration, the workplace continues to consist of individuals who reinvent, do not learn from one another, and may be afraid of trying out new approaches. Good leadership, on the other hand, enables certain administrative structures that encourage collaboration. A case in point is our workplace where conscious steps have been taken to enhance the atmosphere of collaborative working culture, and where the director and other staff have taken an active stance to build structures that allow us to focus on development and research. Our chapter aims to show how removing the barriers of non-collaborative culture, in particular, is essential in breaking down other possible barriers.

The collaborative working culture is a key issue, because we believe, as do socio-cultural theorists (e.g., Wertsch 1993; Wertsch et al. 1993), that individual agency is social in nature. It is this nature that helps us understand and interpret the value of collaboration and good leadership at the Language Centre of the University of Helsinki. Like most university departments, the Language Centre also needs to adapt to constant change in which the action of individuals, when given support and possibilities for interaction, can have a proactive role. Wertsch (1993: 18) notes that 'a socio-cultural approach to mind begins with the assumption that action is mediated and ... cannot be separated from the milieu in which it is carried out'. The mediational tools and language, in turn, shape the action. In other words, people interact with one another and, in this interaction, shape themselves and their environment. Those with more expertise scaffold novices (Vygotsky 1978), and in this process, create shared understandings.

The above idea can also be read into, for example, Lasky's (2005) approach which focuses on human agency. Lasky underlines the importance of analysing how people act and behave as a group in social settings relying on the cultural tools available. She notes that, even though social settings have a specific cultural, social, and historical background, individual agents can have an impact on this context and its practices through interaction, tools, and structures related to this setting. In the context of our Language Centre this means that, although the practices and social roles of the teachers may be highly conventionalized as teachers, they can change into teacher researchers through shared action and forums of interaction triggering further change.

In this chapter, we discuss how our social context and forums of interaction have promoted research engagement in a traditionally teaching-oriented university department. We focus on how teacher research has been made possible in a department with a strong teaching profile. With this aim in mind, we pay particular attention to the role of support, collaboration, and in-house activities.

Context

The University of Helsinki Language Centre

The University of Helsinki is the highest ranking and largest university in Finland with around 37,000 graduate and undergraduate students. The status and size of the university are reflected in the volume of the Language Centre (LC): we offer about 550 courses annually, catering for around 14,000 students. The LC employs 70 full-time teachers and other staff as well as over 130 part-time staff, many of whom are part of our development and research activities.

Teachers at the LC work in a rather unique setting. The reason for the existence of the LC is the University Decree: students need to show their skills in one foreign language and the second national language of the country. In addition to fulfilling their obligatory language requirements at the LC, students are free to study languages as much as they want without extra charge. The LC offers courses from level A1 to level C1 (see Common European Framework of Reference), typically with a focus on academic and professional skills.

The University of Helsinki LC is a sought after place to work in, and it employs a wide range of people with different types of mindsets. The teaching staff mainly come from typical language teacher backgrounds: their major was a language or languages, and they normally have a teaching degree. Among the teachers of some languages especially, we also have less typical backgrounds, from PhDs in biology to ethnology. These various backgrounds amount to different perceptions of what 'proper' research is, and these may occasionally create clashes. At one end, there are staff members who believe that only research that leads to a doctorate is worth doing, whereas, at the other end, some regard teaching development as research. At times, it is also difficult to find an understanding of what constitutes research in the LC context: is it something that arises from individual or from collective needs, and should it be an individual or a collaborative act?

The University of Helsinki (UH) has a general principle that all university teachers should do research, and all researchers should teach. The paradox for the LC teachers is, however, that their annual workload does not normally include any time for research. Our staff sometimes wonder whether everyone ought to be research active (as the general principle of the University implicates) and, if so, what the added value of that activity is.

The status of research engagement

Even though the main tasks of the LC are related to teaching and language support, there is a new emphasis at the LC as well as in other Finnish language centres on in-house research which develops teaching. Rontu and Tuomi (2013), directors of two large Finnish language centres, note:

> While the original tasks still remain, there is a greater demand for more expertise, more variation and flexibility in the contents and modes of teaching, high quality in all processes, provision for new target groups, and more language-related services; but these new tasks are often sought within the context of severe budget restrictions. (Rontu and Tuomi 2013: 342)

Rontu and Tuomi poignantly reveal what is common in many places: more is demanded with no extra funding. Economic matters are, indeed, one of the obstacles to teacher research. In addition, limited resources in terms of time are often seen as one of the main reasons for explaining why some staff members do not carry out research. This was one of the findings in spring 2012, when we arranged a research seminar in order to discuss how to advance research and the research atmosphere at the LC. The outcome was the same in the national Language Centre Days in 2013, where a similar seminar was arranged.

Research related to teaching development by LC staff seems to be on the increase. It is, in part, enabled by small teaching reductions. This research takes place despite the feeling that there is not much extra money or much time for research (the teaching reductions are, on average, the equivalent of 42 teaching hours). However, we hope to show in this chapter that time and money are not the only and not always even the most central barriers to research engagement. Instead, it is the way the staff view research which is of most importance. In the following section, we discuss the structural framework and the institutional support which are likely to increase the drive for research.

Insights

Research and development at the HU Language Centre

Especially in the past three years, the LC has worked to establish a structural framework that takes into account the various levels of research and development activities, lowers the threshold for new projects, increases collaboration, and makes the results more visible. This conscious effort has been led by the LC director, who is keen on making our work transparent and setting strategic goals that are aligned with the university strategy. Without the support of the leadership, we would not be in the current situation that enhances collaboration. The appreciation of research engagement is clearly expressed in our current strategic goals, but, more importantly, while research engagement is encouraged, it is not forced.

Developed institutional structures

One concrete achievement has been the establishment of the Support for Teaching and Learning Unit together with the new position of Senior Lecturer in University Pedagogy that the university granted the LC in 2010. This lecturer represents the network of 16 university pedagogy lecturers, which forms a central resource for the development of teaching and learning at the University of Helsinki (Toom et al. 2013). The network members share tasks in common such as teaching university pedagogy courses for the staff in their faculties, and undertaking research on teaching and learning at faculty or department level. At the LC, it has been agreed that one of the university pedagogy lecturer's duties is also to enhance research and research-based teaching development by providing personal support and by organizing seminars and training in research and writing processes, together with the Research Development group (in more detail below).

Table 13.1 illustrates the current research and development activities at the LC at the organizational level. This structural framework allows for a systematic and cooperative approach. Although the elements in the different parts of the table are separate from one another, they often interact, bridging the themes or topics at different levels.

The activities shown in Table 13.1 have been made possible by a combination of development-oriented atmosphere, critical mass (enough staff), the activities supported and provided by the Unit of Support for Teaching and Learning and the Research Development group, as well as the stable conditions described above.

In practice, the activities presented in Table 13.1 are arranged at regular intervals, according to a pre-established departmental annual timetable. For example, a mini-conference, open to all staff members, is organized once a year; research seminars take place four times a year, twice in each term; and a development day for the whole staff is arranged once a year. These activities attract a fair number of staff members, because our annual timetables have a two-hour time slot allocated for development activities approximately once

Table 13.1: Organisational structures for research and teaching development at the Helsinki University Language Centre

	Teaching development (blurred with research)	Research (blurred with teaching development)
Specific occasions for participants – JOIN US engagement with research	• In-house training • Common room coffee • Development days	• Research seminars (for participants) • Mini-conferences (for participants)
Longer period of time for participants – JOIN US AND WORK engagement in research	• University pedagogy for the staff (5 ECTS course modules) • Peer observation and feedback on teaching • Short in-house training in pedagogy seminars	• Publication series • Publication committee • Reading circle • Research Development group • Research seminars (for presenters) • Mini-conferences (for presenters)
Longer period of time for participants – WORK engagement in research	• Teaching reduction • Conference trips (grants)	• Teaching reduction • Conference trips (grants)

a week. As a rule, full-time teachers do not teach on Thursday afternoons between 2 pm and 4 pm. This is the time slot in which all term-time, development-oriented activities take place, whereas any longer activities, such as the Development day, is planned for days when there is no term-time teaching. Freeing the time to be able to attend is paramount. The following shows how Table 13.1 translates into real life activities that support those interested or potentially interested in research.

Mini-conferences and research seminars

To overcome the barrier posed by 'limitations in teachers' awareness, beliefs, skills and knowledge' (Borg 2010: 409), our regular activities are meant to involve both experienced and less experienced teacher researchers. Good practical examples of this include the low-threshold research seminars and mini-conferences where new teachers have the possibility of presenting and discussing ongoing research and development projects as well as receiving feedback and encouragement from the more experienced teachers before presenting their results later in a conference. The seminars usually engage participants in small group work, which allows them to interact across different language groups. This is also a way for the less experienced participants to interact with the more experienced.

The annual mini-conference allows for engagement with research in a relaxed atmosphere. Typically, the annual afternoon-long mini-conference includes approximately 12 presentations in three parallel sessions with about 80 keen participants, among them colleagues from our partner institutions. The themes have in the past few years ranged from research into advising in language teaching to creative writing and online materials, and a few presentations have been based on doctoral thesis projects which do not necessarily deal with topics most central to LC development work. Allowing a variety of themes carries the message that individual research engagement is encouraged because in a research-intensive university such as the University of Helsinki, it is beneficial for the students to have research-active language teachers who can support their students (directly or indirectly) in research. The mini-conference can initiate the idea that one's endeavours are worth sharing and that engagement in, not only with, research is possible. Naturally, for the presenters, the mini-conference offers a place to share their engagement in research.

The four research seminars a year share more or less the same function as the mini-conference, although they tend to have a different format and a more focused thematic approach. A research seminar is sometimes coupled with a reading circle, deepening the theme of the session further. One of the recent themes, cooperative workplace-related research, attracted a number of staff and invited participants to be engaged in concretely doing some research together as a project.

Steering the organization of our mini-conferences and the workplace-related research project is our Research Development group, headed by the Senior Lecturer in University Pedagogy and consisting of around ten volunteers.

In-house publication series

One of the means for cross-group collaboration and mentoring is the in-house publication series. This is a forum where the staff (teachers as well as administrators) may publish their research or development projects – and find the incentive to carry out research, in the first place. The publication series, available in print and online, was established to promote the idea that we can make our work more visible and learn through the process of peer-reviewing and publishing. In the process of creating the publication, staff members take a variety of collaborative roles as writers and editors, sharing past experience and good practices, turning tacit knowledge into shared practices.

Currently, we have published four books in our publication series, two of which are products of collaborative work consisting of several articles (two are PhD theses). The overarching themes of the two article collections are out-of-classroom language learning (Pitkänen et al. 2011) and the ongoing change at the Language Centre (Matilainen et al. 2013). Topics like these invite and allow a variety of perspectives. For the writers, the publications have enabled engagement with local research that has repercussions on other language centres in Finland, and possibly abroad. The publications serve as institutional records of the past projects for the future (e.g., Lehtonen et al. 2013).

Teaching development seminars and common room coffee afternoons

To inspire engagement with research, the LC has a long tradition in arranging in-house training related to teaching development. The main form is our thematically arranged teaching development afternoons, which offer a low-threshold venue to share ideas and possibly generate ideas that can be approached with the help of research. In these monthly two-hour sessions, the tacit knowledge within the institution becomes more shared among colleagues. An additional venue of a similar nature is our common room coffee afternoons, occasionally arranged by teachers with particular interests or concerns. These coffee afternoons have no regular schedule, attract fewer members of staff than the teaching development afternoons but most likely have the lowest threshold of all the activities available.

University Pedagogy course modules for the staff

The course modules in university pedagogy for the staff are also worth mentioning as forums supporting engagement with and even in research (see Table 13.1). The five-credit modules particularly dedicated to the LC staff have been arranged annually since 2011.[1] These modules have become popular, mainly because they cover language teaching and learning pedagogy, but also because they allow the participants to choose a topic within the general theme announced in advance. The general approach in the university pedagogy modules is interactive, collaborative, and supportive to research; course assignments are designed to promote engagement at least with research (see Evesti et al. 2013). The course module *Advising and counselling in language learning* (currently with 15 teachers and three administrators) also involves engagement *in* research. The participants are carrying out altogether five collaborative projects based on their own teaching or administrative development interests. The projects receive support to be research-based, and, at the end of the term, they will be presented on the Development day of the LC, which most of the staff will attend. Later on, we expect that many of the projects will be presented at conferences and in articles, in the forthcoming LC publication with the same theme, advising and counselling in language learning.

Teaching reductions and travel grants

As mentioned earlier, the two most common practical thresholds related to research are money and time, which also bind together. To encourage engagement in research and teaching development, the LC has created a system that enables teachers to apply for a small teaching reduction. The annual application procedure is relatively simple, but in order for the application to be approved, the research plan has to be feasible.

The teaching reductions within the annual workload are normally of a token character, but they are psychologically important. These reductions, together with reorganized teaching schedules, have enabled both cooperative projects as well as research based on individual interests. So far, they have been financed mainly by different teaching quality awards granted by the university, which also partially cover conference participations. The policy at the LC is to encourage participating in conferences. The condition for conference funding is an accepted paper, and the staff can apply for a conference trip grant once every semester.

A case example of a research-based development project

The collaborative culture prominent at our LC can theoretically be understood using the socio-cultural approach. It seems that there is a fair amount of sharing of know-how, ideas, and teaching materials; those with more expertise in research do research with those with no or less experience; more teachers identify themselves not only as teachers, but teacher researchers. This culture, in turn, enables practices of the type described below.

A way to start

The collaboration of Satu Kattainen (a Study Advisor) and Hanna Vänskä (a teacher of Finnish as a second language; names used with consent) represents an example of engagement in research which was facilitated through university pedagogy training and other support of the community. Satu and Hanna had not, apart from their Master's theses some years earlier, carried out research projects, and thus their collaboration is a good case example of how a research project can be successfully carried out without much previous experience. In our context, it is not rare that members of teaching and administration staff are involved in mutual development through engagement with or in research (see Evesti et al. 2013; Laulajainen et al. 2013), so the work by Satu and Hanna also nicely exemplifies research and development-related collaboration between a teacher and a member of administration. Their collaboration deals with the roles and tasks of those who advise and counsel language learning in the LC context. Their research question was how the students, the teachers and the members of academic administration staff (particularly the study advisors) perceive support in advising and counselling.

Satu attended the five-credit University Pedagogy course *Constructive alignment in course design* in spring 2012, which invited her to development work with the other course participants (mainly teachers), as well as to peer observation of teaching and advising sessions. Hanna did not participate in the same course, but they had previously informally discussed the idea of gaining perspective on each other's work through observation.

Originally, Satu became involved in a mutual observation process with a teacher (rather than a colleague in the administration), because her superior, the Head of Academic Affairs, had encouraged her. The superior had participated in the University Pedagogy course *Teaching and learning in Higher Education* in autumn 2011, where she had gained experience in similar work methods. Along with Satu's course assignment, Satu and Hanna proceeded with the plan to observe each other's work. Soon they discovered that advising and counselling was the ground they both shared in their work. This is how the idea for their mutual project emerged.

At first, Satu and Hanna hesitated because they were not sure if they would have the necessary skills, time and energy to properly explore advising and counselling through a research project. Nearly ready to give up the project idea, they regained their confidence to continue in an informal lunch meeting session with the Senior Lecturer in University Pedagogy (one of the authors of this paper), arranged to briefly discuss the start and plan of the project. This meeting took place in late spring (2012) – the time when most staff members feel tired and more or less looking forward to the summer break. Satu and Hanna became convinced that they would be provided with feedback and support in the different phases of the project. Another inspiring factor was that there was a concrete goal to aim for: to publish an article based on the project in the LC publication due in spring 2013. Satu and Hanna were worried about meeting the deadlines, but then again, they felt positively pushed to work on the project by their superiors and colleagues. The workplace signalled that what Satu and Hanna were doing was important and useful. This way the project had a fertile starting point in the supportive, collegial atmosphere.

The support Satu and Hanna received at this point consisted of various components. The most noteworthy were the supportive attitude towards research and development at the department, encouragement by the superiors and colleagues, interest in sharing differing viewpoints through collaboration, and various forms of interaction. This interaction was both formal (seminars, helpful feedback from the editors) and informal (discussions with peers). All these, combined with personal interest and clear, practical goals, provided a good basis for experimenting with a new idea.

Support in the research process

Satu and Hanna received feedback at all stages of their mutual research project. The project began with Satu and Hanna searching for relevant scientific literature, and designing electronic questionnaires for the target groups: teachers, students and study advisors (the data were collected via e-mail lists). The Senior Lecturer in University Pedagogy gave feedback on the questions, and later helped with the technical design of the electronic questionnaire. Satu and Hanna collected the data during early summer, and started the analysis right away. The deadline for the first drafts for the publication was at the end of August, and Satu and Hanna were able to meet this – they were actually the first ones to deliver a draft, a few days before the deadline. They knew that the article was not quite ready at this point, but they also knew they would receive feedback from four members of the publication committee. Satu and Hanna were open to the feedback, and motivated to improve the text on the basis of the detailed comments from the publication committee members. The feedback included many comments, for example, on the structure of the article and analytical details, and the feedback helped them also further develop the argument of the paper.

Involvement in this type of revision work was new to Satu and Hanna. At first, they had been uneasy about the amount of revision work. However, later on they admitted that the revision process had actually been quite inspiring. One motivating factor was the enthusiastic and constructive feedback on their article idea at an international conference where Satu had presented a paper on a related topic together with two senior colleagues.

Satu and Hanna's article (Kattainen and Vänskä 2013) was published in the fourth LC publication *Language Centre in Change*. In this article, which was based on the questionnaire data gathered among the three target groups, the authors reflect on the perceptions of the roles and tasks in advising and counselling and discuss the findings in relation to relevant literature. This article has further triggered interest in many colleagues, and there is another project currently going on – facilitated by the ongoing University Pedagogy course – which investigates advising and supervising online, partly building on the findings of Kattainen and Vänskä (2013).

The case of Satu and Hanna nicely illuminates how the collegial working culture, development structures and basic investments in resources act as motivating forces in research engagement. It is common in our context that individuals are often insecure about whether their development projects can be considered research and whether their research is worth publishing. Another barrier is, as in the case presented above, a feeling of uncertainty about one's skills. Staff members hesitate because they do not know if they have the methodological skills to carry out proper research projects, particularly within time constraints.

The organizational structures based on collaborative working culture are a starting point in creating a framework for lowering barriers to teacher research. People who have not been engaged in research might believe the threshold and the social risk are too high. Thus, it is of vital importance that people feel there is support available and a great deal to gain but nothing to lose, and whatever the outcome, the process brings some added professional value to both the people involved and the department as a whole. A central factor in creating this atmosphere is that the superiors genuinely allow and appreciate engagement with and in research.

It is essential that the nature of the feedback novice teacher researchers receive on their research and on writing up their research is constructive. Making one's research public in writing is challenging. As shown, Hanna and Satu benefited from the feedback on their writing. Other writers in our context have been treated in the same way when the aim has been to produce a publication. The publication committee members and the editors as peer reviewers have given feedback that is both concrete and encouraging, particularly when major revisions have been requested. The authors in our context are often not used to corrective feedback, and some may even have an attitude that, once submitted, the paper is ready. The feedback process has acted as a scaffold, partly because the starting point has been that none of the articles aimed for the publication series is rejected. The quality of the articles thus has varied in terms of depth of the analysis, methodology, and such, but the peer review processes have guaranteed the basic quality of the texts.

Implications

We have shown that a well-functioning organizational framework based on collaborative culture is a fruitful breeding ground for new ideas. Our framework provides a combination of encouragement, freedom, and flexibility, which grows from positive leadership. This combination allows us to overcome the hurdles of time and money at least to an extent. One of the main strengths in our type of emerging collaboration is related to good practices. Collaboration and scaffolding help create common terminology and create joint practices, making tacit knowledge available to the younger, less experienced teacher researchers, and providing better tools for reflecting and sharing one's teaching-related research and development activities. These practices push us to 'self-assessment and reflective practice', which, according to Heyworth (2013: 301), are seen as qualities of good teachers.

The University of Helsinki LC illustrates an approach that actively invites staff to engage with and in research. For similar developments to take place in other contexts, certain preconditions need to be met. These include:

- freedom to develop ideas emerging out of teaching or other experience;
- support offered at various stages, for example, in methodological approaches and writing processes;
- encouragement, suggesting that research is fun and can glue colleagues together (collaboration with others);
- trust in the teacher's expertise, making it possible to experiment;
- supportive organizational structure, with a head of department and superiors who value research;
- pedagogical development through research orientation; department level and individual engagement in and engagement with research;
- regular, low-threshold activities that invite people who would otherwise not have enough self-confidence, inspiration, experience (e.g. in-house seminars and workshops);
- an annual timetable for research, development, and administration, leaving enough time to focus on relevant issues; and
- research-based development as part of an institution's strategic goals.

Based on our own experiences, a clearly defined and workable institutional support framework will make it easier in any context to encourage research activities. The framework we have in mind combines various activities which, in turn, complement one another. As the different channels feed into one another and reinforce the idea that research – be it engagement with or in research – is valued, the general beliefs and values at the workplace become tuned in with the idea that research is possible and significant. This increases research engagement as a whole.

Conclusion

In this chapter, we have focused on some challenges in teacher research and discussed the different approaches to overcome them at the University of

Helsinki Language Centre. We hope to have shown that institutional support, starting from positive leadership attributes, can affect the development-oriented atmosphere of an institution and encourage the staff in various ways. One (but only one) of these ways is financial support in the form of teaching reductions, because they allow for some extra time on research engagement. Psychologically, even the small reductions create a feeling of inspiration and acknowledgement.

Another, crucially important, way is the development of various types of activities arranged collectively and developed systematically. These are important because they enhance collaborative institutional culture and increase teachers' awareness and knowledge of research, as well as the ownership in their research. These approaches have been beneficial at our LC: they have increased the number of research projects and collaboration within and between different language groups, and they have also brought teaching staff and administration closer. They have also benefited the professional growth of individual teachers and other staff members involved in research and development in keeping up with the trends of the time. All in all, research has become a more cooperative, more visible, and more integrated part of the LC – in other words: more natural, if not yet self-evident.

The socio-cultural approach helps us understand our setting within its cultural, social and historical background – a setting with agents who interact and thus have an impact on our context. This approach hones our belief that we can influence our own setting.

Language centres, like other educational departments, are full of potential: the staff are exposed to various types of data and eager to know more. This potential is wasted if the individuals are not provided with support and encouragement to engage themselves with or in research. When this potential is utilized, they are prone to become more self-reflective, more motivated and less stressed out, through better control of their own work. They also feel more at home because of their improved, extended social networks. These networks lead to a deeper understanding of the current academic trends, providing them with a better sense of why they teach and work the way they do.

Engagement priorities

This chapter has discussed the importance of collaborative working culture as one of the key issues in promoting language teachers' research engagement. The University of Helsinki Language Centre is an example of a community which, through supportive leadership and management procedures, enables an atmosphere conducive to research. Here are some questions for you to discuss:

1. What is the value of language teachers' engagement in and with research? How can research activities promote the quality of teaching? What is the value of collaborative research between academic administration and teachers?

2. Research engagement requires resources from both individuals and the workplace. What kind of activities and structures can you identify in your community that facilitate the staff's research engagement? Who should participate in these activities and how? How is the engagement being supported?
3. In your community, what are the possibilities of promoting research engagement? What are the challenges? What could be done (without increasing funding) at (1) the individual and (2) institutional level?

Notes

1. The credits refer to the European Credit Transfer and Accumulation System. The University of Helsinki Centre for Research and Development in Higher Education offers University Pedagogy courses of up to 60 credits for teaching personnel. The Senior Lecturers in University Pedagogy offer five or ten modules of basic studies (up to 25 credits) in their faculties or departments.

References

Borg, S. (2010). Language teacher research engagement. *Language Teaching*. 43(4): 391–429.

Common European Framework of Reference (CEFR). Available at: http://www.coe.int/t/dg4/linguistic/Source/Framework_en.pdf. [Accessed 28/2/14].

Evesti, L., Kattainen S., and Vaattovaara J. (2013). Enhancing professionalism through teacher–administration collaboration in University Pedagogy training. *Language Learning in Higher Education* 3(1): 191–206.

Heyworth, F. (2013). Applications of quality management in language education. *Language Teaching*, 46(3): 281–315.

Kattainen, S. and Vänskä, H. (2013). Opas, tulkki vai tiedottaja? Opiskelijoiden ohjauksen monet tehtävät Kielikeskuksessa. In M. Matilainen, R. Siddall, and J. Vaattovaara (eds), *Language Centre in Change* (pp. 49–70). Helsinki: Language Centre. Available at: https://helda.helsinki.fi/handle/10138/39261. [Accessed 28/2/14].

Lasky, S. (2005). A Sociocultural approach to understanding teacher identity, agency and professional vulnerability in a context of secondary school reform. *Teacher and Teacher Education*, 21: 899–916.

Laulajainen, T., Vaattovaara J., Wallinheimo K., and Ådjers E. (2013). Hallinnon ja opettajien yhteistyöstä laatua kielikeskustyöhön. In M. Matilainen, R. Siddall, and J. Vaattovaara (eds), *Language Centre in Change* (pp. 71–77). Helsinki: Language Centre. Available at: https://helda.helsinki.fi/handle/10138/39261. [Accessed 28/2/14].

Lehtonen, T., Pitkänen, K., and Siddall, R. (2013). The changing role of English language teaching in Helsinki University Language Centre. In M. Matilainen, R. Siddall, and J. Vaattovaara (eds), *Language Centre in Change* (pp. 33–48). Helsinki: Language Centre. Available at: https://helda.helsinki.fi/handle/10138/39261. [Accessed 28/2/14].

Matilainen, M., Siddall, R., and Vaattovaara, J. (eds). (2013). *Language Centre in Change*. Helsinki: Language Centre. Available at: https://helda.helsinki.fi/handle/10138/39261. [Accessed 28/2/14].

Pitkänen, K. K., Jokinen, J., Karjalainen, S., Karlsson, L., Matilainen, M., Niedling, C., and Siddall, R. (eds). (2011). *Out-of-Classroom Language Learning*. Helsinki: Language Centre. Available at: https://helda.helsinki.fi/handle/10138/25854. [Accessed 28/2/14].

Rontu, H. and Tuomi U. K. (2013). The role of research in teaching-oriented institutions: A case study of university language centres in Finland. *Language Learning in Higher Education* 3(2): 339–354.

Toom, A., Vaattovaara, J., and Myyry, L. (2013). The Senior Lecturers of University Pedagogy: The network as a resource for the development of teaching at the University of Helsinki. Helsingin yliopiston hallinnon julkaisuja 84. Available at: http://www.helsinki.fi/opetus/pedagogisetyolehtorit. [Accessed 28/2/14].

Vygotsky, L.S. (1978). *Mind in Society: The Development of Higher Psychological Processes*. Cambridge, Massachusetts: Harvard University Press.

Wertsch, J. V. (1993). *Voices of the Mind: A Sociocultural Approach to Mediated Action*. Cambridge, Massachusetts: Harvard University Press.

Wertsch, J., Tulviste, P., and Hagstrom, F. (1993). A sociocultural approach to agency. In E. Forman, N. Minick, and C. Stone, *Contexts for Learning* (pp. 336–356). New York: Oxford.

14
Teacher Research: Looking Back and Moving Forward

Hugo Santiago Sanchez and Simon Borg

Introduction

In this concluding chapter we review the work presented in the volume in order to draw some conclusions about the current state of activity and inquiry in teacher research in language teaching. We also identify areas for continued exploration in relation to both doing and facilitating teacher research in our field.

Contexts for teacher research

Excluding our editors' introduction and conclusion, this volume has presented 12 accounts of teacher research from a range of international contexts. Geographically, the following countries have been represented: Japan, Australia, China, the United States, Mexico, Pakistan, Oman, Turkey, Israel, Malaysia and Finland. In one case the author was based in Canada, but worked virtually with students in Europe. The institutional contexts for teacher research have also been varied, with authors coming from private and state universities and colleges, university language centres, adult education institutions, state schools and private language institutions. Overall this volume provides ample evidence that teacher research can be utilized in a wide range of geographical and institutional contexts and by teachers working with diverse groups of learners in terms of age, level of proficiency, and purpose in learning English. The use of teacher research in an online language teaching context was also illustrated.

Characteristics of teacher research

In our Introduction we provided a minimal definition of teacher research as systematic self-study that seeks positive impact and is made public. The different contributions to this volume, though, have illustrated the diverse ways in which, within these broad parameters, teacher research is experienced by ELT professionals in different parts of the world. These experiences highlighted a range of recurrent characteristics which teacher research was seen to have:

- messy and non-linear;
- collaborative;
- reflective;
- pedagogically-driven;
- exploratory;
- self-initiated;
- self-directed;
- ongoing;
- practical;
- flexible.

A practical and pedagogical orientation to teacher research is clear here, and the importance of a reflective mindset was emphasized in several of the chapters as being central to the way teacher researchers think about their work. Teacher research as a self-initiated process emphasizes the relevance of voluntary participation.

It is important to stress that in this context 'messy' is not a negative characteristic, but rather a reflection of the reality that procedures and outcomes in teacher research are very often emergent – i.e. they develop as the inquiry moves forward and this requires teacher researchers to be flexible in making adjustments to any original plans they start off with. The notion of teacher research as an ongoing activity is also important and can be interpreted in at least two distinct ways. One is that teacher research does not provide definitive conclusions; it generates understandings and these will be subject to review as a result of further inquiry. Teacher research may also generate questions, which in turn provide the stimulus for further study. The second sense in which teacher research is ongoing is implied in the notion of lifelong learning; professional development should be an integral part of teachers' lives, not an occasional activity – it is a process rather than an event. Teacher research is a strategy which allows the notion of lifelong learning to be put into practice. This does not imply, of course, that teachers should be doing research all the time. Thinking critically about their work, however, a key disposition that underpins teacher research, is something teachers can do in an ongoing manner.

Strategies for teacher research

We noted in our introductory chapter that, methodologically, teacher research can be approached in many different ways. Action research (see, for example,

Altrichter et al. 2008; Burns 2010) was commonly cited by contributors to this volume as the framework through which teacher research was approached. One case referred specifically to participatory action research, perhaps in the sense that the students the teacher worked with were actively engaged in the study rather than functioning simply as a source of data. We would not say, however, that participatory action research, as defined in the literature we discussed in our Introduction (e.g. Kemmis and McTaggart 2008), is a strong feature of teacher research in language teaching. In fact, the criticism we noted there about the largely practical focus of much teacher research in our field has not been addressed in any significant way by this volume.

Looking more specifically at the data collection strategies used by both teacher researchers and facilitators, a wide range of options emerge: questionnaires, lesson recordings, lesson observations, lesson notes, teacher journals, individual and group interviews, document analysis, tests, e-mail communications, online postings, and transcriptions of professional development meetings. Reading the literature and immersion (i.e. spending time in a new teaching context as a form of professional learning) were also noted. This range reinforces the point we made in our Introduction about the methodological flexibility of teacher research. More critically, though, we would also note that a fairly conventional range of data collection strategies continue to dominate the conduct of teacher research in our field. For example, visual methods, which are emerging as an exciting strategy in research on language teaching and learning (see Borg et al. 2014; Kalaja et al. 2013), do not really feature here and there is clear scope for more exploratory work in which teachers enquire into their own practices and seek to understand their learners and their contexts through the use of photos and drawings. We think that it is perfectly understandable that where teacher research remains an emergent activity, as it is in many language teaching contexts, more familiar and well-established methods of inquiry are adopted. As teacher researchers continue to develop, though, experimentation becomes more feasible and in future we would hope to see a greater range of innovative approaches to data collection being evaluated (and even developed) by teacher researchers in our field.

One other methodological dimension of teacher research which we feel merits more substantial attention, and which we discussed in our Introduction, relates to how its quality can be assessed. We are not suggesting that teacher research be judged against the criteria typically used in evaluating academic research; we do feel, however, that we should be in a position to make judgements about the extent to which teacher research is 'sound'. This will necessarily involve attention to the issues being addressed, the investigative and analytical strategies used, ethics, and real-world benefits/impact of various kinds.

Supporting teacher research

Eight of the chapters in this volume had as their specific focus the facilitation of teacher research and for all but one of these the work described occurred with practising (as opposed to prospective) teachers of English. One point all eight studies combine to emphasize, though, is the positive contribution to teacher research that appropriate support, particularly through a skilled facilitator, can make. Again, action research was the model of teacher research most cited by facilitators, although in some cases the label 'collaborative inquiry' was used instead to define the basic mode of learning that facilitators were seeking to promote (this does not imply, of course, that action research cannot at the same time be collaborative).

The aims of the various teacher research initiatives that have been discussed here were diverse; for example, programmes aimed to:

- create a collaborative culture;
- promote reflection;
- help teachers learn about early literacy;
- expand teachers' understandings of their own practices;
- develop teachers' ability to carry out meaningful teacher research;
- support teachers in conducting systematic self-study in their own working contexts;
- promote change in teachers' beliefs, knowledge, skills and attitudes concerning research as well as in their classroom practices.

One interesting point about these aims is that only one (that on early literacy) has a specific substantive focus; the others address the development of more generic skills and dispositions without defining a focus for these. Both approaches have their benefits; where a group of teachers have a common need to develop understandings of a particular issue, then a collective focus on it can create a strong sense of shared purpose. At the same time, allowing teachers to define their own focus can also be beneficial, especially when teachers from different contexts are taking part in the same teacher research course. In some cases, sponsors may define thematic priorities which teachers wanting to join a scheme will need to address, although the precise ways in which teachers do will not be prescribed.

The amount of explicit insight into principles for supporting teacher research that emerges from the facilitators' chapters varies and this is a reflection of the different emphases in these chapters. For example, while some focus in detail on the experiences of participants, others examine more closely the design and conduct of the teacher research programme. In any case, these chapters highlight, as noted above, the importance of an expert facilitator who can create a framework which is structured while allowing teachers the flexibility to experience teacher research in personal ways. Facilitators also require a range of other attributes: an understanding of research and teacher research, a constructive attitude to teachers' efforts, the ability to facilitate communication and collaboration, skills in dealing with resistance, and transparency in communicating expectations.

Evidence of the factors that contribute to effective language teacher research initiatives is increasingly available (see, for example, Borg 2013; Burns 2014). An awareness of the challenges teachers face in doing research (see below) also has clear implications for the conditions that are required to support their efforts. There remains, though, much scope in our field for more detailed analyses of the practices and cognitions of those who facilitate teacher research.

Benefits

Every chapter in this book has provided evidence of the many ways in which teacher research can have positive impact, and Table 14.1 compiles these in order to emphasize the transformative power that this teacher development strategy has.

Table 14.1 Benefits of teacher research

- Promotes collaboration among teachers
- Gives teachers insight into their own practices
- Promotes innovative solutions to teaching problems
- Extends teacher identities (to include teacher-as-researcher)
- Creates a sense of achievement
- Boosts teachers' self-esteem
- Creates a problem-solving mindset
- Promotes more student-centred perspectives
- Encourages flexibility in teaching
- Raises teachers' awareness of ingrained habits
- Narrows the gap between theory and practice
- Promotes reflective skills
- Creates a sense of community
- Makes teachers more open to feedback
- Increases teachers' knowledge
- Develops 'adaptive expertise'
- Enhances teachers' repertoires
- Enhances professional autonomy
- Improves research skills
- Increases teacher motivation
- Leads to positive changes in what teachers do
- Creates positive attitudes to professional development

The list of benefits that teacher research offers teachers is impressive. While, ultimately, we would hope that teacher research leads to practical changes in classroom practices, this list reminds us that lasting behavioural change of this kind needs be underpinned by changes in less observable facets of teaching – such as attitudes, beliefs, awareness, motivation and confidence. Teacher research, as this volume shows, clearly impacts at these deeper levels. We are not suggesting that deeper cognitive, attitudinal, and emotional changes must always precede behavioural change; changes in behaviour and the observed consequences of these can very often occur first (Guskey 2002). However, as the literature on teacher cognition has established (see, for example, Barnard and Burns 2012), sustained behavioural change is unlikely without accompanying change in what teachers think, believe, know, and feel. Teacher research clearly has the capacity to affect teachers at these levels.

The list of benefits of teacher research extracted from this volume is also interesting in that it makes little explicit reference to benefits to students. It is highly likely that teachers who are experiencing the kinds of benefits we have listed above will become more effective practitioners and that their students will benefit as a result. Documenting how students benefit, though, is challenging for a number of reasons. One is that the benefits to students will very often not be immediate. Another is that students may benefit in ways which are not easily measureable. Showing in a causal manner that students have benefited from teacher research is also problematic given the range of different variables which will affect how students perform. In recent discussions of teacher professional development a focus on the benefits to students has been salient (e.g. Timperley et al. 2008) and this is an issue that we need to engage more robustly with as teacher research in language teaching continues to grow. Experimental solutions (i.e. which require teachers to manipulate variables and to compare treatment and experimental groups) are unlikely to be a feasible option for practising teachers who want to examine how teacher research is impacting on students. Used appropriately, basic quantitative measures of student performance (i.e. test scores) can provide insight into the impact of teacher research, but more participatory, qualitative strategies – e.g. through which teachers and students together construct accounts, over time, of how teacher research is impacting on teaching and learning, may provide options which are more meaningful, feasible, and which can be integrated more naturally into routine teaching and learning practices. Clearly, though, despite the challenges involved in providing evidence that students benefit from teacher research, it is not an issue we can ignore, for ultimately the goal of professional development is enhanced student learning.

The list of benefits listed in Table 14.1 also lacks reference to benefits beyond teachers and their classrooms. For example, what is the impact of teacher research on teachers' organizations and are there benefits which extend even further, beyond organizations and, for example, to students' family lives or to the work of policy makers? (See, for example, Rust and Meyers 2006.) Teacher research clearly has the potential to achieve impacts of this kind; evidence of it in the field of language teaching, though, remains elusive.

Challenges

The factors that hinder teachers' engagement in research have been well-documented in the literature, both in education generally and in language teaching (see Borg 2013). The contributions to this volume have also highlighted a number of challenges that teacher researchers and/or facilitators of teacher research encounter. Table 14.2 summarizes these.

Collectively, such challenges have the power to stifle even the most committed attempts to promote teacher research and an awareness of them is thus important for teachers, teacher educators, and organizations with an interest in promoting this activity. As noted in our Introduction, many language teaching contexts are simply not conducive to teacher research and in such cases, unless key challenges can be addressed prior to or during the process, promoting teacher research can amount to little more than a frustrating experience for all concerned. One point contributors to this volume remind us of is that teacher research is much more than a technical process; teachers do need the skills and knowledge required to design and implement good quality inquiry; however, an exclusive focus on such matters – such as an academic research methods course might encourage – is not an adequate basis for

Table 14.2 Challenges in teacher research

- A lack of research knowledge and skills (in teachers and facilitators)
- Rigid conceptions of what 'research' is
- Limited understandings of what teacher research is
- Tensions between being a teacher and being a researcher
- Sustaining motivation
- Knowing how to disseminate findings
- Knowing how to analyse data
- Finding time
- Managing the threat to self-image
- Lack of institutional support
- Lack of co-operation from colleagues and students
- Lack of a collaborative culture
- No prior experience of reflection
- Limited access to skilled facilitation
- Limited resources
- Low teacher confidence in their ability to do research
- Negative attitudes to professional development

productive teacher research. Very often, there will be more fundamental needs to address in relation to teachers' understandings of what research is, their attitudes to professional development, and their disposition to being self-critical. Teacher research, too, can be a de-stabilizing process which may threaten teachers' self-image as competent professionals and make them feel vulnerable; if teachers are unable or unwilling to expose themselves to such threats, then teacher research will be a less transformative process for them. Clearly, then, the challenges that arise in teacher research relate to a wide range of technical, cognitive, emotional, attitudinal, social, and organizational issues. The conditions that facilitate teacher research, as the chapters in this volume illustrate, will give teachers support in addressing this range of challenges.

Conclusion

The purpose of this volume has been to document, from a range of international language teaching contexts, examples of teacher research, and to highlight the processes, benefits, and challenges that characterize them. Contributors have described what they did (as either teacher researchers or facilitators), reflected on what they learnt, and considered the broader implications of their experiences. In this chapter we have reviewed the key collective insights that have emerged from the volume and noted facets of teacher research which require ongoing systematic study. Teacher research in language teaching has been promoted for many years as a valuable professional development activity; the fact that now it is itself also increasingly the subject of research illustrates, as Rixon (2013) notes, that teacher research has 'arrived'. We hope this volume consolidates this view and serves to stimulate further the productive growth of teacher research in our field.

References

Altrichter, H., Feldman, A., Posch, P., and Somekh, B. (2008). *Teachers Investigate Their Work: An Introduction to Action Research across the Professions* (Second Edition). London: Routledge.

Barnard, R. and Burns, A. (eds). (2012). *Researching Language Teacher Cognition and Practice: International Case Studies*. Clevedon: Multilingual Matters.

Borg, S. (2013). *Teacher Research in Language Teaching: A Critical Analysis*. Cambridge: Cambridge University Press.

Borg, S., Birello, M., Civera, I., and Zanatta, T. (2014). *The Impact of Teacher Education on Pre-Service Primary English Language Teachers*. London: British Council.

Burns, A. (2010). *Doing Action Research in English Language Teaching. A Guide for Practitioners*. New York: Routledge.

Burns, A. (2014). Professional learning in Australian Elicos: An action research orientation. *English Australia Journal*, 29(2): 3–20.

Guskey, T. R. (2002). Professional development and teacher change. *Teachers and Teaching, 8*(3): 381–391.

Kalaja, P., Dufva, H., and Alanen, R. (2013). Experimenting with visual narratives. In G. Barkhuizen (ed.), *Narrative Research in Applied Linguistics*. Cambridge: Cambridge University Press, pp. 105–131.

Kemmis, S. and McTaggart, R. (2008). Participatory action research: Communicative action and public sphere. In N. K. Denzin and Y. S. Lincoln (eds), *Strategies of Qualitative Inquiry* (Third Edition). Los Angeles: Sage Publications, pp. 271–330.

Rixon, S. (2013). Book review: Teacher research in language teaching – a critical analysis, *System, 41*(4): 1086–1088.

Rust, F. and Meyers, E. (2006). The bright side: Teacher research in the context of educational reform and policy-making. *Teachers and Teaching, 12*(1): 69–86.

Timperley, H., Wilson, A., Barrar, H., and Fung, I. (2008). *Teacher Professional Learning and Development: Best Evidence Synthesis Iteration (BES)*. Wellington, New Zealand: Ministry of Education.

Further Reading

Below is an annotated list of recommended reading provided by the contributors to this volume.

Anderson, T. (ed.) (2008). *The Theory and Practice of Online Learning* (2nd edition). Athabasca: AU Press.
This book provides practical examples of quality online learning practices – an excellent impetus for reflection by teacher researchers as they determine issues they wish to pursue through research.

Barkhuizen, G. (2011). Narrative knowledging in TESOL. *TESOL Quarterly, 45*(3): 391–414.
Barkhuizen provides methodological insights from conducting narrative research and explores the concept of 'narrative knowledging', which he describes as 'the meaning making, learning, or knowledge construction that takes place during the narrative research activities of (co)constructing narratives, analyzing narratives, reporting the findings, and reading/watching/listening to research reports' (p. 5).

Ben-Peretz, M., Kleeman, S., Reichenberg, R., and Shimoni, S. (eds) (2013). *Embracing the Social and the Creative: New Scenarios for Teacher Education.* Plymouth, UK: The Mofet Institute and Rowman & Littlefield Publishers, Inc.
This edited volume examines contemporary issues in teacher education in the light of the new challenges of the twenty-first century from a variety of cognitive, social and affective perspectives.

Borg, S. (2013). *Teacher Research in Language Teaching: A Critical Analysis.* Cambridge: Cambridge University Press.
This book provides a theoretical foundation, grounded in empirical evidence, concerning teachers' involvement with action research and its impact on their teaching. The author also provides suggestions for strategies in engaging pre- and in-service teachers in the process of carrying out research.

Borg, S. (ed.) (2014). *Teacher Research in Pakistan: Enhancing the Teaching and Learning of English.* Lahore: British Council.
This volume includes reports from the teacher research course discussed in Chapter 8. Each report is followed by a critical commentary on the methodology of the study.

Bow Valley College (2009). *Learning for LIFE: An ESL Literacy Handbook.* Bow Valley College, Calgary, AB, Canada. Available: www.esl-literacy.com.
For those who work with low-literacy adult ESL students, this handbook and accompanying website are a treasure chest of practical resources and recommendations. Adult English as an Additional Language (EAL) educators in Calgary, Alberta, and Canada have compiled curricula, lesson planning advice, downloadable student readers, and brief videos from actual classrooms into this extensive website, with written explanations easily accessed in the downloadable handbook.

Bruner, J. (1996). *The Culture of Education.* Cambridge, Massachusetts: Harvard University Press.

Bruner's book of essays invites the reader to consider the role of education in a sociocultural setting. It works as an easy-to-read introduction to sociocultural theory.

Burns, A. (1999). *Collaborative Action Research for English Language Teachers*. Cambridge: Cambridge University Press.
This is an excellent analysis of a teacher research programme which places particular emphasis on the importance of collaboration among teachers.

Burns, A. (2010). *Doing Action Research in English Language Teaching: A Guide for Practitioners*. New York: Routledge.
This handbook is an invaluable resource for teachers considering embarking upon an action research project of their own. It provides teachers with a practical step-by-step guide to action research, from what it is, to how it works. The book takes the reader through the process of planning, carrying out, observing, and reflecting upon their own research projects. Examples from real-life studies, along with useful supplemental materials, make this a user-friendly text for both novices and also more experienced researchers.

Check, J. W. and Shutt, R. K. (2011). *Research Methods in Education*. Thousand Oaks: Sage.
This book provides a good overall introduction to educational research. It is broader in scope than Freeman (1998), as it also includes a discussion of quantitative research methods.

Clandinin, D. J. (2006). *Handbook of Narrative Inquiry: Mapping a Methodology*. Thousand Oaks: Sage.
Edited by one of the leading researchers in this emerging field, this book is the definitive guide to using narrative inquiry in educational research for those who wish to learn more about this approach. It outlines the development and theoretical underpinnings of this approach and provides descriptive examples of different forms of narrative research.

Cochran-Smith, M. and Lytle, S. L. (1993). *Inside/Outside: Teacher Research and Knowledge*. New York: Teachers College Press, Columbia University.
This seminal text provides a mixture of historical and theoretical discussion and concrete examples of teacher research conducted by literacy teachers in American schools.

Creswell, J. (2008). *Education Research: Planning, Conducting, and Evaluating Quantitative and Qualitative Research*, Chapter 16 Narrative research designs, pp. 511–550. Upper Saddle River, NJ: Pearson.
Creswell provides a useful overview of narrative research, and different types of narrative designs and their key characteristics. He stresses the importance of collaboration between researchers and participants and offers a useful sample narrative design.

Cummins, J. and Davison, C. (eds) (2007). *The International Handbook of English Language Teaching*. New York: Springer.
This two-volume handbook provides an extensive and international review of issues in the field of language teaching from many of the most respected writers in EFL teaching and research and is an invaluable resource to anyone considering classroom research, including where the use of technology is involved.

Curry, M. and Lillis, T. (2013). *A Scholar's Guide to Getting Published in English: Critical Choices and Practical Strategies*. New York: Multilingual Matters.
This book is a practical guide to those wishing to take part in the social practices, politics, and resources involved in academic publishing and to engage in current debates about them.

Edge, J. (ed.) (2001). *Action Research*. Alexandria, VA: Teachers of English to Speakers of Other Languages.
This is an accessible text about practitioners' experiences of conducting action research in a range of ELT contexts. It provides examples which professionals interested in doing or supporting teacher research will find instructive.

Freeman, D. (1998). *Doing Teacher-Research: From Inquiry to Understanding*. Boston: Heinle & Heinle.
This is a good overall introduction to teacher research and reflective practice. Freeman's five propositions about teacher research are especially helpful for clarifying the scope of the field.

Johnson, K. E. and Golombek, P. R. (2002). *Teachers' Narrative Inquiry as Professional Development*. Cambridge: Cambridge University Press.
This book brings together a number of the themes that we have explored in Chapter 3, including the value of reflective teaching and the use of narrative to make teachers' understanding of their teaching accessible to others with an interest in the profession.

Matilainen, M., Siddall, R., and Vaattovaara J. (eds) (2013). *Language Centre in Change*. Helsinki: Language Centre. Available at: https://helda.helsinki.fi/handle/10138/39261. [Accessed 28/2/14.]

Pitkänen, K. K., Jokinen, J., Karjalainen, S., Karlsson, L., Matilainen, M., Niedling, C., and Siddall, R. (eds) (2011). *Out-of-Classroom Language Learning*. Helsinki: Language Centre. Available at: https://helda.helsinki.fi/handle/10138/25854. [Accessed 28/2/14].
These collections of articles provide a good overview of the current local teacher research activities at the University of Helsinki Language Centre.

Mercer, S. (2013). Working with language learner histories from three perspectives: Teachers, learners and researchers. *Studies in Second Language Learning and Teaching*, 3(2): 161–185.
Mercer examines learner histories from teacher, learner, and researcher perspectives and argues that 'Language learning histories … can reveal valuable insights about our learners' needs, motivations, beliefs, goals and strategies' (p. 164).

Mitchell, R. F. (2009). Current trends in classroom research. In M. H. Long and C. J. Doughty (eds), *The Handbook of Language Teaching*. Oxford: Wiley-Blackwell, pp. 675–705.
Mitchell focuses on teacher and student relationships in the local context of classroom research. She is especially interested in learner experiences inside and outside of the classroom and argues for diversified approaches to second language research.

Moran, J. (2001). *Collaborative Professional Development for Teachers of Adults*. Malabar, FL, USA: Krieger Publishing Company.
This is a step-by-step guide for teachers interested in collaborating with colleagues to grow as educators. The author emphasizes self-directed learning, cooperative learning, and critical reflection as systems for collaborative action research for professional development.

Mullen, C. A. (1999). Anonymity revisited: A case study in mentoring teachers-as-authors. *Teacher Development: An International Journal of Teachers' Professional Development*, 3(1): 171–187.

Mullen, C. A. (2000). Constructing co-mentoring partnerships: Walkways we must travel. *Theory into Practice*, 39(1): 4–12.

These articles describe the processes implemented by an academic to create a collaborative partnership for research and dissemination with teachers in the field.

Patel, A. D. (2008) *Music, Language and the Brain*. New York: Oxford University Press.
This influential work looks at the processing of music and language in the brain from a neuroscientific perspective. Patel challenges the commonly held view that music and language are processed separately and argues that there is, in fact, a deep connection between the two.

Pavlenko, A. and Lantolf, J. P. (2000). Second language learning as participation and the (re)construction of selves. In J. P. Lantolf (ed.), *Sociocultural Theory and Second Language Learning*. Oxford: Oxford University Press, pp. 155–177.
Pavlenko and Lantolf build on the work of Sfard (1998) and extend the participation metaphor to examine the use of personal narratives to reflect the struggle for participation by language learners.

Robson, C. (2011). *Real World Research* (Third Edition). West Sussex: Wiley.
A comprehensive but accessible general textbook on doing research in social science contexts – particularly useful for facilitators of teacher research courses.

Rontu, H. and Tuomi U. K. (2013). The role of research in teaching-oriented institutions: A case study of university language centres in Finland. *Language Learning in Higher Education*, 3(2): 339–354.
This article is an overview of the current state of research and development in the Finnish language centres. It also gives insight into the ongoing strategic planning in them.

Wallace, J. M. (1998). *Action Research for Language Teachers*. Cambridge: Cambridge University Press.
This text provides an easy-to-follow and practical account of action research, supported with numerous practical examples. The book is important for teachers and teacher trainees in that it introduces action research as a form of reflective practice. The author also highlights the role of action research in teachers' professional development.

Warschauer, M. (2011). *Learning in the Cloud*. New York: Teachers College Press.
Mark Warschauer has been a strong proponent of classroom-based research in technology since the mid-90s. This book is a report of his research activities in some of the most privileged and also most struggling schools in the United States.

Wedell, M. and Malderez, A. (2013). *Understanding Language Classroom Contexts: The Starting Point for Change*. London: Bloomsbury.
This volume illustrates how various layers of context influence what happens in the language classroom and the extent that pedagogical change can happen. It reminds us that promoting change in the classroom must take the system that the classroom is part of into account.

Wertsch. J. V. (1991). *Voices of the Mind: A Sociocultural Approach to Mediated Action.* Cambridge, MA: Harvard University Press.
Although at first glance this book might be considered beyond the interests or accessibility of the classroom educator, it has been an essential reference for many in the EFL field in understanding the implications of viewing language learning from a sociocultural perspective.

Wolf, M. (2008). *Proust and the Squid: The Story and Science of the Reading Brain*. New York, NY: Harper Perennial.

Educators interested in the process of learning to read and write will find much to explore in this book by Maryanne Wolf, an expert in dyslexia and reading difficulties. Wolf retells how humanity learned to read and write; provides a layman's introduction to the brain science behind reading; and sheds light on why some learners struggle to develop literacy.

ELTDP Symposium 'teacher as researcher'

In February 2013 ELTDP held a symposium in which 70 teachers from across the project came together to present their work to an audience of peers and colleagues from within the Malaysian Education system. Many of the presentations, and more information on the symposium, are available here: http://teacherasresearcher.weebly.com/index.html.

ELTDP Publications

Available to download at: http://schoolsonline.britishcouncil.org/english-language-teachers-development.

ELTDP (2011). *Project Introduction*

This document outlines the project approach and infrastructure and was written for project stakeholders in 2011. It includes a summary of the conclusions of the baseline survey undertaken by the initial group of mentors in 2011.

Kaplan, I. (2012 and 2013). *Interim and Final External Evaluation Reports.*
The ELTDP undertook a Participatory Impact Monitoring and Evaluation (PIME) which was implemented by EENET CIC. These two reports contain information about the methodology of the participatory evaluation of the ELTDP, commentary, and data to evidence the extent of the project's achievement against stakeholders' indicators of success.

Borg, S. (ed) (2013). *Narratives of Teacher Development.*
This series of three books comprises teachers' accounts of activities undertaken as part of ELTDP. In each book the teachers describe their particular contexts, the focus and process of work, and the impacts which have resulted. The stories were gathered to inspire fellow teachers and others as they see the professional commitment and creativity that these teachers have shown in improving the teaching and learning of English in their schools. The three volumes in this series are:

- Reading and Speaking
- Stories and Songs
- Engaging young learners

The titles are available to download on the 'Engaging Malaysian Schools in English' (EMSE) website: http://www.emse.com.my/. This site also contains KSSR lesson ideas, forums for discussion, teaching tips, and links to other useful websites.

Index

action research, 7, 9, 17, 27, 29, 30, 34, 35, 37, 40, 44, 73, 89, 98, 115, 116, 125, 126, 128, 129, 139, 140, 141, 149, 158, 186, 187, 188, 194, 195, 196, 197
   aims of, 15, 38, 139, 158
   cycles of, 2, 14–15, 127, 129, 144–7
   definitions, 2, 14–15, 38
   facilitating, 44, 128, 136, 141, 144, 145, 148, 149, 150, 158, 165
   impact of, 10, 11, 29, 30, 33, 38, 39, 40, 41, 42, 43, 44, 45, 108, 135, 140, 141–4, 148, 149, 150
   issues, 135
   nature of, 24, 30, 64
   principles of, 10
   projects, 6, 7, 9, 10, 11, 14, 15, 17, 19, 20, 23, 25, 27, 29, 34, 37, 38, 43, 44, 51, 108, 126, 130, 132, 140, 141, 143, 144–7, 148, 149, 150
   quality of, 4, 19
   websites, 140, 144
agency, 58, 60, 167, 171
anxiety, 49, 51, 100, 146, 147
autonomy, 3, 8, 17, 106, 139, 159, 161, 189

beliefs, 1, 6, 26, 34, 48, 62, 74, 99, 101, 102, 103, 106, 108, 114, 115, 118, 119, 145, 146, 149, 155, 157, 160, 164, 167, 170, 175, 181, 182, 188, 190, 196

case study, 11, 116, 152, 153, 156, 158–61, 161–3, 163–4, 165, 168, 196, 197
choir, 29, 33, 36, 39, 41, 42, 43
classroom-based inquiry, *see* classroom research
classroom-based research, *see* classroom research
classroom research, 2, 6, 14, 22, 23, 25, 26, 58, 59, 61, 63–4, 65, 66, 67, 114, 157, 195, 196, 197

collaboration, 6, 26, 33, 37, 38, 45, 64, 73, 77, 81, 84, 123, 143, 144, 149, 152, 160, 170, 171, 173, 176, 177, 178, 179, 181, 182, 189, 195
   collaborative inquiry, 10, 75, 79, 80, 81, 83, 84, 188
   collaborative working culture, 171, 180, 182
constructivism, 153
course design, 7, 44, 98, 121, 178

data analysis, 24, 68, 100, 116, 129
data collection, 2, 4, 20, 24, 25, 35, 65, 94, 100, 113, 116, 127, 129, 132, 133, 167, 187
   methods, 2, 100, 113, 129, 130–1, 131
dissemination, 7, 68, 99, 100, 103, 107, 143, 197
document analysis, 187

education, types of,
   adult, 72, 73, 75, 77, 185
   primary/elementary, 76, 84, 88, 153, 161
   private sector, 10, 14, 16, 89, 91, 126, 185
   secondary/high school, 16, 19, 75, 85, 88
   state sector, 161, 185
   university/higher, 16, 85, 99, 100, 106, 136, 183, 197
empowerment, 33, 40–1, 45, 141, 149
English as a foreign language (EFL), 10, 11, 15–16, 31, 60, 66, 87, 88, 89, 90, 91, 94, 96, 125, 126, 127, 136, 139, 140, 195, 197
English as a lingua franca (ELF), 31, 125
English as a second language (ESL), 10, 71, 72–7, 77–9, 80, 81, 84, 194
English language teaching (ELT), 9, 23, 44, 50, 51, 53, 55, 70, 88, 99, 121, 122, 126, 127, 136, 137, 158, 186, 195, 196
ethics, 62, 107, 116, 187

199

200 Index

facilitative conditions, 109
  see also action research (facilitating)
  see also teacher research (facilitating)

impact, 1, 7, 8, 10, 11, 16, 32, 53, 55, 73, 74, 82, 83, 99, 101, 102, 103, 107, 108, 110, 128, 134, 137, 139, 149, 155, 160, 161, 162, 167, 171, 182, 185, 187, 189, 190, 191, 194, 198
  see also action research (impact of)
  see also teacher research (impact of)
institutional structures, 173–5
interviews, 2, 48, 50, 60, 63, 65, 73, 75, 81, 82, 83, 90, 92, 93, 94, 100, 101, 116, 124, 131, 132, 133, 159, 163, 187

journals, 18, 22, 27, 36, 37, 39, 40, 41, 45, 90, 145, 196
  pedagogical, 144
  reflection, 30, 38, 40, 42
  reflective, 35, 76
  research, 120
  teacher, 35, 45, 187

language as local practice, 95, 96
language centre (LC), 10, 11, 29, 32, 170, 171, 172, 173, 174, 175, 176, 177, 178, 179, 181, 182, 185, 196, 197
language learner histories, 90, 91, 93, 94, 95, 96, 196
leadership, 38, 155, 170, 171, 173, 180, 182
learning community, 80, 143
lesson notes, 19, 187
literacy, 70, 71, 72, 73, 74, 75, 76, 77–9, 80, 81, 83, 84, 188, 194, 195, 198
literature review, 20, 24, 130

mentoring, 3, 51, 144, 155, 156, 165, 166, 176, 196
motivation/demotivation, 8, 15, 17, 19, 23, 42, 55, 58, 73, 93, 101, 105, 109, 115, 117, 121, 125, 127, 143, 159, 160, 161, 164, 165, 166, 189, 190, 191, 196
music, 31–2, 33, 42, 197
  see also singing

narrative inquiry, 35, 195, 196
narratives, 22, 25, 35, 37, 87, 90, 91, 92–4, 92, 93, 94, 95, 107, 194, 195, 196, 197, 198

observations, 1, 3, 9, 20, 30, 42, 45, 63, 74, 75, 81, 116, 144, 145, 146
  classroom, 2, 165, 187
  peer, 174, 178
  personal, 137
  process of, 129
  teacher's, 132

parental involvement, 162, 163, 164
participation metaphor, 90, 91, 92, 93, 95, 96, 197
participatory action research, 64, 187
pilot activities, 100, 163
practicum, 140, 143, 150
practitioner research, *see* teacher research
professional development (PD), 3, 6, 10, 30, 34, 36, 37, 40, 51, 52, 54, 62, 66, 70, 71–4, 75, 79–80, 81, 82, 83, 84, 85, 98, 101, 102, 106, 110, 113, 114, 115, 123, 125, 126–7, 128, 131, 132, 134, 135, 136, 141, 149, 152, 156, 158, 166, 186, 187, 189, 190, 191, 192, 196, 197
  teacher development, 11, 52, 120, 121, 123, 128, 135, 136, 152, 153, 154, 155, 155–6, 157, 164, 167, 168, 189, 196, 198
progress reports, 117, 120, 135
pronunciation teaching, 10, 30–1
publication, 8, 18, 25, 26, 40, 51, 72, 89, 100, 102, 107, 109, 127, 134, 144, 145, 174, 176, 177, 178, 179, 180, 195, 198

questionnaires, 2, 18, 19, 20, 21, 22, 24, 27, 48, 50, 62, 90, 91, 92, 93, 94, 95, 116, 117, 124, 130, 132, 141, 159, 162, 179, 187

reflective practice, 2, 3, 7, 29, 30, 54, 73, 106, 121, 149, 155, 156, 157, 181, 196, 197
  promoting, 118, 120

reflective practitioner, 30, 54, 110, 152, 155, 157, 158, 167
reflective teaching, 25, 30, 35, 196
research courses, 8, 11, 89, 98, 99, 102, 105, 106, 107, 108, 109, 110, 121, 122, 123, 140, 188, 194, 197
research development group, 174, 176
research engagement, 11, 171, 173, 175, 180, 181, 182, 183
  engagement priorities, 26–7, 55–6, 122–3, 172–3, 182–3
research proposals, 48, 49, 51, 54, 100, 104, 116, 124, 127, 131–3
research questions, 4, 19, 24, 83, 103, 116, 119, 130, 131, 132, 133, 134, 158, 159, 160, 161, 178

self-esteem, 8, 15, 16, 51, 101, 189
singing, 31, 32, 33, 37, 42, 45
  see also music
socio-cultural theory, 153, 171, 177, 182, 195, 197
student teacher, 11, 47, 89, 94, 139, 141, 142, 143, 144, 145, 146, 147, 148, 149, 150
study circle, 73, 75, 76, 78, 79, 80, 81, 82, 83

teacher education, 11, 108, 147, 155, 194
  pre-service, 11
  student-teacher learning, 11, 139
  teacher development, *see* professional development (teacher development)
  teacher educator, 127, 128, 139, 143, 156, 191
  teacher trainer, 66, 113, 126, 136, 139, 140, 141, 142, 144, 145, 149
  teacher training, 51, 66, 125, 132, 139, 140, 149
  teaching and, 154–5
  see also student teacher
teacher identity, 33, 34, 37, 43, 44, 143, 189
teacher learning, 6, 11, 48, 51, 74, 82, 99

teacher research, 1, 9, 15, 21, 47, 48, 59, 64, 67, 75, 83, 84, 91, 96, 106, 114, 123, 124, 127, 134, 196
  assessment on, 105–6
  challenges of, 3, 14, 24, 33, 51–53, 55, 56, 68, 71, 73, 107, 114, 152, 170, 171, 173, 175, 180, 181, 191–2
  characteristics of, 1, 2, 3, 4, 5, 6, 14, 55, 185–6
  contexts for, 106, 110, 185
  criticisms of, 8–9
  defining, 1–2, 14, 26–7, 30, 51, 54, 100, 113, 139, 167, 185, 186, 196
  doing, 2, 2–5, 10, 14, 47, 55, 98, 99, 102, 103, 105, 116, 118, 119, 121, 122, 136, 185, 195, 196
  facilitating, 1, 5–7, 10, 11, 53, 54, 55, 56, 89, 90, 95, 98, 99, 101, 106–10, 110, 113, 114, 115, 116, 117, 118–22, 123, 136, 137, 152, 153, 158, 163, 164–6, 167, 168, 185, 188–9, 191, 192, 194, 195, 196, 197
  impact of, 1, 6, 7–8, 9, 14, 60, 61, 65, 71, 72–4, 98, 101, 102, 107, 108, 110, 113, 137, 164, 189–91
  quality of, 4, 8, 104, 105, 110, 187
  schemes, 6, 99
  strategies for, 186–7
teacher trainer, *see* teacher education (teacher trainer)
teacher training, *see* teacher education (teacher training)
teaching methodology, 2, 4, 5, 6, 8, 10, 29, 34, 35, 38, 40, 42, 44, 48, 49, 50, 51, 87, 88, 89, 94, 96, 98, 99, 100, 105, 115–16, 129, 130, 132, 135, 136, 142, 155, 157, 164, 166, 167, 186, 187, 191, 194, 195, 198
technology, 37, 57, 58, 59, 60, 61, 62, 63, 64, 65, 66, 67, 71, 100, 195, 197

university pedagogy, 173, 174, 176, 176–7, 178, 179, 180, 183

videoconference, 60, 64

Printed and bound by CPI Group (UK) Ltd, Croydon, CR0 4YY